BUILDING FOUNDATIONS

BUILDING FOUNDATIONS

Kathleen A Hollowell

Bettyann Daley

Ronald H Wenger

Janson Publications, Inc.

DEDHAM, MASSACHUSETTS

Contents

vii   **Preface**

ix   **Answers to Questions about *Building Foundations***

xii   **Cross-References to Textbook Topics**

1   **Lessons**

3   Conducting a Survey

7   The Meaning of Mean

12   Ratios and Rates

16   Equivalent Fractions

21   Similar Figures

26   Graph Paper Art

29   Capture-Recapture Experiment

33   Getting the Picture

39   Explorations with Prisms

42   Explorations with Pyramids

45   Thinking Graphically I

49   Thinking Graphically II

53   Explorations with Perimeter

58   Explorations with Area

62   Rectangular Garden

65   Counting Cubes

68   Probability I

72   Probability II

76   Coin Toss Experiments

82   What's Your Chance I

87   What's Your Chance II

92   What's Your Chance III

97   Get Ready, Get Set

105   Independent and Dependent Events – Dependent

110   Independent and Dependent Events – Independent

115   Geometry and Probability

123   **Quizzes**

169   **Teaching Notes**

231   **Answers**

Preface

ABOUT THE LESSONS

Building Foundations is a set of independent lessons which promote problem solving, mathematical reasoning, and communication. However, it is not a *random* set of lessons. Rather, lesson topics were specifically chosen to represent the "big ideas" that provide a foundation for secondary school mathematics. The lessons provide students with opportunities to discover the major basic concepts in pre-algebra, geometry, statistics, and combinatorics. Both independent and cooperative learning through small groups are used in the instructional process. The lessons were designed in the spirit of the NCTM's *Curriculum and Evaluation Standards for School Mathematics* and are suitable for use in any Pre-algebra or Algebra class. Students are asked to solve problems and explain their solutions. In some lessons students collect data, create mathematical models to describe the data, and make predictions based on those mathematical models. In other lessons, students construct geometric models and discover geometric relationships. Throughout the year they have the opportunity to work in small groups and to communicate with each other about mathematical ideas.

Some of the lessons cover pre-algebra content that is necessary for success in algebra (Lessons 8–16). In addition, as recommended by the *Standards*, other lessons include content from geometry (Lessons 5, 6, 9, 10, and 13–16), statistics (Lessons 1, 2, and 7) and probability (Lessons 17–19 and 23–26) to broaden students' mathematical backgrounds and illustrate how mathematics can be used in the real world. Students revisit rates, ratios, proportions, and percent in the context of statistics, geometry, and probability (Lessons 1, 3–7, and 23–26). Attention is given to basic concepts in combinatorics (Lessons 20–23), which are connected to basic concepts in probability (Lessons 20–25).

ACKNOWLEDGMENTS

The Delaware Pre-Algebra/Algebra Project began in 1989 supported, in part, by Education for Economic Security Act (EESA) Title II funds. These funds and those provided by the University of Delaware through the Mathematical Sciences Teaching and Learning Center made possible the development and testing of the instructional lessons.

Five individuals in the Mathematical Sciences Teaching and Learning Center, University of Delaware, made significant contributions to this document. Patricia Cleary wrote quizzes and provided answer keys for several lessons. Martha Wilson contributed ideas for new lessons in the second edition and served as an editorial consultant. Eileen Prybolsky, Carolyn Rifino, and Claudia Johnson applied their expert word processing and organizational skills to produce this document.

We wish to thank those Delaware teachers who participated in our workshops, contributed ideas to improve drafts of the lessons, and pilot-tested the lessons in their classrooms.

Answers to Questions about *Building Foundations*

IMPLEMENTATION ISSUES

Question: I hardly have time to complete the year's curriculum now. What do I leave out in order to teach these lessons?
Answer: The lessons can be thought of as "replacement" lessons. They can be used as a different approach or to introduce certain topics replacing the presentation in the regular textbook. For example Lesson #1, "Conducting a Survey", can serve as an excellent introduction to basic concepts in statistics. Some lessons can follow the textbook presentation if reteaching or additional work seem appropriate.

Question: How long should I spend on a lesson?
Answer: Most lessons can be completed in two or three class periods. Some are designed for whole class instruction while others lend themselves to cooperative learning in small groups.

Question: How do these lessons connect to the mathematics I'm teaching now or to other areas of the middle school curriculum?
Answer: Lessons typically integrate mathematical content areas through the use of real-world situations meaningful to students' everyday lives. Teachers can reinforce these content connections by classroom discussions and questions. The correlation chart which follows this introduction shows these connections.

Question: What support do I have for teaching each lesson?
Answer: The "Teaching Notes" for each lesson list the mathematics covered in that lesson, provide suggestions for teaching the lesson with possible questions to ask students, and include extensions for further work (or for those groups which may finish a project ahead of others). Worksheets and patterns are also included in this section.

The set of "Quizzes" allow follow-up assessment on an individual or group basis. Here students can demonstrate what they have learned.

"Answers" to both the assessments and the lessons also are included.

GROUP WORK

Question: What are the advantages of group work?
Answer: Students constantly learn from each other. They are much more likely to ask questions and acknowledge their confusion in a small group than in front of the whole class. Letting them work together on well-defined activities allows room for questioning, explaining, discovering, cooperating, and developing their communication skills. Students clarify their own thinking when they ask questions as well as when they explain an answer. This also shifts the role of the teacher from one of dispenser of knowledge to that of helper or facilitator and places the *responsibility for learning on the students* themselves. It also changes an individual "problem" to a group problem which can be solved by several students collectively instead of an individual working alone.

Once students and teacher are comfortable with group work, both will enjoy the exchange of ideas and discoveries as the classroom becomes a more exciting place to learn.

Question: What is the best way to get started with working in groups?
Answer: Since the lessons are independent of each other and require only a few days to complete, they are an easy way to move into group learning. The first two lessons "Conducting A Survey" and "The Meaning of Mean" together offer a good way to get started. Many of the questions in "Conducting A Survey" provide excellent opportunities for brief periods of working together. If the classroom has movable desks, students can work in groups of four by simply turning their desks to face each other.

The teacher and students should spend time discussing appropriate, productive group behavior, and together they can develop a few simple rules. These might include not disturbing others, making sure all contribute, asking for help only when the entire group agrees, and other common courtesies.

The teacher can determine group membership to assure a mix of abilities, sexes, leadership, *etc.* It is generally a good idea to change group membership from time to time. The introduction of a new lesson is a good time to do this.

Not all educators agree about the best methods for assigning individual roles within the group. Some feel that different roles should be allowed to develop naturally while others feel they should be formally defined and assigned. Such roles include leader, idea person, skeptic, recorder, equipment manager, *etc.* When the teacher is observing group behavior, it is probably most important to make sure all students are contributing and involved actively in the process.

Question: During group work, what is the teacher's role?
Answer: The teacher should circulate actively throughout the room, make sure students are on task, ask questions, answer questions, guide investigations if necessary, and note individual participation to insure each student is contributing.

ASSESSMENT

Question: What are the assessment options provided with these lessons?
Answer: Individual or group learning can be assessed after completion of a lesson by using the "Quizzes". These assessments include questions to assess skills in both computation and applications, and they often require explanation or justification of an answer.

Many lessons can be used as projects that students can do either independently or in groups. Some lessons provide opportunities for groups or individuals to make oral presentations.

A student discovery of a mathematical theorem, such as Euler's Formula (Lesson 9) or the Fundamental Counting Principle (Lesson 20), would be a strong candidate for inclusion in a portfolio.

Question: With students working together in small groups, how do I determine individual grades?
Answer: The simplest way is to give each group member the same grade. This grade can be based on observation, a class presentation or project, and/or grading of a group assignment. This grade will simply be one of many grades and thus a part of the final grade for an individual student.

Column key:
1. Conducting A Survey
2. The Meaning of Mean
3. Ratios and Rates
4. Equivalent Fractions
5. Similar Figures
6. Graph Paper Art
7. Capture-Recapture
8. Getting the Picture
9. Explorations with Prisms
10. Explorations with Pyramids
11. Thinking Graphically I
12. Thinking Graphically II
13. Explorations with Perimeter
14. Explorations with Area
15. Rectangular Garden
16. Counting Cubes
17. Probability I
18. Probability II
19. Coin Toss Experiments
20. What's Your Chance I
21. What's Your Chance II
22. What's Your Chance III
23. Get Ready, Get Set
24. Independent Events
25. Dependent Events
26. Geometry and Probability

Category	Topic	1	2	3	4	5	6	7	8	9	10	11	12	13	14	15	16	17	18	19	20	21	22	23	24	25	26
Rational Nos./ Proportions	Part-whole concept		X					X										X	X	X	X	X	X	X	X	X	
	Rates and ratios			X	X	X	X	X				X															X
	Proportional reasoning			X	X	X	X					X						X	X						X	X	
	Percent	X																	X				X				
Pre-Algebra/Algebra	Variable as pattern generalizer								X	X	X			X	X	X	X										
	Substitution for a variable								X	X	X			X	X	X	X										
	Translations among narrative, table, graph and function rule								X	X	X	X	X	X	X	X	X										
	Intuitive notion of slope											X	X														
	Find maximum or minimum											X	X			X											
Statistics	Frequency of an event	X						X										X	X								
	Relative frequency	X						X										X	X								
	Frequency table	X	X															X	X								
	Bar graph	X																X									
	Mean (arithmetic)		X	X				X					X														
	Sample as population	X						X										X	X								
	Randomization							X										X	X								X
	Pooling sample data							X										X	X								X
	Effect of sample size							X										X	X								X
Probability	Definition																	X	X	X	X	X	X	X	X	X	X
	Theoretical frequency																	X	X	X							
	Experimental frequency																	X	X	X							
	Pascal's triangle																		X								
	$P(A \text{ or } B)$																							X			
	$P(A \text{ and } B)$																							X	X	X	
	Conditional probability																								X	X	
	Dependent and Independent events																								X	X	
	Geometric probability																										X

Column key:

1. Conducting A Survey
2. The Meaning of Mean
3. Ratios and Rates
4. Equivalent Fractions
5. Similar Figures
6. Graph Paper Art
7. Capture-Recapture
8. Getting the Picture
9. Explorations with Prisms
10. Explorations with Pyramids
11. Thinking Graphically I
12. Thinking Graphically II
13. Explorations with Perimeter
14. Explorations with Area
15. Rectangular Garden
16. Counting Cubes
17. Probability I
18. Probability II
19. Coin Toss Experiments
20. What's Your Chance I
21. What's Your Chance II
22. What's Your Chance III
23. Get Ready, Get Set
24. Independent Events
25. Dependent Events
26. Geometry and Probability

Category	Topic	1	2	3	4	5	6	7	8	9	10	11	12	13	14	15	16	17	18	19	20	21	22	23	24	25	26
Geometry	Conceptual similarity				X	X																					
Geometry	Measurement				X	X																					
Geometry	Scale factor				X	X																					
Geometry	"Stretcher" and "Shrinker"					X																					
Geometry	Perimeter													X		X											
Geometry	Area													X	X	X	X										
Geometry	3-dimensional figures									X	X						X										
Geometry	Volume																X										
Geometry	Surface area																X										
Counting Techniques	Tree diagram																			X	X	X		X	X	X	
Counting Techniques	Multiplication Counting Principle																			X	X	X	X			X	X
Counting Techniques	Carefully ordered list																			X	X	X			X	X	
Counting Techniques	Permutation																				X	X					
Counting Techniques	Factorial concept																				X	X					
Counting Techniques	Combination																					X					
Counting Techniques	Elements in A or B																					X					
Counting Techniques	Elements in A and B																					X					
Counting Techniques	Venn diagram																					X			X	X	
Set Theory	Concept of union																					X					
Set Theory	Concept of intersection																					X					
Set Theory	Concept of negation																					X					
Set Theory	Disjoint sets																					X					
Multiple Representations	Table of data	X	X		X	X		X	X	X	X	X	X	X	X	X	X	X	X	X					X	X	X
Multiple Representations	Bar graph	X																			X	X					
Multiple Representations	Number line		X									X															
Multiple Representations	Coordinate plane				X		X	X	X	X	X	X	X	X	X	X	X										
Multiple Representations	Variable expression									X	X	X		X	X	X	X								X		X
Multiple Representations	Tree diagram																				X	X	X	X		X	X
Multiple Representations	Carefully ordered list																				X	X	X			X	X
Multiple Representations	Venn diagram																								X		
Multiple Representations	Picture						X	X	X	X		X			X	X	X										

Lessons

Conducting a Survey

Collecting, Analyzing, and Interpreting Data

A survey may be used to collect data about an entire group.
Then you can display and analyze the data using frequency
tables and bar graphs. After the data are analyzed, you can
interpret the results.

ACTIVITY

Survey the members of your class to determine which of the following flavors of
frozen yogurt they like the most: vanilla, chocolate, or strawberry.

Tally the data as follows:

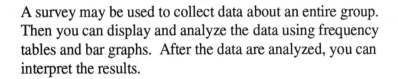

Vanilla   Chocolate   Strawberry

III   ЖЖ ЖЖ II   ЖЖ II

A. Copy and complete a frequency table like the one shown here.

Flavor	Frequency	Relative Frequency Fractional Form		Relative Frequency Decimal Form to nearest 100th	Percent
		Unreduced	Reduced		
Vanilla					
Chocolate					
Strawberry					
Totals					

B. Copy and complete each bar graph below. Fill in the numbers on each
vertical axis in a way which maintains equal intervals. Draw bars with
heights that correspond to the frequency data in your table.

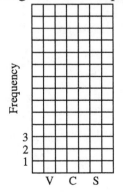

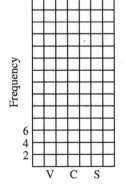

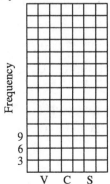

C. Copy and complete the bar graph shown here. Fill in the numbers on the vertical axis in a way which maintains equal intervals. Draw bars with heights that correspond to the relative frequency data in the table.

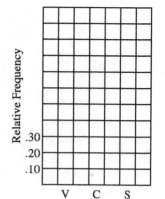

D. i. Which flavor is liked the most in your class?

   ii. Explain how to get this answer from the frequency table.

   iii. Explain how to get this answer from the bar graphs.

E. i. How many more votes does the most liked flavor have than the second most liked flavor?

   ii. Explain how to get this answer from the frequency table.

   iii. Explain how to get this answer from the bar graphs.

F. What is the total of the numbers in the "Frequency" column? What does this total represent?

G. What is the total of the numbers in the "Relative Frequency, Fractional Form" column?

H. i. What is the total of the numbers in the "Percent" column?

   ii. What should the exact total of the numbers in the "Percent" column be?

   iii. Compare your answers to parts i and ii. Explain why they do or do not agree.

EXERCISES

1. Suppose that your school principal decides to purchase one cone of frozen yogurt for each student for an all-school picnic. She decides to use your class data as representative of the entire school.

   a. If there are 326 students in the school, how many vanillas should she buy? How many chocolates? How many strawberries?

   b. Does the total number of cones of frozen yogurt in part a equal 326? Why or why not?

   c. Do you think that your class is truly representative of the entire school population? Explain your answer.

2. Ms. Ryan's class conducted the same survey as your class did. A bar graph of their data appears here.

   In Ms. Ryan's class, how many students prefer vanilla? chocolate? strawberry?

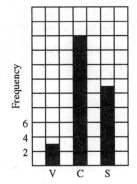

3. How many students responded to the survey in Ms. Ryan's class?

4. Complete a frequency table for Ms. Ryan's class using the data from the bar graph.

5. What is the total of the numbers in the "Relative Frequency, Fractional Form" column in your frequency table for Exercise 4? How does this total compare with your answer to part G of the activity?

6. In any frequency table, the total of the numbers in the "Relative Frequency, Fractional Form" column should equal a certain number.

   a. What is the number?

   b. How could that number be used to check for errors in a frequency table?

7. **a.** What is the total of the numbers in the "Percent" column?

   b. What should the exact total of the numbers in the "Percent" column be?

   c. Compare your answers to parts a and b. Explain why they do or do not agree.

8. **a.** In Ms. Ryan's class how many more students prefer chocolate than prefer strawberry?

   b. In Ms. Ryan's class how many times as many students prefer chocolate as prefer vanilla?

   c. In Ms. Ryan's class how many fewer students prefer vanilla than prefer strawberry?

9. In Mr. Allen's class, 24 students responded to the survey. Copy and complete a table like this one for his class.

Flavor	Frequency	Relative Frequency
Vanilla		$\frac{1}{8}$
Chocolate		$\frac{5}{8}$
Strawberry		$\frac{2}{8}$
Totals		

10. In Ms. Thompson's class, 30 students responded to the survey. A relative frequency bar graph for her class appears here.

Complete a frequency table for Ms. Thompson's class.

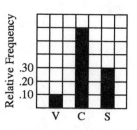

11. Mr. Brown's class also conducted the survey. Copy and complete the table for Mr. Brown's class. **Hint.** First determine the total number of students who responded to the survey.

Flavor	Frequency	Relative Frequency
Vanilla	5	$\frac{1}{4}$
Chocolate		
Strawberry		$\frac{3}{20}$
Totals		

12. Bar graphs for two different classes appear below.

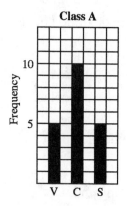
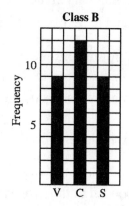

a. How many students in Class A prefer chocolate?

b. How many students in Class B prefer chocolate?

c. What percent of the students in Class A prefer chocolate?

d. What percent of the students in Class B prefer chocolate?

e. Which class has the stronger preference for chocolate? Explain your answer.

The Meaning of Mean

Sometimes people describe a set of numbers using just one number. Often the number they use is the average, also called the mean.

ACTIVITY 1

Work in groups of 3 or 4. Your teacher will distribute index cards to each student in your group. Some students may get more cards than others. Record the names of the group's members and the number of index cards each person receives in a table like the one shown here.

Name	Number of Index Cards

A. Determine the total number of index cards in your group.

B. Redistribute the cards so that each person in your group receives a fair share, that is, so that each person receives the same number of index cards. Describe the method used to redistribute the index cards.

C. Determine the number of index cards in a fair share for your group. The number of cards in a fair share is the *average* or *mean* number of cards for your group.

D. Report to the class the number of cards each member of your group originally had, the total number of cards and the number of cards in a fair share. Describe the method that your group used to give each person a fair share.

E. Summarize the data from all groups in your class in a table like the one shown here.

F. Describe any patterns or interesting features that you see in your table.

Group	Number of Cards for Each Person	Number in Group	Total Number of Cards	Mean Number of Cards
0	12, 5, 1	3	24	8
1				
2				
3				
4				
5				
6				
7				

EXERCISES

1. Describe how to calculate the mean using arithmetic.

2. List three different sets of four numbers that each have a mean of 6. Use sets that are not shown in your table.

3. Return to Activity 1 and redistribute your group's index cards exactly as your teacher originally distributed them. Refer to your table, if necessary, to recall the correct number of cards for each person. Then, the first person listed in your table should get one more index card from your teacher.
   a. What is the new total number of cards for your group?
   b. Distribute the cards so that each person has a fair share. You may have to cut an index card into equal parts. How many cards are in a fair share?
   c. What is the new mean for your group? Show how to get this number using arithmetic.
   d. Do your answers to parts b and c agree?

4. Calculate the mean quiz score for each student. Show how you found each answer.
   a. Mary's quiz grades: 9, 7, 8
   b. BJ's quiz grades: 5, 10, 6, 9
   c. Jason's quiz grades: 8, 8, 8, 8, 8

ACTIVITY 2

Work in groups of 3 or 4.

A. Your group must have a mean of 7 index cards. Determine the total number of cards that your group will need and collect them from your teacher. How many cards did your group have to collect?

B. Distribute the cards so that each person in your group has a fair share. How many cards does each person have?

C. Distribute the cards unevenly to the members of your group. Record results in a table like this one.

D. Calculate the mean using the information in the "Number of Index Cards" column. Show your work. Is the mean still 7?

Name	Number of Index Cards

E. Now distribute the same total number of cards in another way. Is the mean still 7? What could you change so that the mean is not 7?

EXERCISES

5. Five students are in a group. What is the total number of index cards that the group would need so that the mean would be 11 index cards?

6. Carlos, Anita and Michael collect baseball cards. Carlos has 23 cards and Anita has 30 cards. The mean number of cards for all three is 40. How many cards does Michael have? Describe the method you used to find your answer.

7. Myra must get her mid-term math report signed by her parents. She will not be allowed to try out for the basketball team if she has any test grade below 70. Her teacher has recorded her four test scores and the mean of the four scores on the report. However, the report got wet in the rain, and one test score cannot be read. The report shows that the other three scores are 83, 94, and 77, and the mean is 80.

   a. Explain how Myra's parents can determine her missing test score.

   b. Will Myra be able to try out for the basketball team?

8. An activity similar to Activity 1 was conducted with a group of five students. The table below illustrates how the number of index cards originally given to each member of the group "differs" from the mean, or fair share. Notice that Hank received 11 cards and the mean was 6. Therefore, Hank had 5 cards more than the mean, and we recorded a "5" in the column "Number More than the Mean." On the other hand, Sally's 2 cards puts her 4 cards less than the mean, and we recorded a "4" in the column "Number Less than the Mean."

Name	Original Number of Cards	Mean Number	Number More than the Mean	Number Less than the Mean
Hank	11	6	5	
Sally	2	6		4
Jo	3	6		3
Roberto	9	6	3	
Nakia	5	6		1
Totals	30	30	8	8

Make a similar table for your group, based on the data in your table from Activity 1. What do you notice about the totals for "Number More than the Mean" and "Number Less than the Mean"? Check with other groups to see if their results were similar to yours.

9. The *number line diagram* below illustrates the situation in Exercise 8. We plotted the numbers from Hank, Sally, Jo, Roberto and Nakia and calculated the distances between each number and the mean. Notice that the total of the distances to the right of the mean, $5 + 3 = 8$, and the total of the distances to the left of the mean, $4 + 3 + 1 = 8$, are equal.

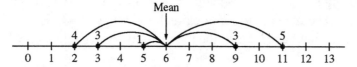

a. Draw a number line diagram for your group based on the data in your table for Activity 1.

b. What is the total of the distances to the right of the mean?

c. What is the total of the distances to the left of the mean?

d. Check your answers to b and c above with the data in the table you made for Exercise 8. Do your answers agree with the table?

10. A group of four students in Mr. Scott's class did the index card experiment. They drew a number line diagram but left out one of the original numbers.

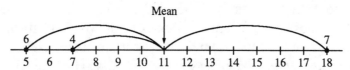

a. What is the missing number? Explain.

b. Calculate the mean of the four numbers. Does this mean agree with the one shown on the number line diagram?

11. The average number of peanuts in a small bag is 33. This means that if all the peanuts in a number of small bags were pooled together and the total divided by the number of bags, you should get 33. Suppose each member of your group were given a bag of peanuts.

a. Can you tell exactly how many peanuts each person in your group would have? Explain.

b. Predict the total number of peanuts that your group would have. If your group does not get exactly the number that you predicted, should you complain to the manufacturer? Why or why not?

12. The average age of the airplanes owned by the Airway Company is 15.14 years.

    a. Does this imply that each airplane owned by Airway is 15.14 years old? Why or why not?

    b. Could some of the airplanes owned by Airway be 15.14 years old?

    c. Describe what two quantities were divided to calculate the average age of the planes.

13. Marvin's last five math quiz grades are 80, 70, 65, 72, 82.

He has another quiz tomorrow. He would like to have an average grade of 75 after he takes tomorrow's quiz. Using three different methods, calculate the quiz score that Marvin will need.

    a. Method 1

    Find the sum of Marvin's grades so far. Copy the table shown here and complete your table by calculating a new mean for each indicated score.

Tomorrow's Quiz Score	New Mean
75	
80	
85	

    From the table, the score that Marvin will need is between what two entries? Choose a score between these scores and calculate the new mean. Continue this process until you find the score needed for an average of 75.

    b. Method 2

    Draw a number line diagram. Use the diagram to determine the quiz score needed for a mean of 75.

    c. Method 3

    Find the total number of points that Marvin would need on his six quizzes in order to have an average of 75. How many points does Marvin have on the first five quizzes? Find the difference between the number of points he has on the first five quizzes and the number that he needs on the six quizzes.

    d. Do your answers to parts a, b, and c agree?

    e. Which of the three methods do you prefer? Explain your choice.

Ratios and Rates

Division can be used to compare two quantities. For example, in a given week, if Yolanda jogged 3 miles for every 2 miles that Tammy jogged, you could write

$$\frac{3 \text{ miles}}{2 \text{ miles}} = \frac{3}{2} \frac{\text{miles}}{\text{miles}} = \frac{3}{2} = \frac{1.5}{1} = 1.5.$$

Yolanda |—|—|—|—|—|—| |—|—|—| |—|—|—|
Tammy |—|—|—|—| |—|—| |—|—|

3 miles to 2 miles $\frac{3}{2}$ miles to 1 mile

Yolanda jogged 1.5 times as far as Tammy.

We can write the *ratio* $\frac{3 \text{ miles}}{2 \text{ miles}}$ as $\frac{3}{2}$ or 1.5 without units. A ratio is a comparison by division of two quantities.

To write the ratio of a number a to a number b, we write $\frac{a}{b}$. Notice that, when we translate from words to mathematical notation, the quantity mentioned immediately before the word "to" becomes the numerator of the fraction. You can also use a colon to write a ratio:

3 miles : 2 miles or 3 : 2.
You read this as "3 to 2".

EXERCISES

1. Write each ratio in fractional form.
   a. 10 points to 6 points
   b. 6 points to 10 points

2. Ms. Thompson has 20 students in her class, and Mr. Arno has 25 students in his class.
   a. Write the ratio of students in Ms. Thompson's class to students in Mr. Arno's class as a fraction.
   b. Write the ratio in part a as a decimal.
   c. Write the ratio in part a using a colon.
   d. Write the ratio of students in Mr. Arno's class to students in Ms. Thompson's class as a fraction.
   e. Write the ratio in part d as a decimal.
   f. Write the ratio in part d using a colon.

3. Ellis complained that it rained 3 out of every 4 days on his vacation.

   a. Write the ratio of rainy days to vacation days as a fraction.

   b. Write the ratio in part a as a decimal.

   c. Write the ratio in part a as a percent.

   d. If Ellis was on vacation for 20 days, how many of those days did it rain?

4. Find the number of girls and the number of boys in your math class. Write each ratio as a fraction without reducing it.

   a. What is the ratio of boys to girls?

   b. What is the ratio of girls to boys?

   c. Describe the relationship between your answers to parts a and b.

   d. What is the ratio of boys to the total number of students?

   e. What is the ratio of girls to the total number of students?

   f. Find the sum of your answers to parts d and e. Explain why this sum makes sense.

A special type of ratio involves comparing two quantities having different units. We call this special type of ratio a *rate*. For example, when planning a party, you might decide to have three cans of soda for every two people present. Using division, you have

$$\frac{3 \text{ cans of soda}}{2 \text{ people}} = \frac{3}{2} \frac{\text{cans of soda}}{\text{person}} = \frac{1.5}{1} \frac{\text{cans of soda}}{\text{person}}$$

3 cans of soda
per 2 people

$\frac{3}{2}$ cans of soda
per person

1.5 cans of soda
per person

The phrase "3 cans of soda per 2 people" is an example of a rate. Rates can be written using a fraction bar or a slash (/), the word "per", or the phrase "for every". Here are some examples of rates written in different ways.

55 miles per hour = $55 \frac{\text{miles}}{\text{hour}}$

70¢/2 cans = 35¢ per can

3 police officers for every 1000 people = $\frac{3 \text{ police officers}}{1000 \text{ people}}$

As an example of a situation using rates, suppose that in the Martin Luther King School there are 2 computers and 25 students in every classroom. Two different

                Building Foundations 13

rates can be used to describe this situation: students per computer and computers per student.

To find the number of students per computer, begin with 25 students per 2 computers.

$$\frac{25 \text{ students}}{2 \text{ computers}} = \frac{25}{2} \frac{\text{students}}{\text{computers}} = \frac{12.5}{1} \frac{\text{students}}{\text{computer}}$$

There are 12.5 students/computer.

To find the number of computers per student, begin with 2 computers per 25 students.

$$\frac{2 \text{ computers}}{25 \text{ students}} = \frac{2}{25} \frac{\text{computers}}{\text{students}} = \frac{0.08}{1} \frac{\text{computers}}{\text{student}}$$

There are 0.08 computers/student.

Notice that, when we translate from words to mathematical notation, the quantity mentioned immediately before the word "per" becomes the numerator of the fraction.

EXERCISES

5. On a recent trip, Kisha traveled 180 miles on 15 gallons of gas.
   a. What two different rates are described?
   b. How many miles per gallon did Kisha get on her trip? Express the rate in fractional form and in decimal form.
   c. How many gallons of gas does Kisha use for each mile that she drives? Express the rate in fractional form and in decimal form.

6. Jon earned $5.00 for 2 hours of babysitting.
   a. What two different rates are described?
   b. How many dollars per hour did Jon earn babysitting?
   c. Write your answer to part b two different ways.
   d. How many hours did Jon have to work to earn one dollar?

7. The local grocery store has a sale on cantaloupes. The sale price is $2.00 for every 4 cantaloupes.
   a. How many cantaloupes can you buy for one dollar?
   b. What is the ratio of dollars spent to canteloupes bought?
   c. How much does the store charge per cantaloupe?
   d. How many cantaloupes could you buy with $3.50?

ACTIVITY

Measure the length of your classroom to the nearest foot. Your teacher will randomly select four students to walk the length of the classroom. For each student, count the number of steps to the nearest counting number and record the data in a table like the one shown below. Compute the number of feet per step for each student. Write each rate in both fractional and decimal form.

	Length of Room in Feet	Number of Steps	Number of Feet per Step	
			Fraction	Decimal
Student 1				
Student 2				
Student 3				
Student 4				

A. Which student took the longest steps?

B. Which student took the shortest steps?

C. What is the average number of feet per step for the four students?

D. Do you think the four students selected are representative of all students in your class? Explain.

Equivalent Fractions

Many real-world problems can be solved using equal, or equivalent, fractions. There are different ways to picture equivalent fractions and to solve problems that involve equivalent fractions.

EXAMPLE 1

Ms. Chang's math class has 3 boys for every 2 girls.

A. Fill in the icon (picture or symbol) boxes to illustrate a ratio of 3 boys to 2 girls.

B. Fill in the table with possible numbers of boys and girls in Ms. Chang's class.

C. Graph the data in the table on graph paper.

SOLUTION

A. Icon

B B	B B	B B
B	B	B
G G	G G	G G
B B	B B	B B
B	B	B
G G	G G	G G
B B	B B	B B
B	B	B
G G	G G	G G

B. Table

Girls	Boys	B/G Fraction	B/G Decimal
2	3	3/2	1.5
4	6	6/4	1.5
6	9	9/6	1.5
8	12	12/8	1.5
10	15	15/10	1.5
12	18	18/12	1.5

C. Graph

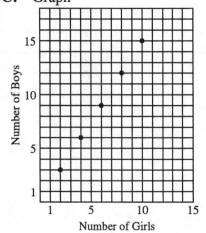

In the solution, notice that the ratio 3 boys for every 2 girls does not mean that there are exactly 3 boys and 2 girls in Ms. Chang's class. Many possibilities exist. For example, if you count all the B's and G's in the icon boxes, you would find 27 boys and 18 girls in the class. The graph shows other possibilities, such as 9 boys and 6 girls or 15 boys and 10 girls. However, the decimal column in the table shows that the ratio of boys to girls is always the same, $\frac{3}{2}$ or 1.5.

You can use the table to find equivalent fractions. Since $\frac{3}{2} = 1.5$ and $\frac{15}{10} = 1.5$, you can write $\frac{3}{2} = \frac{15}{10}$. All the fractions in the table have the same decimal representation, 1.5. Therefore, they are all equivalent fractions.

EXERCISE

1. During the basketball season, the ratio of Charles' foul shots made to foul shots attempted was 4 to 5.

   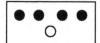 This icon box represents the fact that, out of 5 foul shots attempted, Charles made 4 foul shots and missed 1.

   Use an Icon-Table-Graph Worksheet for Exercises a through f.

   a. Fill in 7 icon boxes like the one above to illustrate the possibilities for foul shots made and foul shots missed.

   b. Copy and complete the following table.

Foul Shots Attempted	Foul Shots Made	Foul Shots Made / Foul Shots Attempted	
		Fraction	Decimal
5	4	5/4	0.8

   c. What was Charles' foul-shooting percentage for the season?

   d. If Charles attempted 30 foul shots, how many did he make?
      Explain how to obtain your answer from the table.
      Explain how to obtain your answer from the icon boxes.

   e. Use graph paper to plot the 7 data points in your table. Label the horizontal axis "Foul Shots Attempted" and the vertical axis "Foul Shots Made." Let each graph paper unit equal 2 shots.

f. Plot two new data points on your graph following the pattern established by the first 7. Include the points in your table. What number of shots attempted and number of shots made does each new data point represent?

You can also use equivalent fractions to answer the question "If Charles attempted 30 foul shots, how many did he make?"

EXAMPLE 2

Step 1 Use the ratio 4 foul shots made to 5 foul shots attempted. Write an equivalent-fraction equation (an equation which states that two fractions are equal).

$$\frac{4}{5}\frac{\text{shots made}}{\text{shots attempted}} = \frac{?}{30}\frac{\text{shots made}}{\text{shots attempted}}$$

Step 2 Find the numerator of the second fraction so that the fractions are equivalent.

Using the icon boxes from Exercise 1, you can see that 6 boxes are required to get 30 shots attempted. 6 boxes times 4 shots made per box gives you 24 shots made. Using mathematics symbols and our equivalent fraction, we could write:

$$\frac{4}{5} = \frac{?}{30} \qquad \text{Since } 5 \cdot 6 = 30, \text{ multiply both 4 and 5 by 6.}$$

$$\begin{array}{c} \times 6 \\ \curvearrowright \\ \frac{4}{5} = \frac{24}{30} \\ \curvearrowleft \\ \times 6 \end{array}$$

The procedure above is the same as multiplying $\frac{4}{5}$ by $\frac{6}{6}$.

$$\frac{4}{5} \cdot \frac{6}{6} = \frac{24}{30}$$

Since $\frac{6}{6} = 1$, the value of the fraction $\frac{4}{5}$ is not changed, so the fractions are equivalent. If Charles attempted 30 foul shots, he must have made 24.

Suppose instead you know that Charles made 24 out of 30 attempted foul shots. Using equivalent fractions, you can also work backwards to find how many foul shots he made for every 5 attempted.

EXAMPLE 3

Step 1 Use the ratio 24 foul shots made to 30 foul shots attempted. Write an equivalent-fraction equation.

$$\frac{?}{5} \frac{\text{shots made}}{\text{shots attempted}} = \frac{24}{30} \frac{\text{shots made}}{\text{shots attempted}}$$

Step 2 Find the numerator of the first fraction so that the fractions are equivalent.

$\frac{?}{5} = \frac{24}{30}$ Since $30 \div 6 = 5$, you should divide both 24 and 30 by 6.

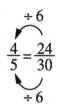

$$\frac{4}{5} = \frac{24}{30}$$

Charles would make 4 foul shots for every 5 attempted.

To decide whether to multiply or divide when finding equivalent fractions, ask yourself the following questions.

$\frac{4}{5} = \frac{24}{?}$ What do I have to do to 4 to get 24?
Answer: **Multiply** by 6

$\frac{4}{?} = \frac{24}{30}$ What do I have to do to 24 to get 4?
Answer: **Divide** by 6.

x 6
$\frac{4}{5} = \frac{24}{30}$ Multiply both numerator and denominator by 6.
x 6

÷ 6
$\frac{4}{5} = \frac{24}{30}$ Divide both numerator and denominator by 6.
÷ 6

When you write equivalent-fraction equations comparing two quantities with different labels, either the numerators should have the same labels and the denominators should have the same labels:

$$\frac{3}{2} \frac{\text{boys}}{\text{girls}} = \frac{12}{8} \frac{\text{boys}}{\text{girls}} \quad \text{or} \quad \frac{2}{3} \frac{\text{girls}}{\text{boys}} = \frac{8}{12} \frac{\text{girls}}{\text{boys}}$$

$$1.5 = 1.5 \qquad\qquad 0.\overline{6} = 0.\overline{6}$$

or the numerator and denominator of each fraction should have the same labels:

$$\frac{3}{12} \frac{\text{boys}}{\text{boys}} = \frac{2}{8} \frac{\text{girls}}{\text{girls}} \quad \text{or} \quad \frac{2}{8} \frac{\text{girls}}{\text{girls}} = \frac{3}{12} \frac{\text{boys}}{\text{boys}}$$

$$0.25 = 0.25 \qquad\qquad 0.25 = 0.25$$

It is incorrect if a label appears in the numerator of one fraction and in the denominator of the other fraction. For example:

$$\frac{3}{2}\frac{\text{boys}}{\text{girls}} \neq \frac{8}{12}\frac{\text{girls}}{\text{boys}}$$

$$1.5 \neq 0.\overline{6}$$

EXERCISES

2. Use the methods from Examples 2 and 3 to find the missing numbers. Show your work.

   a. $\dfrac{7}{10} = \dfrac{?}{80}$ **b.** $\dfrac{4}{3} = \dfrac{36}{?}$ **c.** $\dfrac{?}{5} = \dfrac{16}{20}$

   d. $\dfrac{6}{?} = \dfrac{30}{40}$ **e.** $\dfrac{10}{15} = \dfrac{?}{3}$ **f.** $\dfrac{?}{24} = \dfrac{3}{8}$

3. Seven out of every 10 doctors surveyed preferred Stickem bandages. There were actually 140 doctors in the survey who preferred Stickems.

   a. Use an Icon-Table Worksheet. Fill in 3 icon boxes to illustrate the situation. Choose an appropriate picture or symbol. Each box should have 10 doctors, 7 who prefer Stickems and 3 who do not.

   b. How many icon boxes are required to show 140 doctors who prefer Stickems? Explain.

   c. What is the total number of doctors in the survey?

   d. Replace the appropriate question mark with the number 140 and find the missing number. Show how you found the answer. (**Hint.** Use labels.)

   $$\frac{7}{10} = \frac{?}{?}$$

4. In planning a hike, Levi estimated that he could cover 5 miles in 2 hours. His goal is to hike 20 miles.

   a. How many miles per hour can Levi hike?

   b. How long will it take Levi to achieve his goal of 20 miles? Show how you found your answer.

5. Write a problem that uses a ratio or a rate and involves finding an equivalent fraction. Describe the method you would use to solve the problem.

Similar Figures

If you take a picture of your friend, the picture will have the same shape as your friend, but probably a different size. In geometry if figures have the same shape, they are called *similar*. If similar figures have the same size as well as the same shape, they are called *congruent*.

EXERCISES

1. Draw a single arrow, ↔, between the figures that appear to be similar. Draw a double arrow, ⇔, between the figures that appear to be congruent as well as similar.

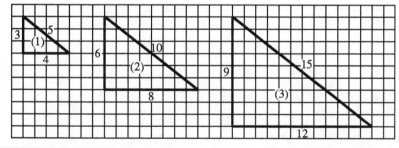

2. The three triangles are similar. Copy and complete the table. Reduce the fractional form of each ratio.

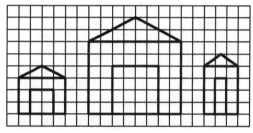

Triangle	Short Side	Medium Side	Long Side	Short Side / Medium Side	Short Side / Long Side	Medium Side / Long Side
(1)	3	4	5	$\frac{3}{4}$		
(2)						
(3)						

3. Describe the patterns you see in the table in Exercise 2.

4. Draw a picture of triangle (4) following the patterns established by the first three triangles. Include a fourth line in the table using the data from triangle (4).

5. a. Use a protractor to measure the angles in triangles (1), (2) and (3). Copy the following table and record the data for the three triangles.

Triangle	Small Angle	Medium Angle	Large Angle
(1)			90°
(2)			
(3)			
(4)			

b. Make a prediction about the measures of the angles in triangle (4). Check your prediction by measuring the angles. Then complete the table using the angle measures.

6. Based upon the data in the table in Exercise 5, what conjecture can you make about corresponding angles of similar triangles?

Suppose you want to draw a triangle similar to triangle (1), but having a short side of 39. To find the other two sides, you can use equivalent fractions.

Find the medium side.

Step 1 Write the ratios as equivalent fractions.

$$\frac{3}{4}\frac{\text{short}}{\text{medium}} = \frac{39}{?}\frac{\text{short}}{\text{medium}}$$

The medium side is 52.

Step 2 Multiply both numerator and denominator by 13.

$$\frac{3}{4}\frac{\text{short}}{\text{medium}} = \frac{39}{52}\frac{\text{short}}{\text{medium}}$$

Find the long side.

Step 1 Write the ratios as equivalent fractions.

$$\frac{\text{short}}{\text{long}}\frac{3}{5} = \frac{39}{?}\frac{\text{short}}{\text{long}}$$

The long side is 65.

Step 2 Multiply both numerator and denominator by 13.

$$\frac{\text{short}}{\text{long}}\frac{3}{5} = \frac{39}{65}\frac{\text{short}}{\text{long}}$$

The number 13 is called the scale factor. The *scale factor* is the number that you multiply the numerator and denominator of one side of the equivalent-fraction equation by to obtain the numerator and denominator of the other side of the equivalent-fraction equation. If you know the scale factor, you can find the missing sides in similar figures.

ACTIVITY

The original triangle was photocopied, producing the new triangle.

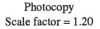

Photocopy
Scale factor = 1.20

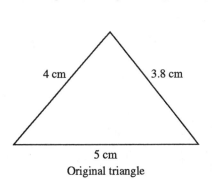

4 cm   3.8 cm

5 cm
Original triangle

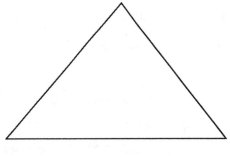

New triangle

A. Use a centimeter ruler to measure the 3 sides of the new triangle.

B. To check to see that the scale factor on the photocopy machine is accurate, the long side of the new triangle was measured and found to be 6 cm. Does this show that the scale factor is accurate? Explain.

C. Calculate the theoretical measurements for the medium side and the short side of the enlarged triangle using the scale factor 1.20.

D. Do your theoretical measurements and actual measurements agree?

If you do not know the scale factor, but you do know the measures of a pair of corresponding sides, you can calculate the scale factor.

EXAMPLE

Find the scale factor.

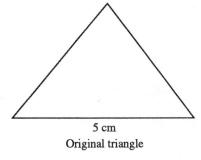

5 cm
Original triangle

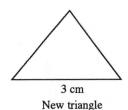

3 cm
New triangle

SOLUTION

Use the corresponding pair of sides that are given: 5 and 3.

Find the ratio $\dfrac{\text{New triangle}}{\text{Original triangle}}$

$\dfrac{3}{5} \dfrac{\text{New triangle}}{\text{Original triangle}} = 0.6$ The scale factor is 0.6.

Notice that to find the scale factor, you should begin with a known number in the new figure and divide it by the corresponding number in the original figure.

EXERCISES

7. Find the missing sides in each pair of similar figures by writing equivalent fractions. Show how you found your answers. Figures are not shown to scale.

a. Original Figure
7, 5, 6, ?, ?, 18

b. 8, 12, Original Figure, 2, ?

c. Find the scale factor for the triangles.

d. Find the scale factor for the rectangles.

e. Change the side in part a measuring 18 to a length of 15. Find the new scale factor. Use the scale factor to find the missing sides.

8. Find the scale factor for each pair of figures. You will need to measure a pair of corresponding sides. Indicate which sides you measured.

a. original figure   photocopy

b. original figure   photocopy

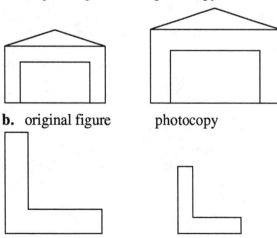

©1995, Janson Publications, Inc.

9. Use arrows to match the scale factor with the appropriate relationship between the original figure and its photocopy.

   a. Scale factor < 1   photocopy is larger than original

   b. Scale factor = 1   photocopy is smaller than original

   c. Scale factor > 1   photocopy is congruent to original

10. Explain why the scale factor for two congruent figures is 1. Use diagrams in your explanation.

11. For figures to be *similar*, that is, to have the same shape, the scale factor for all pairs of corresponding sides must be the same number and corresponding angles must have the same measure. Do all of your similar figures in Exercise 1 meet these conditions? Explain.

Graph Paper Art

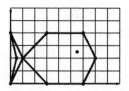

You can create *similar* figures, that is, figures having the same shape, using graph paper. For example, starting with the small triangle below, the coordinates of each vertex were multiplied by 3 to get three new points. These new points were plotted and connected, creating a large triangle similar to the original triangle.

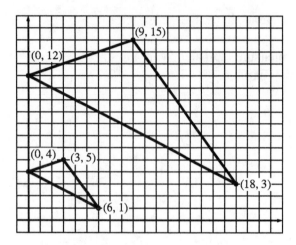

EXERCISES

1. Measure the sides of the two triangles above using a centimeter ruler. Copy and complete the table.

Triangle	Short Side	Medium Side	Long Side	$\dfrac{\text{Short Side}}{\text{Medium Side}}$	$\dfrac{\text{Short Side}}{\text{Long Side}}$	$\dfrac{\text{Medium Side}}{\text{Long Side}}$
Small						
Large						

2. What scale factor can be used to obtain the large triangle from the small triangle? Explain.

3. Compare your scale factor and the number that was used to multiply the coordinates.

4. Use graph paper for parts a through c.

    a. Multiply the coordinates of each point in the figure below by 4. Plot the new points on graph paper and connect them to create a figure similar to the original figure.

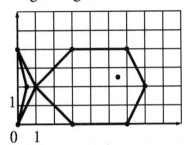

    b. Multiply the coordinates of each point in the figure below by 2. Plot the new points on graph paper and connect them to create a figure similar to the original figure.

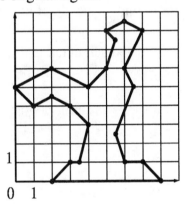

    c. Multiply the coordinates of each point in the figure below by $\frac{1}{2}$ or 0.5. Plot the new points on graph paper and connect them to create a figure similar to the original figure.

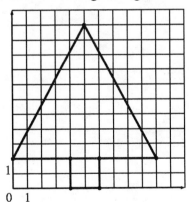

           Building Foundations 27

5. Using shadows and a meter stick, you can estimate the height of a flagpole. You will also need a sunny day!

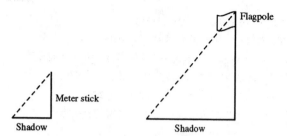

a. Work in pairs or small groups. Place the meter stick perpendicular to the ground and measure the length of its shadow. Measure the length of the shadow of the flagpole.

b. Write equivalent fractions using the heights and shadow lengths.

c. What is the scale factor? Use the scale factor to find the height of the flagpole.

d. Explain why the height of the flagpole is an estimated height rather than the actual height.

6. Using graph paper, create a design that contains at least two similar figures.

Capture-Recapture Experiment

Biologists use a technique called "capture-recapture" to estimate sizes of populations that are difficult to determine directly. For example, to estimate the total number of fish in a pond, a biologist caught 60 fish, tagged them by putting an identifiable mark on each fish, and returned each tagged fish to the pond. After allowing the tagged fish to swim around for a day or two, the biologist caught a sample of 50 fish. The number of tagged fish in the sample was 15.

Since the relative frequency of tagged fish in the sample is approximately equal to the relative frequency of tagged fish in the pond, the biologist can use a *proportion* (an equation which states that two fractions are equal) to estimate the number of fish in the pond.

$$\frac{\text{number of tagged fish in sample}}{\text{total number of fish in sample}} = \frac{\text{number of tagged fish in pond}}{\text{total number of fish in pond}}$$

Let x = total number of fish in the pond.

Step 1 Write a proportion:

$$\frac{15}{50} = \frac{60}{x}$$

Recall that the scale factor is the number that you multiply the numerator and denominator of one side of the equation by to obtain the numerator and denominator of the other side. Here the scale factor is $\frac{60}{15}$, or 4.

Step 2 Use the scale factor:

$$\frac{15}{50} = \frac{60}{200}$$

Since $x = 200$, the approximate number of fish in the pond is 200.

The method described above works even if the scale factor is not a counting number. For instance, if we change the number of tagged fish in the sample from 15 to 16, we would proceed as follows

$$\frac{60}{16} = 3.75 = \text{scale factor}$$

Step 1 Write a proportion:

$$\frac{16}{50} = \frac{60}{x}$$

Step 2 Use the scale factor:

$$\frac{16}{50} = \frac{60}{187.5}$$

Since $x = 187.5$, the approximate number of fish in the pond is 188. To see that this operation is "legal" notice that you are multiplying the original fraction $\frac{16}{50}$ by 1 in the disguise of 3.75/3.75, and therefore are not changing its value.

$$\frac{16}{50} \cdot 1 = \frac{16}{50} \cdot \frac{3.75}{3.75} = \frac{60}{187.5}$$

Check
using a
calculator

$$\frac{16}{50} = 0.32 \qquad\qquad \frac{60}{187.5} = 0.32$$

EXPERIMENT

In this experiment, you will use the capture-recapture technique to estimate the size of a population consisting of an unknown number of pinto beans (brown beans). To do this, you will tag the pinto beans by removing some and replacing them with navy beans (white beans). You will then choose a sample from the population and estimate the size of the population based on the relative frequency of navy beans in the sample.

PREPARATION

1. Work in groups of 4 or 5. Each group should have one bag of pinto beans, approximately 1/4 of a bag of navy beans, and a table of random numbers.

2. Choose a random number from 500 to 999, inclusive. First, choose a random hundreds digit between 5 and 9, inclusive, from the table of random numbers. Use the next two digits in the random number table for the tens and units digits, respectively.

3. Count out exactly the same number of pinto beans as your random number and place them in a coffee can. Report the size of your population to your teacher, who will collect and label each coffee can by group.

PROCEDURE

Your teacher will redistribute the coffee cans, but to different groups. Be sure that your group has a coffee can different from the one that you filled with beans.

1. a. Tag the pinto beans in the coffee can with navy beans as follows:
      Remove ≈ 1/3 cup pinto beans and count the exact number removed.

Replace the removed pinto beans by counting out the exact same number of navy beans and placing them in your coffee can. Shake the coffee can to mix the navy beans in the population.

b. Is the size of your population the same as it was originally?

c. How many navy (tagged) beans are in your coffee can?

2. a. Take a sample, consisting of 100 beans, from your coffee can.

b. How many pinto beans are in your sample?

c. How many navy beans are in your sample?

d. Find the relative frequency of navy beans in your sample.

e. Estimate the total number of beans in your coffee can using the following proportion.

$$\frac{\text{no. of navy beans in sample}}{\text{total no. of beans in sample}} = \frac{\text{no. of navy beans in population}}{\text{total no. of beans in population}}$$

3. Return your sample to the coffee can. Carefully shake the coffee can to randomize the navy beans in the population.

4. Repeat steps 2 and 3 four more times.

Record your information in a table similar to the one below.

Sample Number	Number of Navy Beans in Sample	Total Number of Beans in Sample	Proportion	Estimate of Total Number of Beans in Population
1				
2				
3				
4				
5				

Find the average of your estimates of the total number of beans in the population. Show your work.

5. You can obtain another estimate of the total number of beans in your population by treating all five samples as one large sample. This is called *pooling* your sample data.

a. Find the sum of the numbers in the column "Number of Navy Beans in Sample".

b. Find the sum of the numbers in the column "Total Number of Beans in Sample".

c. Write a proportion using your answers to parts a and b and your original number of tagged beans.

d. Use your proportion to estimate the total number of beans in your population. Show your work.

6. Check with the group that counted the beans in your coffee can to see how your estimates compare to the actual population.

a. What is the actual population?

b. What is the difference between the actual population and the estimated population found by averaging in part 4?

c. What is the difference between the actual population and the estimated population found by pooling in part 5?

d. Are both of your estimates reasonable estimates of the actual population? Explain.

e. Check with other groups in your class to see whether both of their estimates are reasonable estimates of their populations. Describe their findings.

7. Now that you know the actual number of beans in your population, you can investigate the effects of sample size on the accuracy of your estimate.

a. Take 3 more samples, one of size 25, one of size 50 and one of size 200. For sample size = 100, you should use your first sample of size 100 from the previous table. For sample size = 500, use the pooled sample information from part 5. Copy and complete the following table.

Sample size	Number of Navy Beans in Sample	Total Number of Beans in Sample	Proportion	Estimate of Total Number of Beans in Population	Difference: Estimate – Population
25					
50					
100					
200					
500					

b. What effect does a larger sample size appear to have on your estimate of the population? Explain.

c. Check with other groups to see if their data supports your theory. Describe their findings.

Getting the Picture

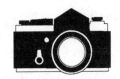

Have you ever heard the expression "A picture is worth a thousand words?" It suggests that a drawing can show a lot of information that would take pages to describe in words. In the study of mathematics, pictures or diagrams can often be used to describe fairly complex mathematical relationships in simple, compact, visual terms.

In this lesson, you will practice drawing pictures to describe relationships among quantities. You will collect data, display your data in a table, look for patterns, and describe patterns using mathematical expressions. You will create graphs to describe relationships in visual terms. You will also interpret pictures, tables, expressions, and graphs and translate from one representation to another. What you learn in this lesson can and should be applied thoughout your study of mathematics.

EXERCISES

1. Each situation is represented by diagrams. Identify the person represented by each diagram.

   a. Abdul has 3 more baseball cards than Sam.

   ▓ ▓   ▓ ▓ ▓ ▓ ▓

   _____   _____

   b. José has 3 times as many pennies as George.

                o o o o
                o o o o
   o o o o   o o o o

   _____   _____

   c. Sally is $\frac{1}{2}$ the age of her brother Jamie.

   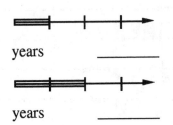

   years _____

   years _____

   d. Tom received twice as many votes as Sari. (Leave one blank empty.)

   √ √ √ √ √   _____

   √ √ √ √ √ √ √   _____

   √ √ √ √ √ √ √ √√   _____

2. Draw a picture to illustrate each situation.

   a. Ann has 4 more books than John.

   b. Jane sold $\frac{1}{3}$ as many boxes of cookies as Rose.

Ann   John

                        Jane   Rose

3. Today is 3 degrees colder than yesterday.

   a. Choose a temperature for today (between 50 and 55) and indicate your choice here.

   b. Copy and color the "Today" thermometer to illustrate your choice.

   c. Based on your choice for today, what was the temperature yesterday?

   d. Copy and color the "Yesterday" thermometer to illustrate the temperature for yesterday.

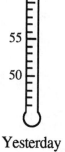

Yesterday   Today

   e. Describe how your thermometers would look if yesterday were 3 degrees colder than today.

4. Circle all descriptions that are represented by the diagrams.

   a.

Ayesha

Mark

   i. Ayesha has 2 more pencils than Mark.

   ii. Mark has 2 pencils fewer than Ayesha.

   iii. Mark has 2 more pencils than Ayesha.

   iv. Ayesha has 2 pencils fewer than Mark.

b.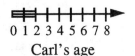

Carl's age   Joan's age

i. Carl is 4 years older than Joan.

ii. Joan is 3 times as old as Carl.

iii. Carl is 4 years younger than Joan.

iv. Joan is 1/3 as old as Carl.

v. Joan is 4 years younger than Carl.

vi. Joan is 4 years older than Carl.

vii. Carl is 1/3 as old as Joan.

viii. Carl is 3 times as old as Joan.

5. Write a sentence that describes the situation represented by the diagrams.

a. $ \$ \quad \$ \quad \$ $

Tom

$ \$ \quad \$ \quad \$ \quad \$ $

Alice

b.

Tanya's age   Darren's age

6. Serafina is 2 years older than Joseph.

a. Copy and complete the table with possible ages for Serafina and Joseph.

b. In the table, a rule can be applied to each number in the first column to get the number in the second column. Describe this rule.

c. If x represents Joseph's age, write an expression using x that represents Serafina's age. Place x and your expression at the bottom of the appropriate columns in the table.

Joseph's age	Serafina's age
1	3
2	
3	
7	9
$8\frac{1}{2}$	
10	
	15
14	

d. If Joseph's age is 20, how old is Serafina? Explain how to get your answer using your expression.

e. If Serafina's age is 20, how old is Joseph? What equation could you solve to obtain the answer?

f. On graph paper, copy the graph shown here. Plot the data points from the table in part a on the graph. The point that corresponds to Joseph's age of 7 and Serafina's age of 9 has been done for you.

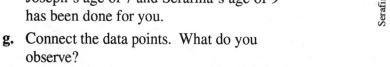

g. Connect the data points. What do you observe?

h. If Joseph is 5 years old, how old is Serafina? Explain how to find the answer using the graph.

i. If Serafina is 11 years old, how old is Joseph? Explain how to find the answer using the graph.

7. The price of a certain type of coffee bean is $3 per pound.

a. Copy and complete the table.

b. In the table, a rule can be applied to each number in the first column to get the number in the second column. Describe this rule.

c. If x represents the number of pounds of coffee beans bought, write an expression using x that represents the total cost. Place x and your expression at the bottom of the appropriate columns in the table.

Number of Pounds Bought	Total Cost (in dollars)
0	
1	
2	
3	
	18.00
7	
$8\frac{1}{2}$	
10	

d. If the number of pounds of coffee beans bought is 15, what is the total cost? Explain how to get your answer using your expression.

e. If the total cost is $60, how many pounds of coffee beans were bought? What equation could you solve to obtain the answer?

f. Using graph paper, plot the data points in the table. Label the horizontal axis "Number of Pounds Bought" and the vertical axis "Total Cost (in dollars)."

g. Connect the data points. What type of geometric shape do you get?

h. If 8 pounds of coffee beans are bought, what is the total cost? Explain how to find the answer using the graph.

i. If the total cost is $15, how many pounds of coffee beans were bought? Explain how to find the answer using the graph.

8. Danielle has a baby-sitting job. The graph shown here describes the relationship between the hours that she works and the money she earns.

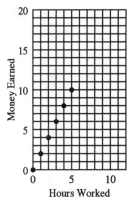

a. Copy and complete the table using the points on the graph.

Time Worked (hours)	Money Earned (dollars)
0	
1	
2	
3	6
4	
5	

b. Include four additional points in the table following the established pattern.

c. In the table, a rule can be applied to each number in the first column to get the number in the second column. Describe this rule.

d. If x represents the number of hours worked, write an expression using x that represents the amount of money earned. Place x and your expression at the bottom of the appropriate columns in the table.

e. If Danielle works 7 hours, how much money will she earn? Explain how you found your answer.

f. Danielle wants to buy a sweater that costs $16. How many hours must she work to earn $16? Explain how you found your answer.

g. How much money does Danielle earn per hour for baby-sitting?

9. Ari and Ned are brothers. If x represents Ari's age, $x - 4$ represents Ned's age.

a. Copy and complete the table with possible ages for Ari and Ned.

b. In the table, a rule can be applied to each number in the first column to get the number in the second column. Describe this rule.

Ari's age	Ned's age
4	
7	
	8
13	
x	$x - 4$

c. If Ari is 10 years old, how old is Ned? Explain how to use x and $x - 4$ to find the answer.

d. If Ned is 5 years old, how old is Ari? What equation could you solve to obtain the answer?

e. Graph the data in the table and connect the points. Label the horizontal axis with "Ari's Age" and the vertical axis with "Ned's Age."

f. If Ari is 11 years old, how old is Ned? Explain how you found your answer.

g. If Ned is 6 years old, how old is Ari? Explain how you found your answer.

h. Fill in the blanks with the correct brother's name.

    i. ____ is 4 years older than ____.

    ii. ____ is 4 years younger than ____.

Explorations with Prisms

1. Cut out and assemble the four prism models. Notice that a prism is named by the shape of its base.

Triangular Prism   Rectangular Prism   Pentagonal Prism   Hexagonal Prism

The features of a prism are:

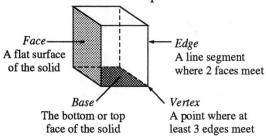

Face — A flat surface of the solid

Edge — A line segment where 2 faces meet

Base — The bottom or top face of the solid

Vertex — A point where at least 3 edges meet

2. Copy and complete the table. Leave space below your table for a line you will add later.

Prisms

Name of Shape of Base	Number of Sides of Base	Number of Faces	Number of Vertices	Number of Edges
	3			
	4			
	5			
	6			

3. A heptagonal prism has a 7-sided base. Predict the number of faces, vertices and edges for this prism.

4. An octagonal prism has an 8-sided base. Predict the number of faces, vertices and edges for this prism.

5. **a.** In the table, a rule can be applied to each number in the "Number of Sides of Base" column to get the number in the "Number of Faces" column. Describe this rule.

   b. If x represents the number of sides of the base of a prism, write an expression using x that represents the number of faces of the prism. Place x and your expression at the bottom of the appropriate columns in the table.

6. **a.** In the table, a rule can be applied to each number in the "Number of Sides of Base" column to get the number in the "Number of Vertices" column. Describe this rule.

   b. If x represents the number of sides of the base of a prism, write an expression using x that represents the number of vertices of the prism. Place your expression at the bottom of the appropriate column in the table.

7. **a.** In the table, a rule can be applied to each number in the "Number of Sides of Base" column to get the number in the "Number of Edges" column. Describe this rule.

   b. If x represents the number of sides of the base of a prism, write an expression using x that represents the number of edges of the prism. Place your expression at the bottom of the appropriate column in the table.

8. Use the information in your table to make three graphs. For each, the horizontal axis should be labelled "Number of Sides of Base". The vertical axes should be "Number of Faces", "Number of Vertices", and "Number of Edges".

9. Is it possible to have a prism with a 2-sided base?

10. On your graph representing "Number of Faces" vs. "Number of Sides of Base", include 5 new data points following the established pattern. Use the graph to answer the following questions.

   a. If the number of sides of the base of a prism is 10, how many faces does the prism have?

   b. If the number of faces of a prism is 9, how many sides does the base of the prism have?

11. On your graph representing "Number of Vertices" vs. "Number of Sides of Base", include 5 new data points following the established pattern. Use the graph to answer the following questions.

    a. If the number of vertices of a prism is 20, how many sides does the base of the prism have?

    b. If the number of sides of the base of a prism is 9, how many vertices does the prism have?

12. On your graph representing "Number of Edges" vs. "Number of Sides of Base", include 5 new data points following the established pattern.

    a. If the number of edges of a prism is 24, what is the shape of the base of the prism?

    b. If the number of sides of the base of the prism is 9, how many edges does the prism have?

13. Imagine a prism with a 20-sided base.

    a. How many faces does this prism have? Explain how you got your answer.

    b. How many vertices does this prism have? Explain how you got your answer.

    c. How many edges does this prism have? Explain how you got your answer.

14. The Swiss mathematician Leonhard Euler (1707-1780, pronounced "oiler") proved a relationship between the number of faces and vertices of a prism and the number of edges of the prism. Try to rediscover Euler's Formula by studying the 2 numbers in the "Number of Faces" and "Number of Vertices" columns and comparing your result with the number in the "Number of Edges" column.

    a. Write Euler's Formula using the words "number of faces," "number of vertices," and "number of edges."

    b. Write Euler's Formula using an equation, where F = number of faces, V = number of vertices, and E = number of edges.

Explorations with Pyramids

1. Cut out and assemble the four pyramid models. Notice that a pyramid is named by the shape of its base.

Triangular Pyramid   Rectangular Pyramid   Pentagonal Pyramid   Hexagonal Pyramid

The features of a pyramid are:

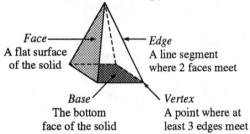

Face — A flat surface of the solid

Edge — A line segment where 2 faces meet

Base — The bottom face of the solid

Vertex — A point where at least 3 edges meet

2. Copy and complete the table. Leave space below your table for a line you will add later.

Pyramids

Name of Shape of Base	Number of Sides of Base	Number of Faces	Number of Vertices	Number of Edges
	3			
	4			
	5			
	6			

3. A heptagonal pyramid has a 7-sided base. Predict the number of faces, vertices and edges for this pyramid.

4. An octagonal pyramid has an 8-sided base. Predict the number of faces, vertices and edges for this pyramid.

5. a. In the table, a rule can be applied to each number in the "Number of Sides of Base" column to get the number in the "Number of Faces" column. Describe this rule.

   b. If x represents the number of sides of the base of a pyramid, write an expression using x that represents the number of faces of the pyramid. Place x and your expression at the bottom of the appropriate columns in the table.

6. a. In the table, a rule can be applied to each number in the "Number of Sides of Base" column to get the number in the "Number of Vertices" column. Describe this rule.

   b. If x represents the number of sides of the base of a pyramid, write an expression using x that represents the number of vertices of the pyramid. Place your expression at the bottom of the appropriate column in the table.

7. a. In the table, a rule can be applied to each number in the "Number of Sides of Base" column to get the number in the Number of Edges column. Describe this rule.

   b. If x represents the number of sides of the base of a pyramid, write an expression using x that represents the number of edges of the pyramid. Place your expression at the bottom of the appropriate column in the table.

8. Use the information in your table to make three graphs. For each, the horizontal axis should be labelled "Number of Sides of Base". The vertical axes should be "Number of Faces", "Number of Vertices", and "Number of Edges".

9. Is it possible to have a pyramid with a 2-sided base?

10. On your graph representing "Number of Faces" vs. "Number of Sides of Base", include 5 new data points following the established pattern. Use the graph to answer the following questions.

   a. If the number of sides of the base of a pyramid is 10, how many faces does the pyramid have?

   b. If the number of faces of a pyramid is 9, how many sides does the base of the pyramid have?

11. On your graph representing "Number of Vertices" vs. "Number of Sides of Base", include 5 new data points following the established pattern. Use the graph to answer the following questions.

   a. If the number of vertices of a pyramid is 11, how many sides does the base of the pyramid have?

   b. If the number of sides of the base of a pyramid is 9, how many vertices does the pyramid have?

12. On your graph representing "Number of Edges" vs. "Number of Sides of Base", include 5 new data points following the established pattern.

   a. If the number of edges of a pyramid is 16, what is the shape of the base of the pyramid?

   b. If the number of sides of the base of the pyramid is 9, how many edges does the pyramid have?

13. Imagine a pyramid with a 20-sided base.

   a. How many faces does this pyramid have? Explain how you got your answer.

   b. How many vertices does this pyramid have? Explain how you got your answer.

   c. How many edges does this pyramid have? Explain how you got your answer.

14. The Swiss mathematician Leonhard Euler (1707-1780, pronounced "oiler") proved a relationship between the number of faces and vertices of a pyramid and the number of edges of the pyramid. Try to rediscover Euler's Formula by studying the 2 numbers in the "Number of Faces" and "Number of Vertices" columns and comparing your result with the number in the "Number of Edges" column.

   a. Write Euler's Formula using the words "number of faces," "number of vertices," and "number of edges."

   b. Write Euler's Formula using an equation, where F = number of faces, V = number of vertices, and E = number of edges.

Thinking Graphically I

Time & Distance

A *line graph* can be used to show changes in data over time. Suppose that you and several of your friends went on a trip in a car driven by your friend's mother, Ms. Veri Swift. She picked you up at your home. The graph below is for the entire trip to your destination. It shows the distance in miles you have traveled from your home after a certain amount of time in hours. For example, after driving for 2 hours (time = 2), you have traveled 110 miles from home (distance = 110).

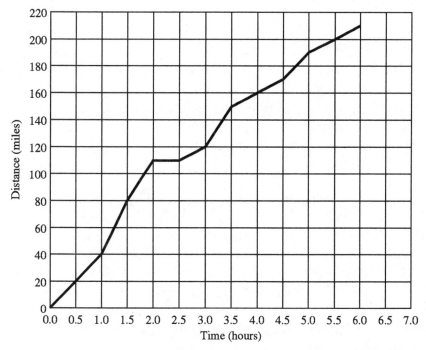

Note. The graph is not a picture of the route you traveled on the trip.

EXERCISES

1. What was the total time needed to reach your final destination? (Note: be sure to include the "units" with each of your answers; for this question the unit is hours.)

2. What was the total distance for the trip?

3. Copy and complete the table using the graph.

4. a. How far did you travel during the time interval from time = 2 hours to time = 2.5 hours?

   b. Write a brief story to explain what Ms. Swift, you, and your friends might have been doing during this time interval.

Time (hours)	Distance (miles)
0	
1	
2	110
3	
4	
5	
6	

5. Estimate the amount of time it took to travel the given distance from home.

   a. 120 miles

   b. 140 miles

   c. Describe how you found the answers to parts a and b.

6. After traveling for 4 hours you saw an amusement park. When you arrived at the destination for your trip, you and your friends tried to convince Ms. Swift to drive back to the amusement park. How far would she have to drive to return to it? Explain how to estimate this distance. Do you think you could convince her to drive you back?

The graph may be thought of as a set of points which can be located by a pair of values, time and distance. For convenience, the values are written in parentheses, (time,distance). For example, the pair of values (2,110) represents the point on the graph which corresponds to time = 2 hours and distance = 110 miles. The numbers 2 and 110 are called the time and distance *coordinates* of the point (2,110). The grid on which the graph is drawn is called a *coordinate plane*. The line along which time is marked off is called the *horizontal axis* and the line along which distance is marked off is called the *vertical axis*. We might also refer to the horizontal axis as the time axis and the vertical axis as the distance axis. When labeling a point on the graph with its coordinates in parentheses, write the horizontal coordinate in the first position and the vertical coordinate in the second position. So the point having coordinates (2,110) on our (time,distance) graph is quite different from the point having coordinates (110,2). If the point (110,2) were on our graph, then at time = 110 hours you would only have traveled distance = 2 miles—pretty slow!

EXERCISES

7. What are the coordinates of the point on the graph which corresponds to time = 1 hour?

8. What are the coordinates of a point on the graph which corresponds to distance = 160 miles?

9. What are the coordinates of a point on the graph which corresponds to distance = 110 miles?

10. If the point (4,100) were on the graph, how far would Ms. Swift have traveled after 4 hours?

11. Is the point (4,100) on the graph?

12. What point having time coordinate 4 is on the graph?

13. Why couldn't (4,100) and (4,160) both be on the graph for your trip with Ms. Swift?

In addition to distance traveled at a given time, it is also interesting to consider distances traveled during various time intervals. The 1st time interval in the figure below is from time = 0 to time = 1 hours. During the 1st time interval, the distance traveled changed from 0 miles at 0 hours to 40 miles at 1 hour, so the distance traveled in the 1st time interval is 40 - 0, or 40 miles. The 5th time interval is from time = 4 to time = 5 hours. During the 5th time interval, the distance traveled changed from 160 miles at 4 hours to 190 miles at 5 hours, so the distance traveled in the 5th time interval is 190 - 160, or 30 miles.

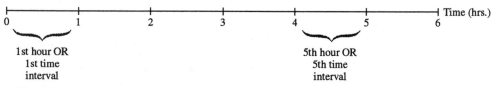

EXERCISES

14. When is the 3rd time interval?

15. Which time interval is given by time = 5 to time = 6 hours?

16. During the 1st hour (from time = 0 to time = 1 hr), what is the distance traveled?

17. During the 2nd hour (from time = 1 to time = 2 hr), what is the distance traveled?

18. During the interval from time = 2 hrs. to time = 4 hrs., what is the distance traveled?

19. Copy and complete the following tables.

Time Interval (hours)	Distance Traveled (miles)
0 – 1	40
1 – 2	
2 – 3	
3 – 4	
4 – 5	30
5 – 6	

Time Interval (hours)	Distance Traveled (miles)
0 – 2	110
2 – 4	
4 – 6	

Thinking Graphically II

Time & Speed

The data in a line graph can sometimes be used to determine additional information. Suppose that you and several of your friends went on a trip in a car driven by your friend's mother, Ms. Veri Swift. She picked you up at your home. The graph below is for the entire trip to your destination. It shows the distance in miles you have traveled from your home after a certain amount of time in hours.

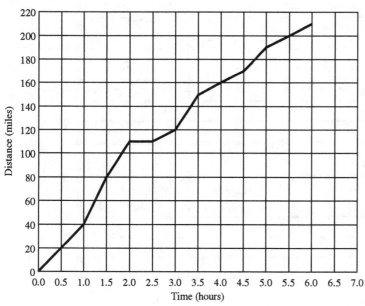

Average speed for an interval of time can be calculated as

$$\text{average speed} = \frac{\text{distance traveled during time interval}}{\text{time elapsed during the interval}}$$

The units used for average speed are simply the units used for distance divided by the units used for time . Always provide the units with your answers. For example, during the first 2 hours of the trip (from time = 0 to time = 2 hours) the graph shows that you traveled 110 miles. So your average speed during that 2 hour time interval was

$$\frac{110 \text{ miles}}{2 \text{ hours}} = 55 \frac{\text{miles}}{\text{hour}} = 55 \text{ miles/hour}.$$

55 miles/hour is an example of a rate, which we may write as 55 miles per hour and abbreviate as 55 mph.

EXERCISES

1. a. What would be your average speed and its units if you traveled 20 feet in 5 seconds?

   b. A particular athlete can run the 100 meter dash in approximately 9.1 seconds. What is the athlete's average speed (include units, of course) for the entire race?

2. Copy and complete Tables I & II by using information on the graph.

Table I. 1-hour time intervals

Time Interval (hours)	Distance Traveled (miles)	Time Elapsed (hours)	Average Speed (miles/hour)
0 – 1	40		
1 – 2			
2 – 3			
3 – 4			
4 – 5	30		
5 – 6			

Table II. 2-hour time intervals

Time Interval (hours)	Distance Traveled (miles)	Time Elapsed (hours)	Average Speed (miles/hour)
0 – 2	110		
2 – 4			
4 – 6			

3. For which time interval in Table I is the average speed largest?

4. For which of the following time intervals does the graph appear to be steepest?

   a. 0 – 1 hrs.   **b.** 1 – 2 hrs.   **c.** 2 – 3 hrs.

   d. 3 – 4 hrs.   **e.** 4 – 5 hrs.   **f.** 5 – 6 hrs.

5. What guess or conjecture would you make about the relationship between steepness of a (time,distance) graph on a time interval and the average speed during that time interval?

6. Examine the steepness of the graph for the following time intervals.

   a. from time = 0 to time = 1 hour

   b. from time = 3 to time = 4 hours

   What do you notice about the steepness of those two portions of the graph?

7. Notice that the graph changes steepness during the time interval time = 3 to time = 4 hours. How can you explain that feature of the graph in terms of Ms. Swift's driving behavior during that time interval?

8. Copy the graph below on graph paper. For each time interval in Table I, plot the corresponding average speed for that interval. For example, from Table I the average speed for the 1st hour (time = 0 hrs. to time = 1 hr.) is 40 miles/hour, so the graph should show a speed of 40 miles/hour for all times between 0 and 1 hours (such as 1/2 hr. or 3/4 hr.). This portion of the graph is already provided. The portion for the 5th time interval (time = 4 to time = 5) is also provided. Plot the remaining intervals.

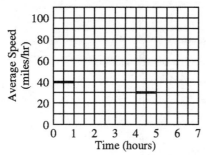

9. For which time interval in your graph from Exercise 8 is the average speed smallest?

10. Could you have predicted the time interval with the smallest average speed by looking at the steepness of the (time, distance) graph? Why or why not?

11. Look at the shape of the (time, distance) graph for your trip and determine for what time interval of length 1/2 hour the graph is least steep.

　a. How far did the car travel during that time interval?

　b. What was the average speed during that time interval?

　c. Describe what Ms. Swift, you and your friends might have been doing during that time period.

12. a. Estimate the distance traveled during the 1/2 hour interval from time = 1/2 hour to time = 1 hour.

　b. What was the average speed during that 1/2 hour interval?

13. a. Copy and complete the following table.

    b. On graph paper, plot the information in the table. Your graph should be similar to the one in Exercise 8.

Time Interval (hours)	Approx. Distance Traveled (miles)	Average Speed (miles/hour)
0 – 0.5		
0.5 – 1		
1 – 1.5		
1.5 – 2		
2 – 2.5		
2.5 – 3		
3 – 3.5		
3.5 – 4		
4 – 4.5		
4.5 – 5		
5 – 5.5		
5.5 – 6		

14. A (time, distance) graph for a school bus trip you took to the "Awesome Amusement Park" is provided here.

a. Examine the steepness of the graph to select a .5-hour time interval during which the bus traveled at its highest average speed.

b. Determine a second .5-hour time interval during which the bus traveled at its highest average speed.

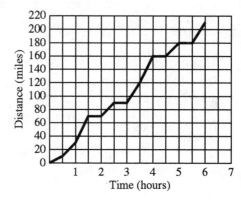

c. How many stops did the bus make? During what time intervals were they made?

d. What was the total distance for the entire trip? What was the total time required for the trip? What was the average speed for the entire trip?

©1995, Janson Publications, Inc.

Explorations with Perimeter

A rectangle is a closed four-sided figure in which the two pairs of opposite sides are equal in length and all four angles are right angles. A square is a rectangle in which all four sides are equal in length.

EXAMPLE 1

A baseball diamond is a square with a distance of 90 feet between corners (bases). If you hit a home run and run around the bases how far will you have run?

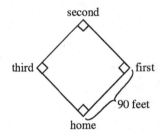

SOLUTION

The distance around the bases is 90 + 90 + 90 + 90 or 360 feet. This is called the *perimeter* of the square.

EXERCISES

1. Copy each square below and label the remaining sides. Then determine the perimeter.

   a. **b.** **c.**

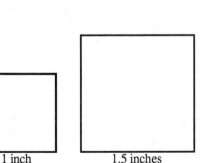 

1 inch   1.5 inches   2 inches

2. a. Copy and complete the table below.

Length of One Side (in inches)	Perimeter of the Square (in inches)
0.5	
1	
1.5	
2	
	10
	12

b. In the table, a rule can be applied to each number in the first column to obtain the number in the second column. Describe this rule.

c. If *x* represents the length of one side of a square, write an expression using *x* that represents the perimeter of the square. Place *x* and your expression at the bottom of the appropriate columns in the table.

d. Determine the perimeter of a square if the length of each side is 5 feet. Explain how to find the answer using your expression in part c.

e. Plot the data points in the table on graph paper. Plot perimeter on the vertical axis and the length of a side on the horizontal axis. Make sure the vertical scale goes up through 20 inches.

f. Connect the data points. Describe the graph.

g. Use the graph to determine the perimeter if the length of a side is $3\frac{1}{2}$ inches. Use the graph to determine the length of a side if the perimeter is 16 inches.

h. Since a square has four sides of equal length, when you know the perimeter you can determine the length of each side. If the perimeter is represented by *P*, write an expression that represents the length of the side. Place *P* and your expression at the bottom of the appropriate columns in the table in part a.

EXAMPLE 2

A rectangular swimming pool has a length of 18.2 yards and a width of 6.4 yards. If you swim once around the edge of the pool, how many yards will you swim?

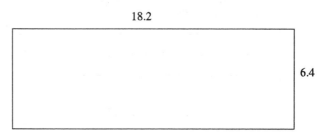

18.2

6.4

SOLUTION

The distance around the pool can be calculated by adding the lengths of each side.

$$18.2 + 6.4 + 18.2 + 6.4 = 49.2 \text{ yards}$$

This is called the *perimeter* of the rectangle.

You can find the perimeter of any closed figure composed of line segments by adding the lengths of the sides.

EXERCISES

3. Copy each rectangle below and label the remaining sides. Then determine the perimeter.

a.
10

4

b.
8

3

4. a. Make a table with three columns; label them Width, Length and Perimeter. Complete the table by choosing at least three different values for width and length.

   b. If w represents the width and l represents the length, write an expression for the perimeter in terms of w and l. Place w and l and your expression at the bottom of the appropriate columns in the table.

5. a. If the width of a rectangle is 4 units and the length is 5 units, determine the perimeter.

   b. Draw this rectangle on graph paper and find the perimeter by counting units.

   c. Does your calculated perimeter agree with your drawing?

                                          Building Foundations

d. If the width of a rectangle is 5 units and the length is 4 units, determine the perimeter. Draw a picture of this rectangle on graph paper.

e. What do you notice about the rectangles and their perimeters drawn in parts b and d?

The perimeter formula you developed in Exercise 4, part b, might look like

Perimeter $= w + l + w + l$

   or

Perimeter $= 2l + 2w$.

As you can see, in order to find the perimeter (the distance around the figure) we must count the width twice and the length twice and add these together. Remember that when swimming around the pool you must swim along each side, which means you will have covered the length twice and the width twice.

Suppose we have a rectangle with a perimeter of 36 units and a width of 8 units. If we know the perimeter and the width how can we determine the length? Using our formula above, substitute 8 for width and 36 for the perimeter.

$$36 = 2(l) + 2(8)$$

If we subtract two times the width (16) from the perimeter, the remaining distance must be twice the length. Therefore, two times the length is $36 - 16 = 20$, so the length must be 10 units long. Thus, if the perimeter is 36 units and the width is 8 units the length is 10 units.

EXERCISES

6. On graph paper, draw a picture of a rectangle whose perimeter is 36 units and whose width is 8 units.

7. If the perimeter of a rectangle is given as 36 units, fill in the table below for values of width and length.

Width	Length	Perimeter
8		36
12		36
	3	36

8. On graph paper, draw a picture of the last two rectangles described in the table above. Note that rectangles with the same perimeter can look different!

9. For the last rectangle in the table for Exercise 7, what equation could you solve to determine its width?

10. Plot the data points from the table with length on the vertical axis and width on the horizontal axis.

11. Connect the data points. Describe the graph.

12. Using your graph, determine the width of a rectangle if the length is 4 units. What is the length if the width is 4 units?

Explorations with Area

The area of a closed figure is a measure of its surface. Area is measured in *square units*, which are squares whose sides are one unit long.

1 square centimeter

1 square inch

To find the area of a closed figure, find the number of square units that it takes to cover the figure exactly.

EXERCISES

1. Suppose you have several square posters that each have a length of 1 foot. You want to cover a rectangular portion of wall with these posters. The measurements of the portion you want to cover are 3 feet by 5 feet.

    a. What is the area of each poster?

    b. Determine the area of the wall to be covered by counting the number of square feet in the diagram. (Be sure to indicate units.)

    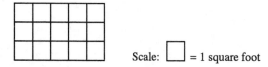

    Scale: ☐ = 1 square foot

    c. How many posters will be needed?

2. Determine the area of each rectangle. (Be sure to indicate units.)

a.

5 inches

3 inches

b.

4 feet

4 feet

c.

1 inch

8 inches

d.

5 yards

4 yards

3. Draw a rectangle on graph paper whose sides are different than the rectangle in Exercise 2, part c, but still has an area of 8 square inches.

4. a. Describe how to find the area of a rectangle given its length and width.

  b. If the length of a rectangle is l and its width is w, write an expression for its area, A.

5. If one side of a rectangle is 3.5 inches and another side is 4 inches, determine the area using your description in Exercise 4.

6. The following rectangles have areas of 36 square inches.

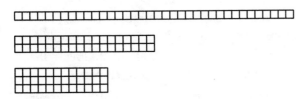

  a. Draw the next three rectangles on graph paper whose area is 36 square inches following the pattern of increasing the width by one unit.

Building Foundations 59

b. Assume the area of a rectangle is 36 square inches. Copy and complete the table below.

Width inches	Length inches	Area square inches
1		36
1.5		36
2		36
	4	36
	5	36
	1.5	36

c. On graph paper, plot at least six data points from the table in part b. Let the vertical axis represent length and the horizontal axis represent width.

When you plot your data points, notice that they do not all fall on one straight line. Draw a rounded curve that connects the points as in the figure, not a series of lines.

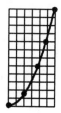

d. If a rectangle has an area of 36 square inches and a width of *w* inches, determine an expression for the length. Place *w* and your expression at the bottom of the appropriate columns in the table.

e. From the graph, determine the width of a rectangle with length 12 inches. From the graph, determine the length of a rectangle with width 12 inches.

7. Determine the area of a square with sides of length 3 inches.

8. a. Make a table in which the first column represents the length of a side of a square and the second column represents the area of the square. Complete the table using sides of length 0.5, 1, 1.5, and 2 units. Calculate the length of a square with an area of 16 square units and place it in the table.

b. If *s* represents the length of one side of a square, write an expression using *s* that represents the area of the square. Place *s* and your expression at the bottom of the appropriate columns in the table. Describe this expression, and explain how this expression works if the side of the square is 6 inches.

c. On graph paper, plot the data points in the table with area on the vertical axis and the length of a side of the square on the horizontal axis. Connect the data points with a smooth curve. (Do not draw line segments.)

d. Using the graph, determine the area of a square with sides of length 5 inches. Describe how to get this answer using the graph.

e. Using the graph, approximate the length of a side of a square with an area of 12 square inches.

9. Use the floor plans for the rectangular apartment shown below to answer the following.

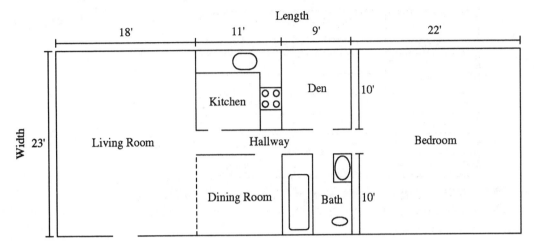

a. What is the total length of the apartment?

b. What is the total area of this apartment? (Be sure to include units.)

c. Suppose you want to carpet part of the apartment. The carpet you want costs $5.50 per square foot.

    i. How much would it cost to carpet the living room?

    ii. How much would it cost to carpet the hallway?

    iii. How much would it cost to carpet the bedroom?

    iv. If A represents the area of a room, write an expression using A that represents the cost of carpeting the room.

    v. Suppose you have $5,000. Is this enough money to carpet the living room, the hallway, and the bedroom? Why or why not?

    If you need more money, how much more do you need?

d. Baseboard is a molding that goes around the bottom of a wall. You decide to put a new baseboard along the walls that divide the bedroom from the den and the bath. The baseboard you choose costs $1.25 per foot. How much will the cost be?

e. You decide to renovate the bathroom. It is estimated that it will cost $20 per square foot for the renovation.

    i. If A represents the number of square feet of the room to be renovated, write an expression using A that represents the cost of the renovation.

    ii. Using the formula that you wrote, how much will this renovation cost?

        Building Foundations 61

Rectangular Garden

In this lesson, you will make use of your ability to find patterns and to graph data to solve the following maximization problem.

Mrs. Wilson has 40 ft of fencing. She wants to make a rectangular vegetable garden and enclose it with the fencing.

a. What width and length should the garden be in order to maximize its area?

b. What is the maximum possible area of the garden?

Since Mrs. Wilson has 40 ft of fencing to surround the garden, the perimeter of the rectangle must be 40 ft.

EXERCISES

All rectangles in this lesson should have a perimeter of 40 ft.

1. a. Copy and complete the table. On graph paper, draw the rectangles corresponding to each entry.

Width (ft)	Length (ft)	Area (ft^2)
1	19	19
2		
3		
4		
5		
6		
7	13	91
8		
9		
10		
11		
12		
13		
14		
15		
16		
17		
18		
19		
x		

b. What patterns do you see in the table?

c. Explain how to get the length of a rectangle if you know the width.

d. Explain how to get the area of a rectangle if you know the width.

e. As the entries in the "Width" column increase, what happens to the entries in the "Length" column?

f. As the entries in the "Width" column decrease, what happens to the entries in the "Length" column?

g. What are the width and length of the rectangle of maximum area?

h. What is the area of the rectangle of maximum area?

i. What type of figure is the rectangle with maximum area?

j. Suppose Mrs. Wilson uses her 40 ft of fencing to build a rectangular garden whose area is 70 ft^2. The width lies between what two consecutive counting numbers? Give two answers.

2. Use the data in the table to make a graph with width on the horizontal axis and length on the vertical axis. Connect the data points.

a. If you know that the width of a rectangle is 7 ft, explain how to find the length by using the graph. What is the length?

b. If you know that the length of a rectangle is 17 ft, explain how to find the width by using the graph. What is the width?

c. If the width of a rectangle is $8\frac{1}{4}$ ft, use the graph to estimate the length. What is the exact length?

d. If the length of the rectangle is $3\frac{1}{2}$ ft, use the graph to estimate the width. What is the exact width?

e. Copy and complete the table, then answer the related questions.

Width (ft)	Length (ft)	Area (ft^2)
1		
$\frac{1}{2}$		
$\frac{1}{10}$		
$\frac{1}{100}$		
0		

i. As the width approaches 0, what happens to the length?

ii. As the width approaches 0, what happens to the area?

iii. Add these data points to your graph. Do they follow the pattern established by your other points?

f. Copy and complete the table, then answer the related questions.

Width (ft)	Length (ft)	Area (ft^2)
19		
$19\frac{1}{2}$		
$19\frac{9}{10}$		
$19\frac{99}{100}$		
20		

   i. As the width approaches 20, what happens to the length?

   ii. As the width approaches 20, what happens to the area?

   iii. Add these data points to your graph. Do they follow the pattern established by your other points?

3. Use the data in the table from Exercise 1 to make a graph with width on the horizontal axis and area on the vertical axis. Draw a smooth curve through the data points.

   a. From the graph, can you determine the area of the rectangle of maximum area? If so, explain how.

   b. From the graph, can you determine the width of the rectangle of maximum area? If so, explain how.

   c. From the graph, can you determine the length of the rectangle of maximum area? If so, explain how.

   d. Suppose Mrs. Wilson uses her 40 ft of fencing to build a rectangular garden whose width is $5\frac{3}{4}$ ft. Use the graph to estimate its area. What is the exact area?

   e. Suppose Mrs. Wilson uses her 40 ft of fencing to build a rectangular garden whose area is 70 ft^2. Explain how to use the graph to estimate the width of the garden. Give two different approximations for the width.

Counting Cubes

Small cubes can be used to build larger cubes. To distinguish between the small and large cubes, each large cube will be called a block. A pattern of blocks is started below. What would the next block look like?

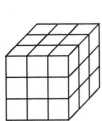 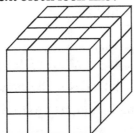

The first block is 3 cubes long, 3 cubes wide and 3 cubes high. We call this a $3 \times 3 \times 3$ block.

Suppose the entire surface of a $3 \times 3 \times 3$ block is painted. Then the block is broken apart into its original cubes. Some cubes will be painted on 3 sides, some on two sides, some on one side and some will not be painted on any side.

The cubes with one painted face are the middle cubes of each face of the $3 \times 3 \times 3$ block. There is one middle cube in each face and 6 faces in each block and thus, there are 6 cubes with one painted face.

The cubes with two painted faces would occur in the middle of an edge of the block. Each edge has one middle cube and there are 12 edges of the block. Thus, there are a total of 12 cubes with 2 painted faces.

The cubes with three painted faces must be on corners (vertices) of the block. The block has 8 vertices. Thus, there would be a total of 8 cubes with 3 painted faces.

The cubes that are not painted would be in the interior of the block where no sides would be exposed to paint. Thus, there is one cube in that position.

EXERCISES

1. Will there be any cubes painted on 4 sides? 5 sides? 6 sides (all sides)?

2. A $4 \times 4 \times 4$ block is shown here. Suppose the surface of this block were also painted and then broken apart into its original cubes.

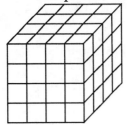

a. Describe where the cubes with 0 painted faces are located in this block. How many of these cubes are there?

b. Describe where the cubes with only one painted face would be in this block. How many of these cubes are there?

c. Describe where the cubes with two painted faces would be in this block. How many of these cubes are there?

d. Describe where the cubes with three painted faces would be in this block. How many of these cubes are there?

3. a. Copy and complete the following table. Leave two extra lines at the bottom.

Length of Edge	Block Dimensions	Number of Cubes in Block	Number of Cubes with Paint On			
			3 Faces	2 Faces	1 Face	0 Faces
2	$2 \times 2 \times 2$					
3	$3 \times 3 \times 3$	27	8	12	6	1
4	$4 \times 4 \times 4$					
5	$5 \times 5 \times 5$					
6	$6 \times 6 \times 6$					

b. Describe any patterns that you see in the table.

4–8. For each of these exercises, do the following.

a. Use the data in the table to create a graph. Label the horizontal axis "Length of Edge" and the vertical axes as indicated for each exercise. Allow room for 7 units on the horizontal axis.

b. If the length of an edge is 7, predict the number of cubes with the indicated number of painted faces. Place the 7 and your prediction at the bottom of the appropriate columns in the table.

c. Plot the corresponding data point on your graph. If you extend your curve, will your new point lie on it?

4. The vertical axis is "Number of Cubes with Paint on 0 Faces." Allow room for at least 150 units.

5. The vertical axis is "Number of Cubes with Paint on 1 Faces." Allow room for at least 150 units.

6. The vertical axis is "Number of Cubes with Paint on 2 Faces." Allow room for at least 60 units.

7. The vertical axis is "Number of Cubes with Paint on 3 Faces." Allow room for at least 350 units.

8. The vertical axis is "Number of Cubes with Paint on 4 Faces."

9. Let n represent the length of an edge of a block. The dimensions of the block would then be $n \times n \times n$.

   a. Place n and $n \times n \times n$ at the bottom of the appropriate columns in the table.

   b. A rule can be applied to n to get the number in the "Number of Cubes in Block" column. Describe this rule.

      Write an expression using n that represents the number of cubes in a block. Place your expression at the bottom of the appropriate column in the table.

   c. Describe the pattern in the "Number of Cubes with Paint on 3 Faces" column. Place an appropriate expression at the bottom of the appropriate column in the table.

   d. A rule can be applied to n to get the number in the "Number of Cubes with Paint on 2 Faces" column. Describe this rule.

      Write an expression using n that represents the number of cubes with 2 painted faces. Place your expression at the bottom of the appropriate column in the table.

   e. An appropriate expression to represent the number of cubes with 1 painted face is $6(n - 2)^2$. Use this expression to predict the number of cubes with 1 face painted for a $10 \times 10 \times 10$ block. Show your work.

   f. Look for a relationship between the numbers in the "Number of Cubes in Block" column and the "Number of Cubes with Paint on 0 Faces" column. Describe this relationship.

      A rule can be applied to n to get the number in the "Number of Cubes with Paint on 0 Faces" column. Describe this rule.

      Write an expression using n that represents number of cubes with 0 painted faces. Place your expression at the bottom of the appropriate column in the table.

        Building Foundations 67

Probability I

In English, the word "probable" means "likely to occur". If the weather forecaster says "It will probably rain today," you might want to carry an umbrella because it is likely that it will rain today. Sometimes, the forecasters attempt to quantify how likely it is by saying things such as "There is a 70% chance that it will rain today." This means that, based on current weather conditions and past experience with similar weather conditions, approximately 70 out of 100 times it rains and 30 out of 100 times it does not rain.

In this lesson, you will learn how to determine the probability for certain events. For example, if you toss one coin, only two possible outcomes can occur: heads or tails. Because 1 of the 2 possible outcomes is a head, the probability of tossing a head is 1 out of 2, or $\frac{1}{2}$. Similarly the probability of tossing a tail is 1 out of 2, or $\frac{1}{2}$.

EXAMPLE 1

Suppose you roll one die.

A. What is the probability that you will roll a 3?

B. What is the probability that you will roll a 1 or a 5?

C. What is the probability that you will roll an even number?

SOLUTION

First list all of the possible outcomes. In this case, the experiment is rolling one die. The possible outcomes are: 1 2 3 4 5 6.

A. Since a 3 occurs once out of the 6 possible outcomes, the probability of rolling a 3 is $\frac{1}{6}$.

B. Since a 1 or a 5 account for 2 of the 6 possible outcomes, the probability of rolling a 1 or a 5 is $\frac{2}{6}$, or $\frac{1}{3}$.

C. The even numbers that occur in the possible outcomes are 2, 4 and 6, so there are 3 even numbers out of the 6 possible outcomes. So the probability of rolling an even number is 3/6, or 1/2.

A particular type of occurence is called an *event*. Rolling a 1 or 5 on a die is one example of an event. The probability of an event is defined as

$$P(\text{Event}) = \frac{\text{Number of outcomes in the event}}{\text{Total number of possible outcomes}}$$

In Example 1, we may write

$P(\text{rolling a 3}) = \frac{1}{6}$ or $P(3) = \frac{1}{6}$

$P(\text{rolling a 1 or a 5}) = \frac{2}{6} = \frac{1}{3}$ or $P(1 \text{ or } 5) = \frac{1}{3}$

$P(\text{rolling an even number}) = \frac{3}{6} = \frac{1}{2}$ or $P(\text{even}) = \frac{1}{2}$

EXERCISES

1. Suppose you roll one die.
    a. What is the probability of rolling a 6?
    b. What is the probability of rolling a number less than 3?
    c. Find $P(\text{rolling an odd number})$.
    d. Find $P(\text{rolling a number greater than 2})$.

2. A standard deck of 52 cards has 2 black suits (clubs and spades) and 2 red suits (hearts and diamonds). Each suit has 13 cards in it, A (Ace) 2 3 4 5 6 7 8 9 10 J (Jack) Q (Queen) K (King). Suppose you choose one card from a standard deck of 52 cards.
    a. What is the probability that you will choose a red card?
    b. What is the probability that you will choose a diamond?
    c. Find $P(\text{Ace})$.
    d. Find $P(\text{the card is }not\text{ an Ace})$.

3. A multiple choice question has 5 choices for an answer. What is the probability that you will guess the correct answer, assuming that you have no knowledge about the question?

EXAMPLE 2

A. Suppose you roll one die. What percent of the time would you expect to roll a 5?

B. Suppose you roll one die 120 times. How many times would you expect to roll a 5?

SOLUTION

A. Find the probability of rolling a 5. Write the fraction as a decimal, then convert the decimal to a percent.

$$P(\text{rolling a 5}) = \frac{1}{6} = 0.\overline{16} \approx 0.167 = 16.7\%$$

B. We have two correct ways to answer this question.

i. Since $P(\text{rolling a 5}) = \frac{1}{6}$, we expect that $\frac{1}{6}$th of the rolls would be a 5.

Thus, $\frac{1}{6} \cdot 120 = 20$ times

ii. Approximately 16.7% of the time we expect a 5: 16.7% of 120
$= 0.167 \cdot 120 = 20.04 \approx 20$ times.

If you actually roll one die 120 times, must you obtain exactly twenty 5's? No! The theoretical frequency is twenty, but the actual number of 5's may vary. The difference between the theoretical number of 5's and the actual number of 5's is due largely to chance.

When a probability is calculated using an experimental frequency the result is called the *experimental probability*. The probabilities we have been calculating are sometimes called *theoretical probabilities* to distinguish them from experimental probabilities.

EXPERIMENT

Work in groups of size 2 or 3. Copy the table. Each group should roll one die 18 times and record the outcomes in the "Experimental Frequency with 18 rolls" column. Complete the table.

Group Data

Outcome	Theoretical Probability		Theoretical Frequency with 18 rolls	Experimental Frequency with 18 rolls	Experimental Probability with 18 rolls	
	Fraction	Percent			Fraction	Percent
1	$\frac{1}{6}$	16.7%	$\frac{1}{6} \cdot 18 = 3$			
2						
3						
4						
5						
6						
Total						

A. i. Copy and complete the bar graph of the theoretical frequencies in the table.

ii. Make a bar graph of the experimental frequencies in the table.

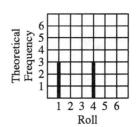

Now pool your class data and fill in a new table. What is the total number of rolls for your class?

Class Data

Outcome	Theoretical Probability		Theoretical Frequency	Experimental Frequency	Experimental Probability	
	Fraction	Percent			Fraction	Percent
1	$\frac{1}{6}$	16.7%				
2						
3						
4						
5						
6						
Total						

B. i. Make a bar graph of the theoretical frequencies in the Class Data table.

ii. Make a bar graph of the experimental frequencies in the table.

C. Which bar graphs are more alike?
Theoretical and experimental frequency with your group data
   or
Theoretical and experimental frequency with your class data?

D. Suppose you roll one die 1000 times and make two bar graphs, one for the theoretical and one for the experimental frequency. Which two bar graphs would you expect to be more alike—the two new ones or the two for the class data?

E. In which table, Group Data or Class Data, are the "Theoretical Probability" and "Experimental Probability" columns more alike?

F. Suppose you roll one die 1000 times and make a new table. Which two columns would you expect to be more alike—"Theoretical Probability" and "Experimental Probability" for the class data or for 1000 rolls?

Probability II

An Experiment

If you have ever played a game that requires rolling 2 dice, you might have noticed that certain sums, such as 7, seem to come up more frequently than other sums, such as 2 or 12. To see why this happens, we can use a chart to show the possible outcomes for rolling two dice and finding the sum.

First Die	Second Die					
	1	2	3	4	5	6
1	2	3	4	5	6	7
2	3	4	5	6	7	8
3	4	5	6	7	8	9
4	5	6	7	8	9	10
5	6	7	8	9	10	11
6	7	8	9	10	11	12

Notice that there are a total of 36 possible outcomes.

EXAMPLE 1

2 dice are rolled.

A. What is the probability of rolling a sum of 7?

B. What is the probability of rolling a sum of 2?

C. What is the probability of rolling doubles, that is, both dice have the same number on them?

SOLUTION

A. Remember that *probability* means *theoretical probability*. Look through all of the possible outcomes and count the number of times that a sum of 7 occurs. The 7's occur along a diagonal of the chart and there are 6 of them. Since there are 36 possible outcomes in our chart, 7 occurs 6 out of 36 times, so the probability of rolling a 7 is $\frac{6}{36}$, or $\frac{1}{6}$.

B. There is only one outcome of 2 in our chart. Thus, the probability is $\frac{1}{36}$.

C. The doubles are listed here.

The event "rolling doubles" occurs 6 times. Thus, the probability of rolling doubles is 6/36, or 1/6.

1st Die	2nd Die
1	1
2	2
3	3
4	4
5	5
6	6

EXPERIMENT

Work in groups of 2. One person should roll 2 dice 36 times, while the partner carefully records the number of 2's, 3's, ..., 12's. Then switch jobs so that the recorder now has an opportunity to roll.

A. Copy and complete the table using your group data. Check to be sure that you have a total of $2 \cdot 36 = 72$ rolls.

Group Data

Sum	Theoretical Probability		Theoretical Frequency 72 Rolls	Experimental Frequency 72 Rolls	Experimental Probability 72 Rolls	
	Fraction	Percent			Fraction	Percent
2	$\frac{1}{36}$	2.8%	$\frac{1}{36} \cdot 72 = 2$			
3						
4						
5						
6						
7	$\frac{1}{6}$	16.7%	$\frac{1}{6} \cdot 72 = 12$			
8						
9						
10						
11						
12						
Total						

B. Now pool the data from your class. Copy and complete the following table using the class data. What is the total number of rolls for your class?

Class Data

Sum	Theoretical Probability		Theoretical Frequency	Experimental Frequency	Experimental Probability	
	Fraction	Percent			Fraction	Percent
2						
3						
4						
5						
6						
7						
8						
9						
10						
11						
12						
Total						

Compare your group data to the class data. In which case does the "Theoretical Probability" column more closely match the "Experimental Probability" column?

Use the tables to complete the following.

C. If you roll 2 dice 100 times, how many times do you expect to get a sum of 5? Show your work.

D. Make a bar graph of the theoretical frequencies for the class data.

E. Make a bar graph of the experimental frequencies for the class data.

F. Does the experimental probability match the theoretical probability more closely for the Group Data or the Class Data?

EXERCISES

4. What do you notice about the total of the numbers in the "Theoretical Probability: Fraction" column?

5. What do you notice about the total of the numbers in the "Theoretical Probability: Percent" column?

6. What do you notice about the total of the numbers in the "Theoretical Frequency" column?

7. What do you notice about the sum of the numbers in the "Experimental Frequency" column?

8. What do you notice about the sum of the numbers in the "Experimental Probability: Fraction" column?

9. What do you notice about the sum of the numbers in the "Experimental Probability: Percent" column?

10. The probability (experimental and theoretical) of an event is always between two numbers, inclusive. What are the two numbers?

Coin Toss Experiments

In this lesson, do not reduce probability fractions.

COIN TOSS GAME

You will play a game that involves tossing coins. Each game consists of 20 trials. Each person in your group will choose an event. The winner is the student whose event occurs most frequently.

EXPERIMENT 1

Work in groups of 2 students. For each trial, toss a coin. Remember, 20 trials are needed to complete a game.

A. Each student should choose an event, Heads or Tails. One student can toss the coin and the second student can record the results in a table similar to the one here. At the end of Game 1, students must switch events and switch recorder and tosser.

Toss A Coin—Game Data

Event	Game 1 Frequency	Game 2 Frequency
H(Head)		
T(Tail)		
Winning Outcome		
Winning Student		

Which event occurs most often? Check your results with other groups of students. If you ever play this game again, which event will you choose to be?

B. Copy and complete the following table.

Look back at the experimental frequencies from Games 1 and 2. How closely do they match the theoretical frequencies in your table?

Toss A Coin

Event	Probability	Theoretical Frequency with 20 Trials
H	$\dfrac{1}{2}$	$\dfrac{1}{2} \cdot 20 = 10$
T		

C. Pool your class data for the 2 games. Each group of students made 40 trials. How many groups are there in your class? What is the total number of times that a coin was tossed?

D. Copy and complete the following table using the pooled data.

How closely do your pooled experimental frequencies match the theoretical frequencies?

Toss A Coin—Pooled Data

Event	Probability	Theoretical Frequency	Experimental Frequency
H			
T			

EXPERIMENT 2

Work in groups of 3 students.

This time you will toss a coin twice for each trial. Remember, 20 trials are needed to complete a game.

A. Each student in your group should choose an event (2 Heads, 1 Head and 1 Tail, or 2 Tails). For each trial, two students can each toss the coin and the third student can record the results in a table similar to the one here. At the end of each game, students must switch events and choose a new recorder.

Toss a Coin 2 Times—Game Data

Event	Game 1 Frequency	Game 2 Frequency	Game 3 Frequency
2H's			
1H & 1T			
2T's			
Winning Outcome			
Winning Student			

Which event occurs most often? Check your results with the results of other groups of students. If you ever play this game again, which event will you choose to be?

B. Theoretically, the event 1 Head and 1 Tail will occur more frequently than 2 Heads or 2 Tails. To determine the probability of getting 1 Head and 1 Tail when you toss a coin 2 times, we construct a tree diagram to describe the possible outcomes.

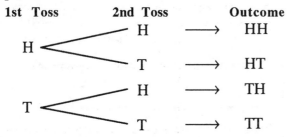

Notice that outcomes HT and TH can be grouped under the event "1H and 1T."

Copy the following table and use the information from the tree diagram to complete it.

Look back at the experimental frequencies from Games 1, 2 and 3. How closely do they match the theoretical frequencies?

C. Pool your class data for all 3 games. Each group of students made 60 trials. How many groups are there in your class?

What is the total number of times that two coins were tossed?

D. Copy and complete the table using the pooled data.

How closely do your pooled experimental frequencies match the theoretical frequencies?

Toss a Coin 2 Times

Event	Probability	Theoretical Frequency with 20 Trials
2H's		
1H and 1T	$\frac{2}{4}$	$\frac{2}{4} \cdot 20 = 10$
2T's		

Toss a Coin 2 Times—Pooled Data

Event	Probability	Theoretical Frequency	Experimental Frequency
2H's			
1H and 1T			
2T's			

EXPERIMENT 3

Work in groups of 4 students.

This time you will toss a coin 3 times for each trial. Remember, 20 trials are needed to complete a game.

A. Divide the events (3H's, 2H's and 1T, 1H and 2T's, or 3T's) among the group. Three students can each toss the coin once and the fourth student can record the results in a table similar to the one here. At the end of each game, students must switch events and choose a new recorder.

Toss a Coin 3 Times—Game Data

Event	Game 1 Frequency	Game 2 Frequency	Game 3 Frequency
3H's			
2H's and 1T			
1H and 2T's			
3T's			
Winning Outcome			
Winning Student			

Which outcome occurs most often?

Check your results with other groups of students. If you ever play this game again, which outcome will you choose to be?

B. To determine the probabilities of the 4 outcomes in the table, copy and complete the following tree diagram. To keep things consistent, you should always put H above T for a given toss.

Toss 1 Toss 2 Toss 3   Outcome

How many different outcomes are listed in the final column above?
Copy the following table and use the information from the tree diagram to complete it.

Toss a Coin 3 Times

Event	Probability	Theoretical Frequency with 20 Trials
3 H's		
2H's and 1T		
1H and 2T's		
3T's		

Look back to your experimental frequencies from Games 1, 2, and 3. How closely do they match the theoretical frequencies?

C. Pool your class data for all 3 games. Each group of students made 60 trials. How many groups are there in your class?

What is the total number of trials?

D. Copy and complete the table using your pooled data.

Toss a Coin 3 Times—Pooled Data

Event	Probability	Theoretical Frequency	Experimental Frequency
3H's			
2H's and 1T	$\frac{3}{8}$		
1H and 2T's			
3T's			

How closely do your experimental frequencies match the theoretical frequencies?

ACTIVITY 1

A. Make a tree diagram for tossing 4 coins. How many different outcomes are listed in the final column?

B. Copy and complete the table.

Suppose you and your classmates toss 4 coins 640 times. How many times do you expect to get 2 Heads and 2 Tails? Show your work.

Toss a Coin 4 Times

Event	Probability
4H's	
3H's and 1T	4/16
2H's and 2T's	
1H and 3T's	
4T's	

ACTIVITY 2

The tree diagram for 5 coins is large. Instead of actually drawing the tree diagram, you can predict the number of different outcomes in the final column by looking for a pattern in the table to the right.

To fill in the probability table for tossing 5 coins, again we look for a pattern. This pattern was originally discovered by the French mathematician, Blaise Pascal, and so it is called *Pascal's Triangle*.

Number of Coins	Number of Different Outcomes
1	2
2	4
3	8
4	16
5	
6	

		Number of Different Outcomes
Toss a Coin 0 Times	1	1
Toss a Coin 1 Times	1 1	2
Toss a Coin 2 Times	1 2 1	4
Toss a Coin 3 Times	1 3 3 1	8
Toss a Coin 4 Times	1 4 6 4 1	16
Toss a Coin 5 Times		
Toss a Coin 6 Times		

A. In the interior of the triangle, each number is related to the 2 closest numbers in the row above itself. What is the relationship?

B. Copy Pascal's Triangle and complete the next two rows.

Hint. What do you notice about the first and last entries in each row?

C. Notice that the numbers in the "Toss a Coin 4 Times" row correspond to the numerators in the probability column of the table for that experiment. Check to see that this pattern holds for tossing a coin 2 or 3 times. Notice that the number of different outcomes in the "Toss a Coin 4 Times" row corresponds to the denominator in the probability column of the table. Does this pattern holds for tossing a coin 2 or 3 times?

D. Complete the following table based on your numbers in the "Toss a Coin 5 Times" row of Pascal's Triangle.

E. Suppose you and your classmates toss a coin 5 times for 640 trials. How many times do you expect to get 3H's and 2T's? Show work.

Toss a Coin 5 Times

Outcome	Probability
5H's	
4H's 1T	
3H's 2T's	
2H's 3T's	
1H's 4T's	
5T's	

What's Your Chance I

The Multiplication Counting Principle

1	2	3	4	5	6
9	10	11	12	13
16	17	18	19	20
23	24	25	26	2
21	32	33		

Cash Stash Problem: To win the Cash Stash lottery you must choose 6 numbers out of 36 and match the combination of numbers that the computer chooses. If you buy one combination of 6 numbers, what is the probability that you will win the lottery?

To answer this question you need to know the number of possible combinations of 6 numbers from the 36 numbers. You could count these combinations by making a carefully ordered list of combinations such as the following.

1	2	3	4	5	6
1	2	3	4	5	7
1	2	3	4	5	8
1	2	3	4	5	9

etc.

However, this process would take a huge amount of time and paper. Fortunately, there are three basic counting principles that will make the task of counting the combinations easy. Each of the three What's Your Chance lessons introduces one of the principles. By the end of What's Your Chance III, you will have the counting tools necessary for solving the Cash Stash problem.

In this lesson, we investigate the first of the basic counting principles. Try to answer the problem below and explain your reasoning before reading ahead.

EXAMPLE 1

How many different outfits can be made from 5 blouses and 3 skirts?

SOLUTION

You can solve this problem by a number of methods. One way to solve the problem is by drawing a tree diagram.

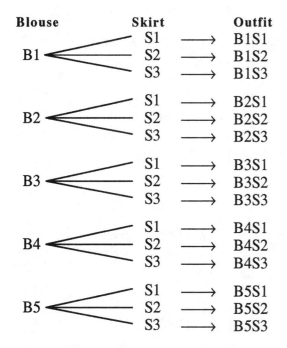

By counting we can see that there are 15 different outfits or outcomes. Notice that you could obtain the answer of 15 using multiplication.

$$5 \text{ blouses} \cdot \frac{3 \text{ outfits}}{\text{blouse}} = 15 \text{ outfits.}$$

EXAMPLE 2

We can extend this problem by introducing 4 different pairs of socks. How many different outfits can be made with 5 blouses, 3 skirts, and 4 pairs of socks?

METHOD 1

Add a column to the tree diagram from Example 1.

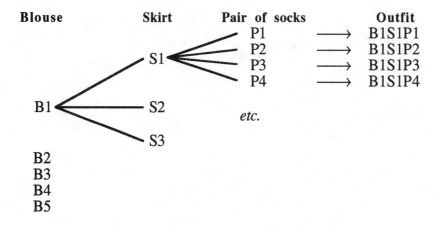

As you can see, this method would be time consuming.

METHOD 2

You may choose to make a carefully ordered list. Don't change an item until you must.

B1S1P1
B1S1P2
B1S1P3
B1S1P4   No socks left. To get a new outfit, you must change S1.
B1S2P1
B1S2P2
B1S2P3
B1S2P4   No socks left. To get a new outfit, you must change S2.
B1S3P1
B1S3P2
B1S3P3
B1S3P4   No socks left. To get a new outfit, you want to change to a new skirt. But there are no more skirts. So, you must change B1. To keep consistent, let's start over with S1 and P1 also.
B2S1P1   *etc.*

Notice that this list is identical to the "outfit" column in the tree diagram.

METHOD 3

The *Multiplication Counting Principle.*

Think of the act of creating an outfit as a sequence of 3 events.

Event 1	**Event 2**	**Event 3**
Choose a blouse	Choose a skirt	Choose a pair of socks
5 possibilities	3 possibilities	4 possibilities

In Example 1 we saw that for each blouse we could choose from 3 skirts, giving $5 \cdot 3 = 15$ outfits. For each of these, we can now choose from 4 pairs of socks. Thus the number of possible outcomes can be found by multiplying the number of possibilities for each of the events.

$$5 \cdot 3 \cdot 4 \quad = 60 \text{ outcomes}$$
$$= 60 \text{ outfits}$$

We recommend using a blank line for each event and then filling in each blank with the number of possibilities for the event.

Choose a blouse   Choose a skirt   Choose a pair of socks

$$\underline{3} \quad \cdot \quad \underline{5} \quad \cdot \quad \underline{4} \quad = \quad 60$$

EXERCISES

1. Make a tree diagram to answer the following question. A frozen yogurt store has 4 flavors of yogurt and 7 toppings. How many different sundaes could be made, assuming 1 flavor of yogurt and 1 topping per sundae? Use F1, F2, F3 and F4 for flavors and T1, T2, T3, T4, T5, T6, and T7 for toppings.

2. A particular model of car has 6 possible exterior colors and 10 possible interior colors. How many different color combinations does a customer have to choose from?

3. 52 boys and 87 girls are attending the 7th grade class dance. Boys' names will be placed in one hat and girls' names will be placed in another. A single name will be drawn from each hat. The lucky couple whose names are chosen will be crowned king and queen.

   a. How many different couples could be chosen?

   b. If Ned and Sarah are among the boys and girls at the dance, what is the probability that they will be the couple chosen as king and queen?

4. A local restaurant has 3 appetizers, 4 entrees, and 2 desserts. Make a carefully ordered list of the different possible meals that could be ordered, assuming that each meal consists of 1 appetizer, 1 entree and 1 dessert. Use A1, A2, and A3 for appetizers, E1, E2, E3, and E4 for entrees, and D1 and D2 for desserts.

   a. How many different meals are in your list?

   b. Find the number of different meals using the Multiplication Counting Principle. Show your work.

   c. Do your answers to parts a and b agree?

5. Two hats, each containing digits 0 through 9, are sitting on a table. One number is drawn from each hat. A new number is formed by putting the first number drawn into the ones place and the second number drawn into the tens place.

   a. How many different new numbers could be formed?

   b. What is the probability that the number 48 will be formed?

6. Three hats, each containing the digits 0 through 9, are sitting on a table. One number is drawn from each hat. A new number is formed by putting the first number drawn into the ones place, the second number drawn into the tens place and the third number drawn into the hundreds place.

   a. How many different new numbers could be formed?

   b. What is the probability that the number 481 will be formed?

What's Your Chance II

Permutations

$$\boxed{\text{ABC}} \quad \boxed{\text{ACB}} \quad \boxed{\text{BAC}}$$

$$\boxed{\text{BCA}} \quad \boxed{\text{CAB}} \quad \boxed{\text{CBA}}$$

The Multiplication Counting Principle can be used to investigate the *permutations*, or arrangements, of a set of objects. For example, if 3 students, Aaron, Brian, and Charles, run a race, they can finish in the following different orders.

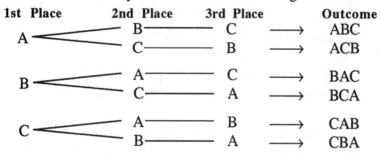

Since there are 6 different arrangements, we say that there are 6 permutations of 3 objects. Notice that to choose a name for 1st place, you have 3 choices. However, to choose a name for 2nd place, you only have 2 choices because one name has already been used for 1st place. To choose a name for 3rd place, you only have one choice because one name has already been chosen for 1st place and another name has already been chosen for 2nd place.

Using the Multiplication Counting Principle, we have the following.

Event 1	**Event 2**	**Event 3**
Choose 1st place	Choose 2nd place	Choose 3rd place
3 possibilities	2 possibilities	1 possibility

$$\underline{\;3\;} \quad \cdot \quad \underline{\;2\;} \quad \cdot \quad \underline{\;1\;} = 6 \text{ outcomes}$$

EXERCISES

1. Make a tree diagram to answer the following question.
   Tanya is planning a party. She will play her 4 favorite CD's but needs to decide upon the best order.

   a. How many different possible permutations are there for the 4 CD's? Use letters D(Dance), R(Rap), H(Hard Rock) and S(Soft Rock) to identify the CD's in your tree diagram.

   b. If Tanya decides to choose the order by pulling the 4 styles out of a hat, what is the probability that the order will be Hard Rock, Soft Rock, Rap, Dance?

2. Five finalists are announced for the Miss Teen U.S.A. contest. The contestants are announced alphabetically by state–California, Delaware, Illinois, New York and Texas.

   a. How many different possible arrangements are there for 1st place through 5th place?

   b. In how many of the possible arrangements is Delaware listed first? What fraction of the total number of arrangements does this represent?

3. The coach of the Little League state champions has an important decision to make. He must make up a batting order for the national tournament.

   a. He has his 9 starting players set. How many different batting orders can be made with his 9 starting players?

   b. The coach decides to put Joe, the best hitter, in the 4th position and the pitcher, Roger, in the 9th position. How many possible batting orders does he now have?

   Hint. First, figure out how many of the 9 starters could bat 1st.

   $$\underline{} \quad \underline{} \quad \underline{} \quad \underset{\text{4th}}{\overline{\text{Joe}}} \quad \underline{} \quad \underline{} \quad \underline{} \quad \underline{} \quad \underset{\text{9th}}{\overline{\text{Roger}}}$$

   1st   2nd   3rd   4th   5th   6th   7th   8th   9th

4. For the questions below, first write your answer as an expression involving multiplication, then evaluate the expression.

   a. A local DJ has 2 songs to play. In how many different orders can the 2 songs be played?

   b. A local DJ has 3 songs to play. In how many different orders can the 3 songs be played?

   c. A local DJ has 4 songs to play. In how many different orders can the 4 songs be played?

   d. A local DJ has 5 songs to play. In how many different orders can the 5 songs be played?

   e. A local DJ has 6 songs to play. In how many different orders can the 6 songs be played?

5. The exclamation point, !, has a special meaning in mathematics. If you see the symbol 5!, it means $5 \cdot 4 \cdot 3 \cdot 2 \cdot 1$, which has a value of 120 and is read "5 factorial." Similarly,

   $$6! = 6 \cdot 5 \cdot 4 \cdot 3 \cdot 2 \cdot 1 = 720 \qquad 7! = 7 \cdot 6 \cdot 5 \cdot 4 \cdot 3 \cdot 2 \cdot 1 = 5040$$

a. Copy and complete the following table.

Factorial	Expression	Value
1!		
2!		
3!		
4!		
5!		
6!		
7!		
8!		
9!		
10!		

b. Return to Exercise 4 and write your answers using factorial notation.

4a. ____ **4b.** ____ **4c.** ____ **4d.** ____ **4e.** ____

6. A local DJ has identified 7 song titles containing the word "summer." On Saturday night, beginning at 9:00 PM, she will play the songs in a certain order. Listeners are invited to send in a postcard with their best guess of the order. Winners will each be given a free CD. You and your friends decide to send in one postcard for each possible guess. Postcards cost 19¢ each.

a. How much will it cost to send one postcard per guess?

b. Suppose the average cost of a CD is 13 dollars. Is your plan to send in one postcard per guess a good one from a financial point of view?

If the prize were changed to an all-expenses-paid vacation for four people, would your plan be a good one from a financial point of view?

c. What is the probability that a single guess will be correct?

EXAMPLE 1

The student council chooses a president, secretary and treasurer from among its 5 eighth grade members. How many slates of officers are possible?

SOLUTION

We have 5 people from which we must choose a president, secretary and treasurer. Illustrate the situation by naming the 5 eighth grade members A, B, C, D, and E, and by constructing a partial tree diagram.

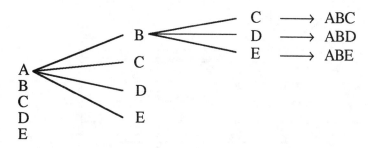

The Multiplication Counting Principle can also be used. Once a president has been chosen, only 4 candidates remain for secretary, and once a president-secretary pair has been chosen, only 3 candidates remain for treasurer.

Event 1	**Event 2**	**Event 3**
Choose a president	Choose a secretary	Choose a treasurer
5 possibilities	4 possibilities	3 possibilities
5 ·	4 ·	3

Thus we have $5 \cdot 4 \cdot 3 = 60$ slates of officers.

We describe the situation in Example 1 by saying that the number of permutations of 5 things taken 3 at a time is 60. We use the notation $_5P_3 = 60$.

Notice that the slate "ABE" means that A is the president, B is the secretary and E is the treasurer. The slate "BEA" means that B is the president, E is the secretary and A is the treasurer. Thus, although slates ABE and BEA contain the same people, they are considered to be different slates of officers because the arrangement of the people is different. This is characteristic of problems involving permutations: a different order of the same objects makes a different permutation. The order in which things are chosen makes a difference.

EXAMPLE 2

Suppose 10 records are nominated for play on a local radio program, but that time allows only 4 records to be played. How many different arrangements of 4 records chosen from the 10 are possible?

SOLUTION

Event 1	**Event 2**	**Event 3**	**Event 4**
Choose 1st Record	Choose 2nd Record	Choose 3rd Record	Choose 4th Record
10 ·	9 ·	8 ·	7

Thus, there are 5040 permutations of 10 records taken 4 at a time, and we would write $_{10}P_4 = 10 \cdot 9 \cdot 8 \cdot 7 = 5040$.

EXERCISES

7. Work in groups of 5 students. Each group should make a carefully ordered list of the possible slates of officers—President, Secretary, Treasurer—using students from their group. Each person is responsible for the slates in which he/she is the President. How many slates of officers should each group have?

8. Copy and complete the table below.

Number of Records Nominated for Play	Number of Records Played	Number of Permutations (Expression)	Number of Permutations (Value)	Notation
10	1			
10	2			
10	3			
10	4	$10 \cdot 9 \cdot 8 \cdot 7$	5040	$_{10}P_4$
10	5			
10	6			
10	7			
10	8			
10	9			
10	10			

9. The last row in the above table describes a situation that is different from all the others. In what way is it different?

10. **a.** What is the expression for $_8P_3$?

b. What is the value for $_8P_3$?

c. In the symbol $_8P_3$, how many objects are there to choose from? How many objects are actually chosen? The corresponding expression contains how many consecutive counting numbers? What is the largest of these counting numbers?

11. 12 Olympic contestants are competing for the gold, silver and bronze medals in womens' figure skating. How many different outcomes are possible?

12. **a.** Write a problem of your own whose solution is $_7P_3$.

b. Write a problem of your own whose solution is $_7P_7$.

What's Your Chance III

Combinations

The last of the fundamental counting principles involves the concept of *combination*. A combination is a subset of elements chosen from a given set. This idea is illustrated below.

EXAMPLE 1

The student council has 5 eighth grade members. How many different 3-member committees can be chosen from these five members?

SOLUTION

Each 3-member committee is a 3-member subset chosen from the set of 5 eighth graders. Name the 5 people A, B, C, D, and E, and write down a carefully ordered list of the different 3-member subsets.

ABC	Begin with alphabetical order
ABD	
ABE	Must change B
ACD	
ACE	Must change C
ADE	Must change A
BCD	
BCE	Must change C
BDE	Must change B
CDE	

Thus, there are 10 3-member committees, and we say that the number of *combinations* of 5 things taken 3 at a time is 10. We use the notation $_5C_3 = 10$.

When you are listing different combinations of objects, you need to be aware of an important difference between combinations and permutations. To illustrate this difference, compare Example 1 with the following example from What's Your Chance II: Permutations.

EXAMPLE 2

The student council chooses a president, secretary and treasurer from among its 5 eighth grade members. How many different slates of officers are possible?

SOLUTION

Choose president   Choose secretary   Choose treasurer
    5   ·   4   ·   3

Thus, there are 60 slates of officers, and we may write

$$_5P_3 = 5 \cdot 4 \cdot 3 = 60.$$

In both examples, we have 5 students from which to choose groups of 3 students. However, consider the following.
ABC
ACB
BAC
BCA
CAB
CBA

All of these represent 1 combination (committee) but 6 different permutations (slates of officers).

A different arrangement of the same objects **does** represent a new permutation, but **does not** represent a new combination.

ACTIVITIES

A. Divide your class into groups of 5 students. Each group should make a carefully ordered list of the 2-member committees from their group.

   i. How many 2-member committees can be formed from 5 students?

   ii. What is the relationship between $_5C_3$ and $_5C_2$? Explain.

B. Divide your class into groups of 6 students. Use the letters A, B, C, D, E, and F to name the students in your group.

   i. Make a carefully ordered list of the 1-member committees from your group. What is $_6C_1$?

   ii. Make a carefully ordered list of the 2-member committees from your group. What is $_6C_2$?

   iii. Make a carefully ordered list of the 3-member committees from your group. What is $_6C_3$?

    iv. Make a carefully ordered list of the 4-member committees from your group. What is $_6C_4$?

    v. Make a carefully ordered list of the 5-member committees from your group. What is $_6C_5$?

    vi. Make a carefully ordered list of the 6-member committees from your group. What is $_6C_6$?

    vii. Of the numbers $_6C_1$, $_6C_2$, $_6C_3$, $_6C_4$, $_6C_5$ and $_6C_6$, which pairs are equal? Explain why each pair is equal.

C. Divide your class into groups of 7 students. Use the letters A, B, C, D, E, F, and G to name the members of your group.

    i. Make a carefully ordered list of the 3-member committees from your group. What is $_7C_3$?

    ii. Predict the number of 4-member committees from your group.

Listing combinations becomes very tedious when the numbers get large. Fortunately, there is a simple relationship between permutations and combinations, and the number of permutations is easy to compute. Compare Examples 1 and 2, whose solutions are $_5C_3$ and $_5P_3$, respectively. In the table below, each combination (3–member committee) is listed across the first row and the possible permutations of the members of each committee are listed in committee's column.

```
ABC  ABD  ABE  ACD  ACE  ADE  BCD  BCE  BDE  CDE
ACB  ADB  AEB  ADC  AEC  AED  BDC  BEC  BED  CED
BAC  BAD  BAE  CAD  CAE  DAE  CBD  CBE  DBE  DCE
BCA  BDA  BEA  CDA  CEA  DEA  CDB  CBE  DBE  DCE
CAB  DAB  EAB  DAC  EAC  EAD  DBC  EBC  EBD  ECD
CBA  DBA  EBA  DCA  ECA  EDA  DCB  ECB  EDB  EDC
```

Notice that each column has 6 entries, representing the fact that there are $6 = 3 \cdot 2 \cdot 1 = 3!$ permutations of 3 elements. The rectangular arrangement suggests the following rule.

number of combinations · number of permutations per combination
$$= \text{total number of permutations}$$

In our example, this becomes $10 \cdot 6 = 60$, or $_5C_3 \cdot 3! = _5P_3$
If we want to find $_5C_3$, we can first compute $_5P_3$ and divide by 3!

$$_5C_3 = \frac{_5P_3}{3!} = \frac{5 \cdot 4 \cdot 3}{3 \cdot 2 \cdot 1} = 10$$

You are now ready to solve the Cash Stash lottery problem from What's Your Chance I: The Multiplication Counting Principle. Recall that, to win the Cash

Stash lottery, you must choose 6 numbers out of 36 and match the combination of numbers that the computer chooses. How many possible combinations could the computer choose?

$$_{36}C_6 = \frac{_{36}P_6}{6!} = \frac{36 \cdot 35 \cdot 34 \cdot 33 \cdot 32 \cdot 31}{6 \cdot 5 \cdot 4 \cdot 3 \cdot 2 \cdot 1} = 1{,}947{,}792$$

If you buy one combination of numbers, what is the probability that you will win the lottery? Since only one combination out of 1,947,792 wins, the probability of winning is

$$\frac{1}{1947792} \approx .000000513.$$

In other words, you have about a 1 in 2 million chance of winning.

EXERCISES

1. The yearbook staff has 10 members. A 3-member advertising committee must be chosen.

   a. How many possible 3-member committees could be formed?

   b. What symbol would you use to describe the fact that you have 10 people from which to choose committees of size 3?

2. **a.** Describe what the symbol $_{17}C_5$ means.

   b. Write the expression described above.

   c. Evaluate the expression in part b.

3. Copy and complete the table.

Combinations	Expression	Value
$_6C_1$		
$_6C_2$		
$_6C_3$		
$_6C_4$	$\frac{6 \cdot 5 \cdot 4 \cdot 3}{4 \cdot 3 \cdot 2 \cdot 1}$	15
$_6C_5$		
$_6C_6$		

4. Check the numbers in the "Value" column in Exercise 3 with your answers to Activity B, parts i through vi. Do your answers agree? If your answers do not agree, correct your errors.

5. The cheerleading squad will practice 2 of the 5 weekdays after school.

   a. Make a carefully ordered list of the pairs of days using the letters M, T, W, R and F.

   b. How many different combinations of days are possible?

   c. Write your answer to part b using the notation for combinations.

   d. Use a fraction similar to the one used to solve the Cash Stash lottery problem to calculate the number of combinations of days. Does your calculation agree with your answer to part b?

   e. Janice has piano lessons after school on Wednesday. What is the probability that cheer leading practice will conflict with her piano lesson, assuming that the pairs of practice days are equally likely to be chosen?

6. The Eastern Basketball League has 8 teams. During the season, each team plays every other team in the league exactly once.

   a. Name the teams A, B, C, D, E, F, G, and H. Make a carefully ordered list of the league games for a season.

   b. Think of the teams as if they were people. The list of games can then be thought of as a list of committees. How many members are in each committee? How many people are there to choose from?

   c. How many league games must be scheduled for the season?

   d. Write your answer to part c by using the notation for combinations.

   e. Use a fraction to calculate the number of games. Does the value of your fraction agree with your answer to part c?

7. To win the Mounds o' Money lottery, you must choose 6 numbers out of 40 and match the winning combination.

   a. How many different combinations are possible?

   b. If you buy just one ticket, what is the probability of winning the Mounds o' Money lottery?

   c. If you buy just one ticket for each, do you have a better chance of winning the Cash Stash lottery or the Mounds o' Money lottery? Explain your answer.

Get Ready, Get Set

The diagram below shows a seating chart for Ms. King's class.
Each small square represents one student.

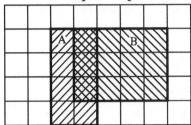

Members of the art club are seated together and are indicated by ▨.

Members of the band are seated together and are indicated by ▧.

EXERCISES

Refer to the seating chart of Ms. King's class. Count the appropriate squares to answer each question below.

1. What is the total number of students in the class?

2. a. How many students in the class are members of the art club?
   b. What fraction of the students in the class are members of the art club?
   c. What percent of the class are members of the art club?
   d. How many students in the class are not members of the art club?
   e. What percent of the class are not members of the art club?

3. a. How many students in the class are members of the band?
   b. How many students in the class are not members of the band?

4. How many students in Ms. King's class are members of either the art club or the band?

5. How many students in Ms. King's class are members of both the art club and the band?

6. Which word best describes the sets of band and art club members: separate or overlapping?

7. How many students in the class are members of the art club but are not members of the band?

8. How many students in the class are members of the band but are not members of the art club?

9. How many students in the class belong to neither the art club nor the band?

10. Suppose the names of the students in Ms. King's class are put into a hat and one name is chosen to be the class representative to the Student Council.

  a. What is the probability that the student will be a member of the art club?

  b. What is the probability that the student will be a member of the band?

  c. What is the probability that the student will be a member of either the art club or the band?

  d. What is the probability that the student will be a member of both the art club and the band?

There are some important relationships among the answers to Exercises 1 through 10. By knowing the answers to a few of the questions, you should be able to use simple arithmetic to calculate the answers to other questions without actually having to count students.

To simplify our work, we will use the following notation.

  A = the set of students in the art club
  B = the set of students in the band

The notation N(a set) is used to mean the number of members of the set.

  $N(A)$ = the number of students in the art club
  $N(B)$ = the number of students in the band

Thus we may write $N(A) = 8$ (Answer to Exercise 2, part a) and $N(B) = 12$ (Answer to Exercise 3, part a)

To describe the set of students who are members of either the art club **or** the band, we use the word "OR".

  A OR B

We also have a special symbol in mathematics that is equivalent to "OR". That symbol is $\cup$, which stands for "union".

  $A \cup B$

$A \cup B$ unites, or joins together, the members of sets A and B. If you see "A OR B" or "$A \cup B$", they mean the same thing–namely, the set of all students who belong to either the art club or the band. The set consists of all students in the shaded region in the diagram.

Thus,

$N(A$ OR $B) = 17$ (Answer to Exercise 4)

$N(A \cup B) = 17$.

To describe the set of students who are members of both the art club **and** the band, we use the word AND:

A AND B.

We also have a special symbol in mathematics that is equivalent to "AND". That symbol is $\cap$, which stands for "intersection":

$A \cap B$.

$A \cap B$ consists of the students in common to both A and B–it is the overlap between the two sets, which is the double-shaded region in the diagram. If you see "A AND B" or "$A \cap B$", they mean the same thing. The word "intersection" has the same meaning in this context as it does when two streets intersect. The intersection is the region in common to both streets.

Thus,

$N(A$ AND $B) = 3$ (Answer to Exercise 5)

$N(A \cap B) = 3$.

Notice that the word AND has a highly specialized meaning when it is used with sets, as illustrated by our example of A AND B. When used with sets, AND means "and at the same time". Therefore, a student in A AND B must be a member of A (art club) and at the same time must be a member of B (band), that is, the student must be a member of both A and B. In this context, AND does **not** mean "add". To see this, note that $N(A) = 8$ and $N(B) = 12$, but $N(A$ AND $B) \neq 20$. In fact, $N(A$ AND $B) = 3$.

To describe the set of students who are **not** in the art club, we use NOT A. Thus $N($NOT $A) = 32$.

Notice that there are two ways that you can get this answer.

1. Count the squares outside the art club.

2. The number of students who are not in the art club is the total number of students in the class minus those who are in the art club.

$N($NOT $A) = N($Ms. King's Class$) - N(A) =$

$$40 - 8 = 32$$

The information in our original diagram can be presented using ovals to indicate the sets and numbers to indicate the size of each set.

This type of diagram is called a *Venn diagram*, named after the 19th century English mathematician John Venn. The 5 indicates that there are 5 students in the art club who are not in the band. To determine the total number of students in the Art Club, you must add up the students in the different parts of the art club oval: $5 + 3 = 8$. If you add all the numbers in the Venn diagram, $5 + 3 + 9 + 23$, you get 40, which is the total number of students in the class.

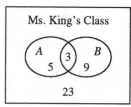

You should be familiar with the notation $P(A)$, which means "the probability of event A". Sets also can be considered to be events as well. For example, if a student is chosen at random from Ms. King's class, the probability that the student is a member of the art club is written $P(A)$.

Thus,

$P(A) = 8/40 = 1/5.$

EXERCISES

11. Refer to the Venn diagram shown here for this exercise.
    C = the set of cheerleaders in Mr. Nolan's class
    H = the set of honor roll students in Mr. Nolan's class

    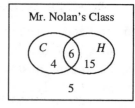

    a. What is the total number of students in Mr. Nolan's class?
    b. Find the following numbers.

$N(C)$	$N(C \text{ AND } H)$	$N(C \text{ OR } H)$	$N(\text{NOT } C)$
$N(H)$	$N(C \cap H)$	$N(C \cup H)$	$N(\text{NOT } H)$

    c. A student is chosen at random from Mr. Nolan's class. Find the following probabilities.

$P(C)$	$P(C \text{ AND } H)$	$P(C \text{ OR } H)$	$P(\text{NOT } C)$
$P(H)$	$P(C \cap H)$	$P(C \cup H)$	$P(\text{NOT } H)$

    d. Helen is a member of the set $C \cap H$. What does this tell you about Helen?
    e. Tanya is a member of $C \cup H$. What does this tell you about Tanya?
    f. i. What is $N(C) + N(H)$?
        ii. Is your answer greater than or less than the total number of students in Mr. Nolan's class? Explain why.

12. Refer to the Venn diagram shown here for this exercise.
C = the set of cheerleaders in Mr. Nolan's class
F = the set of football players in Mr. Nolan's class

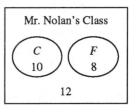

a. Find the following numbers.

$N(C \cup F)$ $N(C \cap F)$

b. A student is chosen at random from Mr. Nolan's class. Find the following probabilities.

$P(C \cup F)$ $P(C \cap F)$

c. Is the set of cheerleaders separate from the set of football players, or are the two sets overlapping?

13. Draw a Venn diagram for the following. Ms. Jackson's class has 25 students. 10 of her students are taking Spanish; 7 of her students are taking Home Economics; 4 of her students are taking both Spanish and Home Economics. How many students are taking either Spanish or Home Economics? **Hint.** Start with the students taking both courses.

14. This Exercise is designed to help you discover a rule for finding $N(A \cup B)$ if you know $N(A)$, $N(B)$ and $N(A \cap B)$.

a. Copy and complete the table using the data in the Venn diagrams.

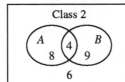

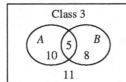

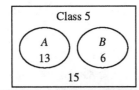

Class	N(A)	N(B)	N(A ∩ B)	N(A ∪ B)
1				
2				
3				
4				
5				
6				

b. A rule can be applied to the numbers in the 3 middle columns to produce the number in the right-most column. Describe this rule.

c. Write an equation for the rule using $N(A)$, $N(B)$, $N(A \cup B)$, and $N(A \cap B)$. **Hint.** $N(A \cup B) = ?$

d. When is subtraction necessary? Explain why.

15. If A and B do not overlap, we say that A and B are *disjoint* sets and we may write $A \cap B = \emptyset$ (empty set).

a. If A and B are disjoint sets, then $N(A \cap B) =$

b. If A and B are disjoint sets, the rule in Exercise 14 can be simplified. Write a new equation for the simplified rule.

16. a. This Exercise is designed to help you discover a rule for finding $P(A \cup B)$ if you know $P(A)$, $P(B)$ and $P(A \cap B)$. For each class in Exercise 14, a student is chosen at random. Copy and complete the table using the Venn Diagrams in Exercise 14. Do not reduce fractions.

Class	$P(A)$	$P(B)$	$P(A \cap B)$	$P(A \cup B)$
1				
2				
3				
4				
5				
6				

b. A rule can be applied to the numbers in the 3 middle columns to produce the number in the right-most column. Describe this rule in words.

c. Write an equation for the rule using $P(A)$, $P(B)$, $P(A \cup B)$, and $P(A \cap B)$. **Hint.** $P(A \cup B) = ?$

17. If A and B are disjoint sets, the rule for $P(A \cup B)$ can be simplified. Write an equation for the simplified rule.

18. A Class Survey

a. By show of hands, collect the following data.

i. How many students made the honor roll in the last marking period?

ii. How many students ride a bus to school?

iii. How many students made the honor roll in the last marking period and ride a bus to school?

iv. How many students made the honor roll in the last marking period or ride a bus to school?

v. What is the total number of students surveyed?

b. Make a Venn diagram to display the data collected in the survey.
H = the set of honor roll students
B = the set of bus riders

    i.   What percent of the students surveyed made the honor roll?

    ii. What percent of the students surveyed ride the bus to school?

c. Assume that a student is chosen at random from those who responded to the survey and find the following probabilities.

    $P(H)$ $P(B)$ $P(H \cap B)$ $P(H \cup B)$

d. Identify each of the following as true or false. Show your arithmetic.

    i. $N(H \cup B) = N(H) + N(B) - N(H \cap B)$

    ii. $P(H \cup B) = P(H) + P(B) - P(H \cap B)$

19. A standard deck of 52 playing cards consists of 2 red suits (hearts and diamonds) and 2 black suits (spades and clubs) with 13 cards in each suit: A (Ace) 2 3 4 5 6 7 8 9 10 J (Jack) Q (Queen) K (King). Make a Venn diagram for the following sets, then complete the exercise using your diagram.

D = A standard deck of 52 playing cards
R = the set of red cards
F = the set of face cards (JQK)

a. Find the following numbers.

    $N(R)$ $N(F)$ $N(R \cap F)$ $N(R \cup F)$

b. A card is chosen at random from the deck. Find the following probabilities.

    $P(R)$ $P(F)$ $P(R \cap F)$ $P(R \cup F)$

c. Identify each of the following as true or false. Show your arithmetic.

    i. $N(R \cup F) = N(R) + N(F) - N(R \cap F)$

    ii. $P(R \cup F) = P(R) + P(F) - P(R \cap F)$

20. A Group Activity
Work in groups of 3 or 4 students. Each group should choose two sets, such as "the set of students with brown eyes" or "the set of students who have a cat". Survey your class by show of hands to determine the number of students in the first set, the number of students in the second set, and the number of students in both sets.

a. Make a Venn diagram with the two sets from your group.

b. Determine the number of students who are in either the first set or the second set.

c. Make a report to the class about the results of the survey.

d. Check the answer to part b by asking for a show of hands.

          Building Foundations 103

21. Repeat Exercise 20 with one change:

If your two sets were disjoint in Exercise 10, choose two sets that will overlap.

If your two sets overlapped in Exercise 10, choose two sets that will not overlap.

22. Venn Diagram Detective Stories

For each part below make a Venn diagram to help you answer the question.

a. The following data was collected from Ms. Dee's class.

14 students have a dog.

3 students have both a dog and a cat.

20 students have either a dog or a cat.

How many students have a cat?

b. The following data was collected from Mr. Morris' class.

15 students have a cat.

7 students have a dog.

20 students have either a cat or a dog.

How many students have both a cat and a dog?

c. The following data was collected from Ms. Chen's class.

There are 28 students in Ms. Chen's class.

12 students do not have a cat or a dog.

6 students have a cat.

4 students have both a cat and a dog.

How many students have a dog?

23. A school newspaper conducted a survey about extracurricular activities. A report on the findings of the survey states the following.

40% of the students surveyed participate in a musical activity.

60% of the students surveyed participate in a physical education activity.

Does this mean that all students surveyed either participate in a musical activity or a physical education activity? Explain.

Independent and Dependent Events

Dependent

In the real world, events can happen that affect the outcome of other events. For example, if you get A's in math, your chances of getting into college will improve. We could say that grades in math and getting into college are *dependent*. However, your grades in math will not affect the chances of rain tomorrow. We could say that grades in math and the weather are *independent*.

In mathematics, we can decide whether two events are dependent or independent by looking at the probabilities of the two events. If the probability of one event changes as a result of the other event occurring, we say that the two events are dependent. If the probability of one event does not change as a result of the other event occurring, we say that the two events are independent. In this lesson and the next, you will perform experiments that illustrate both of these ideas. You will calculate experimental probabilities and compare them with theoretical probabilities. In addition, you should discover a way to calculate $P(A \cap B)$ without having to draw a tree diagram or count outcomes one at a time.

SITUATION 1

Ms. Dep has divided her mathematics class into 7 groups. She has the names of 7 group leaders, 4 girls and 3 boys, in a hat. She will choose the names of 2 group leaders, who will each have to explain a different problem to the class. However, she does not want the same student to be chosen twice. Therefore, once the first name is chosen, she puts it aside and chooses the second name from among the remaining 6 names. She wants to know the probability of choosing 2 girls.

The experiment below is designed to determine an experimental probability for choosing 2 girls. Since choosing two girls requires choosing a girl 1st AND a girl 2nd, the probability of choosing 2 girls is written as $P(\text{girl 1st} \cap \text{girl 2nd})$.

EXPERIMENT 1

Work in groups of 3 or 4 students. Each student should conduct the following experiment.

Put the names of 4 girls (G1, G2, G3, and G4) and 3 boys (B1, B2, and B3) into a container. Play the role of Ms. Dep 10 times.
• Shake the container.

- Choose the first name, record it and put it aside.
- Choose the second name and record it.
- Return both names to the container.

Repeat 9 more times.

A. What is the number of times that you chose a girl 1st AND a girl 2nd?

B. What is your experimental probability, P(girl 1st $\cap$ girl 2nd)?

C. Group members should pool their counts. What is the group experimental probability?

D. Your teacher will pool the data from each group. What is the class experimental probability?

EXERCISES

1. Copy and complete the following diagram. It is like a tree diagram, except that we wrote the entries under "Choose 2nd Name" and "Outcome" as horizontal lists separated by commas rather than as vertical lists. Notice that when you choose a 2nd name, only 6 names are left to choose from.

Choose 1st Name	Choose 2nd Name	Outcome
G1	G2, G3, G4, B1, B2, B3	G1G2, G1G3, G1G4, G1B1, G1B2, G1B3
G2	G1, G3, G4, B1, B2, B3	G2G1, G2G3, G2G4, G2B1, G2B2, G2B3
G3		
G4		
B1	G1, G2, G3, G4, B2, B3	B1G1, B1G2, B1G3, B1G4, B1B2, B1B3
B2		
B3		

2. a. Circle all outcomes with 2 G's. How many times does the event 2 G's occur?

   b. What is the total number of possible outcomes?

   c. What is the value of P(girl 1st $\cap$ girl 2nd)?

   d. What is the difference between your class' experimental probability and the theoretical probability?

3. The Multiplication Counting Principle can be used to check your answers to Exercise 2, part c. Answer the questions below using the Multiplication Counting Principle.

    a. What is the number of outcomes with girl 1st AND girl 2nd?

1st Event	2nd Event	Outcome
Choose a Girl	Choose a Girl	Choose 2 Girls

$$\underline{\qquad} \quad \cdot \quad \underline{\qquad} \quad = \quad \underline{\qquad}$$

    b. What is the number of possible outcomes?

1st Event	2nd Event	Outcome
Choose a Name	Choose a Name	Choose 2 Names

$$\underline{\qquad} \quad \cdot \quad \underline{\qquad} \quad = \quad \underline{\qquad}$$

    c. Answer the questions below using the Multiplication Counting Principle.

4. Do your answers to Exercise 2, part c, and Exercise 3, part c, agree?

An interesting question to think about is the following:

    What is the probability that the 2nd name chosen is a girl's name if you already know that the first name chosen is a girl's name?

To answer this question, notice that if a girl's name was chosen first, then only 3 girls' names remain out of 6 names. Therefore, the probability is $\frac{3}{6}$. The question can be written using any of the following.

    P(2nd name is a girl's name, given that the 1st name is a girl's name)

    P(girl 2nd, given girl 1st)

    P(girl 2nd $\mid$ girl 1st)

In our example, P(girl 2nd $\mid$ girl 1st) $= \frac{3}{6}$. This is an example of a new type of probability called a *conditional* probability. You are being asked to find the probability of choosing a girl 2nd based on the condition that a girl was chosen first.

    Be very careful not to confuse $\mid$ with $\cap$. As we already noted,

P(girl 1st $\cap$ girl 2nd) = probability of both events occurring $= \frac{12}{42}$

P(girl 2nd $\mid$ girl 1st) = probability of girl 2nd occurring,

        given that girl 1st has already occurred $= \frac{3}{6}$

Thus, the two probabilities mean very different things. However, there is an important relationship between them, as illustrated by the following.

$$P(\text{girl 1st} \cap \text{girl 2nd}) = \frac{4 \cdot 3}{7 \cdot 6}$$
$$= \frac{4}{7} \cdot \frac{3}{6}$$
$$= P(\text{girl 1st}) \cdot P(\text{girl 2nd} \mid \text{girl 1st})$$

In fact, this situation generalizes as follows.

For any two events A and B,

$$P(A \cap B) = P(A) \cdot P(B \mid A)$$

You can think of this rule in the following way.

The probability of both A and B occurring is the probability that A occurs, multiplied by the probability that B occurs, given that A has already occurred.

EXERCISES

Refer to the diagram in Exercise 1 to answer the following.

5. a. What is the number of outcomes with boy 1st AND boy 2nd? What is $P(\text{boy 1st} \cap \text{boy 2nd})$?

  b. What is the number of outcomes with girl 1st AND boy 2nd? What is $P(\text{girl 1st} \cap \text{boy 2nd})$?

  c. What is the number of outcomes with boy 1st AND girl 2nd? What is $P(\text{boy 1st} \cap \text{girl 2nd})$?

6. a. Write the symbol that means "the probability that the 1st name chosen is a boy's name and the 2nd name chosen is a boy's name."

  b. Explain what the symbol $P(\text{boy 2nd} \mid \text{girl 1st})$ means and give its numerical value.

7. Find the following probabilities.

  a. $P(\text{girl 1st})$?

  b. $P(\text{boy 1st})$?

  c. $P(\text{girl 2nd} \mid \text{girl 1st})$?

  d. $P(\text{girl 2nd} \mid \text{boy 1st})$?

  e. $P(\text{boy 2nd} \mid \text{girl 1st})$?

  f. $P(\text{boy 2nd} \mid \text{boy 1st})$?

8. Use the probabilities that you found in Exercises 5 and 7 to help you decide whether the following statements are true or false. Show your work.

a. P(girl 1st $\cap$ boy 2nd) $= P$(girl 1st) $\cdot P$(boy 2nd $\mid$ girl 1st)

b. P(boy 1st $\cap$ boy 2nd) $= P$(boy 1st) $\cdot P$(boy 2nd $\mid$ boy 1st)

9. P(boy 1st $\cap$ girl 2nd) is equal to the product of what two probabilities? Check your answer by using the probabilities found above.

10. What is the probability that Ms. Dep will choose 2 boys' names? Explain.

11. Suppose Ms. Dep chooses a new set of group leaders with 5 girls' names and 2 boys' names. Again, she chooses 2 leaders to explain problems to the class and uses the same method that she used in Situation 1.

a. What is the probability that she will choose 2 girls? Show work.

b. What is the probability that she will choose 2 boys? Show work.

c. What is the probability that she will choose a girl 1st and a boy 2nd? Show work.

d. What is the probability that she will choose a boy 1st and a girl 2nd? Show work.

e. What is the sum of the probabilities in parts a through d?

Independent and Dependent Events

Independent

SITUATION 2

Mr. Indy has divided his mathematics class into 7 groups. He has the names of 7 group leaders, 4 girls and 3 boys, in a hat. He will choose the names of 2 group leaders, who will each have to explain a different problem to the class. In order to keep students on their toes, he wants to choose the names in such a way that one student could be chosen twice. Therefore, once he chooses the first student, he puts the name back into the hat, shakes the hat and chooses the second student. He wants to know the probability of choosing 2 girls.

The experiment below is designed to determine an experimental probability for choosing 2 girls, that is, P(girl 1st $\cap$ girl 2nd).

EXPERIMENT 2

Work in groups of 3 or 4 students. Each student should conduct the following experiment.

Put the names of 4 girls (G1, G2, G3 and G4) and 3 boys (B1, B2 and B3) into a container. Play the role of Mr. Indy 10 times.

- Shake the container
- Choose the 1st name, record it, return it to the container
- Shake the container
- Choose the second name, record it, return it to the container.

Repeat 9 more times.

A. What is the number of times that you chose a girl 1st AND a girl 2nd?

B. What is your experimental probability, P (girl 1st $\cap$ girl 2nd)?

C. Group members should pool their counts. What is the group experimental probability?

D. Your teacher will pool the data from each group. What is the class experimental probability?

EXERCISES

1. Complete the following diagram.

Choose 1st Name	Choose 2nd Name	Outcome
G1	G1, G2, G3, G4, B1, B2, B3	G1G1, G1G2, G1G3, G1G4, G1B1, G1B2, G1B3
G2	G1, G2, G3, G4, B1, B2, B3	G2G1, G2G2, G2G3, G2G4, G2B1, G2B2, G2B3
G3		
G4		
B1	G1, G2, G3, G4, B1, B2, B3	B1G1, B1G2, B1G3, B1G4, B1B1, B2B2, B2B3
B2		
B3		

2. **a.** On your paper, circle all outcomes with 2 G's. How many times does the outcome 2G's occur?

   b. What is the total number of possible outcomes?

   c. What is the value of $P(\text{girl 1st} \cap \text{girl 2nd})$?

   d. What is the difference between your class' experimental probability and the theoretical probability?

3. The Multiplication Counting Principle can be used to check your answers to Exercise 2. Answer the questions below using the Multiplication Counting Principle.

   a.

1st Event		2nd Event		Outcome
Choose a Girl		Choose a Girl		Choose 2 Girls
____	·	____	=	____

   b.

1st Event		2nd Event		Outcome
Choose a Name		Choose a Name		Choose 2 Names
____	·	____	=	____

   c. What is the value of $P(\text{girl 1st} \cap \text{girl 2nd})$? (Use answers to a and b above.)

4. Do your answers to Exercise 2, part c, and Exercise 3, part c, agree?

5. Refer to the experimental probabilities in Experiment 2 to answer the following questions.

   a. What is the value of $P(\text{girl 1st})$?

   b. What is the value of $P(\text{girl 2nd} \mid \text{girl 1st})$?

   c. What is the value of $P($girl 1st $\cap$ girl 2nd$)$?

   d. Is the following statement true or false?

      $P($girl 1st $\cap$ girl 2nd$) = P($girl 1st$) \cdot P($girl 2nd $\mid$ girl 1st$)$

6. What is the major difference between Ms. Dep's and Mr. Indy's methods for choosing students? Which method do you prefer? Why?

In Mr. Indy's class, the chances of choosing a girl 2nd are not affected by what happens on the 1st choice. After the first name is chosen, no matter what that choice is, it is returned to the hat. For the second choice, there are 7 names in the hat, 4 of which are girls' names. Therefore, $P($girl 2nd$)$ is $\frac{4}{7}$. In Exercise 5, part b, you should have discovered that $P($girl 2nd $\mid$ girl 1st$)$ is also $\frac{4}{7}$. Thus, in Mr. Indy's class,

    $P($girl 2nd $\mid$ girl 1st$) = P($girl 2nd$)$.

In general, for any two events A and B, whenever $P(B \mid A) = P(B)$ we say that events A and B are *independent*. The equation says that the probability of B, given A is the same as the probability of B. In other words, A does not affect the chances of B occurring. Thus, in Mr. Indy's class, we can say that "choosing a girl 1st" and "choosing a girl 2nd" are independent events.

   If A and B are independent, since $P(B \mid A) = P(B)$, the rule $P(A \cap B) = P(A) \cdot P(B \mid A)$ simplifies to $P(A \cap B) = P(A) \cdot P(B)$.

   On the other hand, if $P(B \mid A) \neq P(B)$ we say that events A and B are *dependent*. To see an example of dependent events, we return to Ms. Dep's class and compare $P($girl 2nd $\mid$ girl 1st$)$ with $P($girl 2nd$)$. Recall that $P($girl 2nd $\mid$ girl 1st$) = \frac{3}{6}$. To find $P($girl 2nd$)$, we refer to the diagram in Exercise 1 and count the outcomes in which a girl appears 2nd. Since the count is 24 and the total number of possible outcomes is 42, $P($girl 2nd$) = \frac{24}{42}$. Thus, in Ms. Dep's class, $P($girl 2nd $\mid$ girl 1st$) \neq P($girl 2nd$)$ and we can say that "choosing a girl 1st" and "choosing a girl 2nd" are dependent events. This should make sense to you on the grounds that, in Ms. Dep's class, the chances of choosing a girl 2nd are affected by what was chosen 1st.

EXERCISES

7. Show that in Mr. Indy's class $P($girl 1st $\cap$ girl 2nd$) = P($girl 1st$) \cdot P($girl 2nd$)$.

8. What is the probability that Mr. Indy will choose 2 boys' names? Explain.

9. Suppose Mr. Indy chooses a new set of group leaders with 5 girls' names and 2 boys' names. Again he chooses 2 leaders to explain problems to the class and uses the same method that he used in Situation 2.

   a. What is the probability that he will choose 2 girls? Show your work.

   b. What is the probability that he will choose 2 boys? Show your work.

   c. What is the probability that he will choose a girl 1st and a boy 2nd? Show your work.

   d. What is the probability that he will choose a boy 1st and a girl 2nd? Show your work.

   e. What is the sum of the probabilities in parts a, b, c, and d?

10. The diagram shows a seating chart of Mr. King's class.
A = the set of students in the art club
B = the set of students in the band
Each small square represents one student.

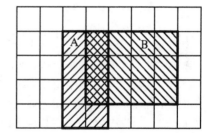

   a. What do you know about a student who is in the set $A \cap B$?

Suppose that a student is chosen at random from Mr. King's class. Count the appropriate squares to answer parts b through e.

   b. What is the value of $P(A \cap B)$?

   c. What is the value of $P(A)$?

   d. What is the value of $P(B)$?

   e. What is the value of $P(B \mid A)$?

     Hint. This means "the probability that the chosen student is in the band, given that the student is in the art club". To find the correct probability, you will need to restrict your attention to students in the art club (how many?) and ask how many students in the art club are also in the band.

   f. Does $P(A \cap B) = P(A) \cdot P(B)$? Show your work.

   g. Does $P(A \cap B) = P(A) \cdot P(B \mid A)$? Show your work.

   h. Are A and B dependent or independent events? Explain.

                                          Building Foundations 113

11. **Rule 1:** $P(X \cap Y) = P(X) \cdot P(Y)$
    Rule 2: $P(X \cap Y) = P(X) \cdot P(Y \mid X)$
    Which rule works for any two events X and Y? What must be true about X and Y to use the other rule?

12. Suppose that, in order to play softball today, you must get at least a B on today's math quiz AND it must not be raining. You estimate that the probability of getting at least a B on the quiz is $\frac{3}{4}$ and the weather report says that you have an 8 out of 10 chance that it will not rain. What is the estimated probability that you will play softball today?

13. What is the significance of the teachers' names in Situations 1 and 2?

Geometry and Probability

In Figure 1, notice that the area of the shaded region is one square unit and that the area of the whole figure is 9 square units. Thus, the ratio of the shaded area to the area of the whole figure is $\frac{1}{9} \approx 0.11$.

In Figure 2, the dots have been randomly distributed throughout the figure.

Figure 1

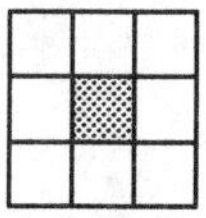

Figure 2

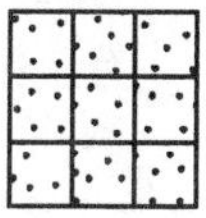

EXERCISES

The following questions refer to Figure 2.

1. Answer the following without actually counting the dots. Give both fraction and decimal forms for your answer.

    a. Estimate the ratio of the dots in the top row to the dots in the whole figure.

    b. Estimate the ratio of the dots in the 4 unit squares found in the corners to the dots in the whole figure.

    c. Estimate the ratio of the dots in the center square to the dots in the whole figure.

2. Answer the following by actually counting the dots. Give both fraction and decimal forms for your answers.

    a. Calculate the ratio of dots in the top row to dots in the whole figure.

    b. Calculate the ratio of dots in the 4 unit squares found in the corners to dots in the whole figure.

    c. Calculate the ratio of dots in the center square to dots in the whole figure.

3. Give both fraction and decimal forms for your answers.

    a. Calculate the ratio of the area of the top row to the area of the whole figure.

    b. Calculate the ratio of the area of the 4 unit squares found in the corners to the area of the whole figure.

    c. Calculate the ratio of the area of the center square to the area of the whole figure.

4. Compare your answers to Exercises 2 and 3. What do you observe?

5. A speck of dust lands on Figure 2. What is the probability that the speck is in the center square?

ACTIVITY 1

Work in groups of 3 or 4 students. Each student should place a random dot transparency over Figure 3 and count the number of dots in the shaded region and in the whole figure.

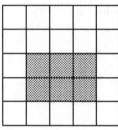

Figure 3

A. Pool your group data to calculate a ratio for the sum of group members' dots in the shaded region to the sum of group members' dots in the whole figure. Give both fraction and decimal forms.

B. Compute the ratio of area of shaded region to area of whole figure for Figure 3. Give both fraction and decimal forms.

C. Compare your answers to parts A and B. What is the difference between the dot ratio and the area ratio (round your answer to the nearest 1/100th)?

D. What is the probability that a speck of dust landing on Figure 3 will land in the shaded region?

E. Compare your answers to parts B and D.

F. If 400 dots are spread randomly throughout Figure 3, how many do you predict will land inside the shaded region?

Activity 1 was designed to suggest the two most basic and important ideas in geometric probability. If dots are spread randomly throughout a figure,

$$\frac{\text{dots in shaded region}}{\text{dots in whole figure}} \approx \frac{\text{area of shaded region}}{\text{area of whole figure}}$$

and

$$\frac{\text{area of shaded region}}{\text{area of whole figure}} = \begin{array}{l}\text{probability that a dot selected at random} \\ \text{from the whole figure is in the shaded} \\ \text{region.}\end{array}$$

EXERCISES

6. A local carnival has two different dart games. In both games, you win if you get the dart inside the shaded region. The game boards, shown here, are identical in size.

Which game would you rather play?

Explain your answer.

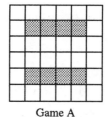

Game A

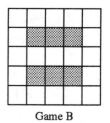

Game B

You can use the basic ideas of geometric probability to estimate the area of a figure even if you do not know how to calculate the area exactly. Example 1 illustrates how to do this.

EXAMPLE

Estimate the area of the triangle.

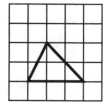 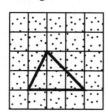

With Transparency

SOLUTION

We placed a random dot transparency over the figure and counted the dots in the triangle as well as in the whole figure. If a dot appeared to be exactly on a border, we omitted it from our counts. Dots that appeared to be more than halfway into a region were considered to be in that region.

Number of dots in the triangle = 19

Number of dots in the whole figure = 167

We then reasoned as follows.

$$\frac{\text{dots in triangle}}{\text{dots in whole figure}} \approx \frac{\text{area of triangle}}{\text{area of whole figure}}$$

Thus, we have

$$\frac{19}{167} \approx \frac{x}{25}$$

$$2.84 \approx x$$

The actual area of the triangle is 3 square units, so our estimate was fairly accurate.

EXERCISES

7. Estimate the areas of the given triangles using a method similar to the one described in Example 1. Work in groups of 3 or 4 students. Each student should be responsible for 2 of the following figures and use a random dot transparency to count dots in the triangle and in the whole figure. The group is responsible for computing an area estimate for each figure.

Give both fraction and decimal forms for your ratios. Round your decimal answers to the nearest $\frac{1}{100}$ th.

a. 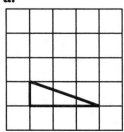   **b.** 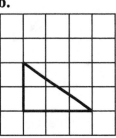   **c.** 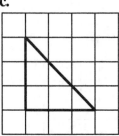   **d.**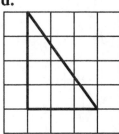

e. 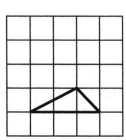   **f.** 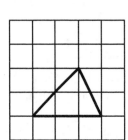   **g.** 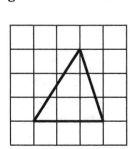   **h.**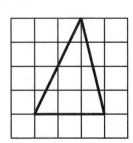

8. List 4 pairs of triangles in Exercise 7 that might have equal areas.

9. The area of a triangle can be computed if its base and height are known.

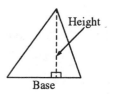

Copy and complete the table using data from Exercise 7. For each triangle find the mean of the area estimates from each group in your class. Each mean will serve as the class area estimate.

Figure	Class Area Estimate	Base	Height
a			
b			
c			
d			
e			
f			
g			
h			

10. What rule can you apply to the base and height of a triangle to get its area?

11. Write a formula for the area of a triangle using the variables A for area, b for base, and h for height.

12. Check your formula in a mathematics textbook. Use the correct formula for the area of a triangle to calculate the areas of the given triangles.

a.

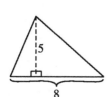

b.

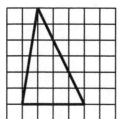

c.

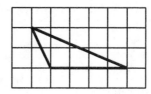

13. Use a random dot transparency to estimate the areas of the given circles. Estimate your answers to the nearest 1/100th.

a.

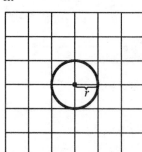

b.

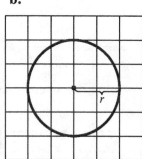

c.

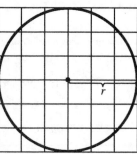

14. a. Copy and complete the following table using data from Exercise 13. For each circle, find the mean of the area estimates from each group in your class. Each mean will serve as the class area estimate. Leave an extra row at the bottom of the table.

Figure	Radius	(Radius)^2	Class Area Estimate
a			
b			
c			

b. Predict the area of a circle of radius 4 based on the data in your table. Place the information at the bottom of the appropriate columns in the table.

c. The area of a circle is approximately how many times the square of the radius?

d. The formula for the area, A, of a circle of radius r is

$$A = \pi r^2, \quad \text{where } \pi \approx 3.14.$$

To obtain your own experimental approximation for π, add one column labeled $\dfrac{\text{Area}}{(\text{radius})^2}$ to the table in part a. Complete the table by computing $\dfrac{\text{Area}}{(\text{radius})^2}$ to the nearest $\dfrac{1}{100}$th.

Find the average of the first 3 numbers in your new column (to the nearest $\dfrac{1}{100}$th.) This number is your estimate for π.

What is the difference between your estimate for π and the decimal approximation 3.14?

e. Compute the area of a circle of radius 4 using the correct formula with $\pi \approx 3.14$ (round to the nearest $\frac{1}{100}$th).

Compare your answer with your answer for part b.

ACTIVITY

A particular carnival game uses a mat consisting of $1\frac{1}{2}$" squares that has been placed on the ground. The object of the game is to drop a penny onto the mat so that it lands completely inside one of the squares.

Take an $8\frac{1}{2}$" x 11" sheet of graph paper and mark off as many $1\frac{1}{2}$" squares as will fit on your paper. Drop a penny 20 times onto the paper.

A. How many times did you win (the penny landed inside a square)? How many times did you lose (the penny touched one or more lines)?

B. Pool your class data and calculate the ratio of winning trials to the total number of trials.

C. Based on your answer to part B, what is the experimental probability of winning the game?

D. To calculate the theoretical probability of winning the game, you must decide where the "safe" regions are for the penny to land. To do this, think about the safe points for the **center** of the penny to land on. Four "just barely safe" locations are shown in this figure.

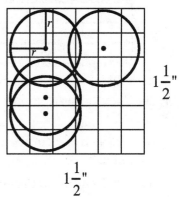

$1\frac{1}{2}$"

$1\frac{1}{2}$"

i. Place a penny inside the square and push it around the four sides. Notice the location of the center. Remove the penny and shade in the safe region for the center to land on.

ii. The radius of a penny is approximately $\frac{3}{8}$" = 0.375".

Calculate the area of the shaded region.

iii. Calculate the probability of winning the game.

E. Change the mat to 2" squares. Compute the theoretical probability of winning the game.

F. Change the mat to 1" squares. Compute the theoretical probability of winning the game.

G. Change the mat to $\frac{3}{4}$" squares.

Compute the theoretical probability of winning the game.

Quizzes

Conducting a Survey
Quiz

Name _____

Students in Mr. Snover's class were surveyed to determine their favorite type of pet. The results of the survey are tallied below:

Dog	Cat	Gerbil
ﬆﬅﬅ ﬆﬅﬅ	ﬆﬅﬅ ￨￨￨	ﬆﬅﬅ
￨		

1. Fill in the following frequency table.

Pet	Frequency	Relative Frequency Fractional Form		Relative Frequency Decimal Form	Percent
		Unreduced	Reduced	to nearest 100th	
Dog					
Cat					
Gerbil					
Totals					

2. Use the information in the table to construct a *frequency* bar graph and a *relative frequency* bar graph.

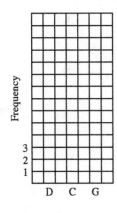
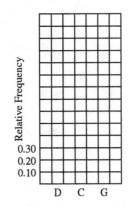

3. **a.** What is the favorite pet in Mr. Snover's class?

   b. The favorite pet received how many more votes than the second favorite pet?

   c. In Mr. Snover's class how many fewer students prefer gerbils than dogs?

4. The local pet store owner plans to stock his store with a *total* of 40 new pets. He plans to buy only dogs, cats, and gerbils, but needs to decide how many of each to buy. If he uses Mr. Snover's class as representative of pet-buyer preferences, how many dogs should he buy? Show your work.

5. Mr. Jensen's class conducted the same survey. A frequency bar graph of the results appears here.

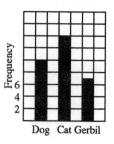

The students in Mr. Jensen's class all had to fill out a frequency table just like the one in problem 1.

   a. What should the total in the "Frequency" column be?

   b. What should the total in the "Relative Frequency, Fraction Form" column be?

   c. What should the total in the "Percent" column be?

6. In Ms. Adam's class, 30 students responded to the same survey. If the relative frequency of "Cat" is $\frac{2}{5}$, how many students in Ms. Adam's class prefer cats? Show your work.

BONUS

Ms. Washington's class conducted the same survey. If the "Frequency" for Gerbil is 4 and the "Relative Frequency" for Gerbil is $\frac{1}{7}$, what is the total number of students who responded to the survey in Ms. Washington's class? Show your work.

The Meaning of Mean
Quiz

Name _____

1. At the Savoy Theater, the mean amount of money spent per person at the snack bar is $2.93.

   a. Does this imply that every person who attends the Savoy Theater spends $2.93 at the snack bar? Explain.

   b. Evan and Barry went to a movie. Evan spent $2.50 at the snack bar, and the average amount spent by the two boys was $2.93. Did Barry spend more or less than Evan? Explain.

2. Joan's three exam grades are 83, 85, and 75.

   a. What is the mean of Joan's exam grades? Show your work.

   b. Joan has another exam tomorrow. She would like to raise her mean to 85. What score will she need on tomorrow's exam to raise her mean to 85? Show your work.

3. Give a list of four exam scores that have a mean of 75.

4. a. Calculate the mean of the following numbers: 1, 5, 7, 10, 17.
   b. Draw a number line diagram for the numbers in part a.

   c. What is the total of the distances above the mean?
   d. What is the total of the distances below the mean?

Ratios and Rates
Quiz

Name _____

1. The telephone company is offering a special rate to those who call long distance between the hours of 11 PM and 7 AM. Customers pay just 60 cents for every 5 minutes that they talk long distance during these hours.

   a. How many cents per minute does the customer pay?

   Fraction ____ $\dfrac{\text{cents}}{\text{minute}}$ Decimal ____ $\dfrac{\text{cents}}{\text{minute}}$

   b. How many minutes per cent can a customer talk long distance between the hours of 11 PM and 7 AM?

   Fraction ____ $\dfrac{\text{minutes}}{\text{cent}}$ Decimal ____ $\dfrac{\text{minutes}}{\text{cent}}$

2. At Camp Blue Lake there are 20 girls and 30 boys. One activity that the campers really enjoy is canoeing. The camp has 10 canoes.

   a. How many campers are there per canoe?

   Fractional form ____   Decimal form ____

   b. How many canoes are there per camper?

   Fractional form ____   Decimal form ____

   c. How many girls are there per canoe?

   Fractional form ____   Decimal form ____

   d. How many boys are there per canoe?

   Fractional form ____   Decimal form ____

   e. How many girls are there per boy?

   Fractional form ____   Decimal form ____

   f. How many boys are there per girl?

   Fractional form ____   Decimal form ____

3. Explain why you would (or would not) like to go to Camp Blue Lake based on the rates and ratios found in Question 3.

4. At the Newtown Community Pool there are 3 lifeguards for every 45 swimmers in the pool. At the Midvale Community Pool there are 2 lifeguards for every 28 swimmers in the pool.

    a. Find the number of swimmers per lifeguard at the Newtown Community Pool.

    b. Find the number of swimmers per lifeguard at the Midvale Community Pool.

    c. Which pool would you consider safer? Explain.

5. Fifteen dentists were asked to name their favorite type of music for the office. Ten said soft rock and five said jazz.

    a. Write the ratio, in fractional form, of the number of dentists who prefer soft rock to the number of dentists who prefer jazz.

    b. Write the ratio of the numbers of dentists who prefer jazz to the total number of dentists surveyed.

    c. Write the ratio of the number of dentists who preferred soft rock to the total number of dentists surveyed.

Equivalent Fractions
Quiz

Name _____

Mrs. Lanko's class has collected money for charity and has decided that 2 out of every 5 dollars will be donated to the Special Olympics and the rest will be donated to the Save the Whales Foundation.

1. **a.** Out of every 5 dollars collected by the class, how many will be donated to the Special Olympics?

   b. Out of every 5 dollars collected by the class, how many will be donated to the Save the Whales Foundation?

2. Fill in the boxes to illustrate possibilities for Mrs. Lanko's class. Each box represents $5. Use an "S" to represent each dollar donated to the Special Olympics and a "W" to represent each dollar donated to the Save the Whales Foundation.

3. Fill in the missing entries in the table.

Total	Special Olympics
$ 5	$2
$10	
$15	

4. Graph the data in the table. Label the horizontal axis "Total" and the vertical axis "Special Olympics." Then add 2 new points to the graph by following the pattern established by the first 3 points.

5. Using the graph, find an approximate answer to the following question. If the class donated $8 to the Special Olympics, how much money was collected by the class?

6. a. What is the ratio of dollars donated to the Special Olympics to dollars collected by the class?

   b. What is the ratio of dollars donated to the Save the Whales Foundation to dollars collected by the class?

7. If $80 was collected by the class, how much was donated to the Special Olympics? Show your work.

8. If $40 was donated to the Special Olympics, how much money was collected by Mrs. Lanko's class? Show your work.

9. If the class collected $40, how much was donated to the Save the Whales Foundation? Show your work.

10. If $12 was donated to the Save the Whales Foundation, how much money was collected by the class? Show your work.

BONUS

If $15 was donated to the Save the Whales Foundation, how much was donated to the Special Olympics? Show your work.

Similar Figures
Quiz

Name _____

1. What does it mean to say that two figures are similar?

2. What does it mean to say that two figures are not only similar but also congruent?

3. The two figures shown below are similar (but not drawn to scale).

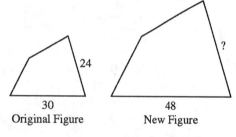

30
Original Figure

48
New Figure

24

?

    a. Determine the scale factor. Show your work.

    b. Find the length of the side with the question mark. Show your work.

4. The two figures shown below are similar (but not drawn to scale).

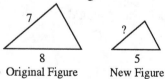

7

8
Original Figure

?

5
New Figure

    a. Determine the scale factor. Show your work.

    b. Find the length of the side with the question mark. Show your work.

Graph Paper Art
Quiz

Name _____

1. Multiply the coordinates of the emphasized points by 2. Plot the new points on $\frac{1}{4}$ inch graph paper and connect them as indicated below.

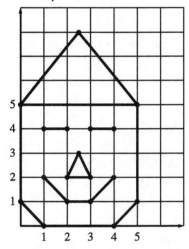

2. **a.** The hat in the original figure has two slanting lines. Find the length of one of them using a centimeter ruler.

   b. Measure the corresponding slanting line in your drawing.

   c. What is the ratio of the length found in part b to the length found in part a?

   d. What is the scale factor from the original figure to your new, enlarged figure?

   e. What is the relationship between the scale factor and the number that was used to multiply the coordinates?

Capture-Recapture Experiment Quiz

Name _____

The Environmental Protection Agency wishes to estimate the number of fish in Crescent Pond. They catch and tag 60 fish, and return them to the lake.

1. A sample consisting of 80 fish is caught. Each fish is examined for a tag and is then returned to the lake. Six of those fish caught have tags on them. Based on this sample, estimate the number of fish in the lake. Show your work.

2. The next day, a sample of 100 fish are caught. Again, each fish is examined for a tag and is then returned to the lake. Eight of those fish caught have tags on them. Based on this sample, estimate the number of fish in the lake. Show your work.

3. Which sample, the sample with 80 fish or the one with 100 fish, is more likely to give you the better population estimate? Explain why.

BONUS

Average the two population estimates to find a new population estimate. Show your work.

Pool the data from the two samples to find a new population estimate. Show your work.

Getting the Picture
Quiz

Name _____

1. Fill in the blanks with the correct person's name.

Alex has 4 times as many stamps as Andrew.

_____   _____

2. Complete the picture to illustrate the following sentence.

Maria is 3 cm taller than Miguel.

150 cm   150 cm

_____   _____

3. Write a sentence that describes the situation.

√ √ √ √   √ √ √ √ √ √ √ √ √ √

Votes for Brand *X*   Votes for Brand *Y*

4. Circle all correct descriptions of the given situation.

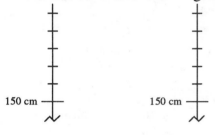

0 1 2 3 4 5 6 7 8   0 1 2 3 4 5 6 7 8
    Emily's age   JoAnn's age

a. JoAnn is 2 times as old as Emily.   **b.** Emily is 3 years older than JoAnn.

c. JoAnn is $\frac{1}{2}$ as old as Emily.   **d.** JoAnn is 3 years older than Emily.

e. Emily is 2 times as old as JoAnn.   **f.** Emily is 3 years younger than JoAnn.

g. JoAnn is 3 years younger than Emily.   **h.** Emily is $\frac{1}{2}$ as old as JoAnn.

5. Juan has two times as many baseball cards as Lamar.

   a. Fill in the table of possible values.

Number of Cards Owned by Lamar	Number of Cards Owned by Juan
1	
2	
3	
	10
8	

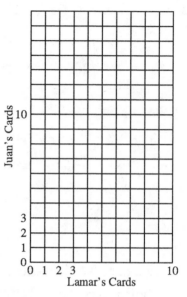

   b. Plot the data points in the table on the graph paper.

   c. In the table above, a rule can be applied to each number in the first column to get the number in the second column. Describe this rule.

   d. If x represents the number of cards owned by Lamar, write an expression using x that represents the number of cards owned by Juan.

   e. If the number of cards owned by Lamar is 20, what is the number of cards owned by Juan?

   Explain how to get your answer using x.

   f. If the number of cards owned by Juan is 14, what is the number of cards owned by Lamar?

   What equation could you solve to obtain your answer?

6. Isabella and Antonio work in two different stores. If x represents the weekly salary in dollars of Isabella, $x + 4$ represents the weekly salary in dollars of Antonio.

   a. Fill in the table of possible salaries for Isabella and Antonio.

   b. In the above table, a rule can be applied to each number in the first column to get the number in the second column. Describe this rule.

Isabella's Weekly Salary	Antonio's Weekly Salary
25	
	40
x	$x + 4$

   c. If $x = 10$, what is $x + 4$?

   d. If $x + 4 = 20$, what is x?

   e. Fill in the blanks with the correct person's name.

   i. _____ earns more money per week than _____.

   ii. _____ earns less money per week than _____.

7. Megan and Paulette are sisters. The graph below describes the relationship between their ages in years.

   a. Use the points on the graph to fill in the table.

Megan's Age	Paulette's Age

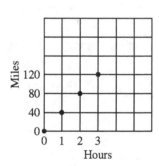

   b. Add four points to the graph following the established pattern.

   c. In the above table, a rule can be applied to the number in the first column to get the number in the second column. Describe this rule.

   d. If x represents Megan's age, write an expression using x that describes Paulette's age.

   e. If Megan is 8 years old, how old is Paulette? Explain how to get your answer using the graph.

   f. If Paulette is 4 years old, how old is Megan? Explain how to get your answer using the graph.

BONUS

A car is traveling at a constant speed on a highway. The graph shown here describes the relationship between the number of hours traveled and the number of miles traveled.

   a. If the car travels for 3 hours, how many miles will it go?

   b. How many hours does it take for the car to go 200 miles?

   c. What is the speed of the car, that is, how many miles does it travel per hour?

Explorations with Prisms
Quiz

Name _____

1. Fill in the table referring to the given prisms.

   a.   **b.**   **c.**

	Name of Shape of Base	Number of Sides of Base	Number of Faces	Number of Vertices	Number of Edges
a.					
b.					
c.					

2. a. If the base of a prism has 3 sides, how many faces would the prism have?

  b. In the table a rule can be applied to each number in the "Number of Sides of Base" column to get the "Number of Faces" column. Describe this rule.

  c. If the base of the prism has x sides, how many faces would the prism have?

3. a. If the base of the prism has 3 sides, how many vertices would it have?

  b. In the table a rule can be applied to each number in the "Number of Sides of Base" column to get the "Number of Vertices" column. Describe this rule.

  c. If the base of a prism has x sides, how many vertices would it have?

4. a. If the base of a prism has 3 sides, how many edges would the prism have?

b. In the table a rule can be applied to each number in the "Number of Sides of Base" column to get the "Number of Edges" column. Describe this rule.

c. If the base of a prism has x sides, how many edges would the prism have?

5. Using the table, plot 3 data points on each of the following grids.

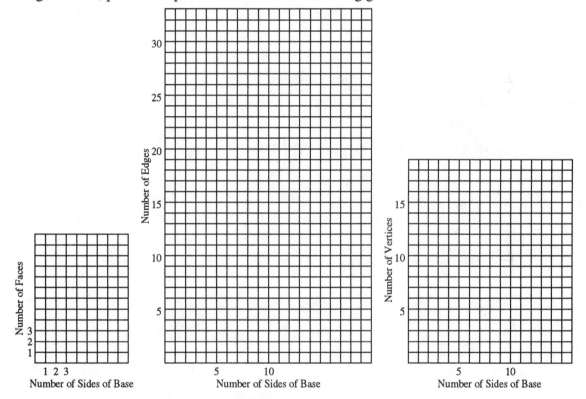

Add 3 new points to each graph following the established pattern.
Use the graphs to answer the following questions:

a. If the base of the prism has 7 sides, how many edges does it have?

b. If the prism has 8 vertices, how many sides does the base have?

c. If the number of faces of the prism is 6, how many sides does the base have?

6. Imagine a prism with 12 faces. How many sides does the base have? Explain.

7. Imagine a prism with 12 vertices. How many sides does the base have? Explain.

8. Imagine a prism with 12 edges. How many sides does the base have? Explain.

9. Euler's formula for pyramids states that for a given pyramid the number of faces plus the number of vertices is the same as the number of edges plus two. Therefore, if

F = the number of faces,

V = the number of vertices, and

E = the number of edges, then

$F + V = E + 2.$

Does this rule also hold true for these prisms?

Explorations with Pyramids
Quiz

Name _____

1. Fill in the table referring to the given pyramids.

a.   **b.**   **c.**

	Name and Shape of Base	Number of Sides of Base	Number of Faces	Number of Vertices	Number of Edges
a.					
b.					
c.					

2. a. If the base of a pyramid has 6 sides, how many faces would the pyramid have?

   b. In the table a rule can be applied to each number in the "Number of Sides of Base" column to get the "Number of Faces" column. Describe this rule.

   c. If the base of the pyramid has x sides, how many faces would the pyramid have?

3. a. If the base of the pyramid has 6 sides, how many vertices would it have?

   b. In the table a rule can be applied to each number in the "Number of Sides of Base" column to get the "Number of Vertices" column. Describe this rule.

   c. If the base of a pyramid has x sides, how many vertices would it have?

4. a. If the base of a pyramid has 6 sides, how many edges would the pyramid have?

    b. In the table a rule can be applied to each number in the "Number of Sides of Base" column to get the "Number of Edges" column. Describe this rule.

    c. If the base of a pyramid has x sides, how many edges would the pyramid have?

5. Using the table, plot 3 data points on each of the following grids.

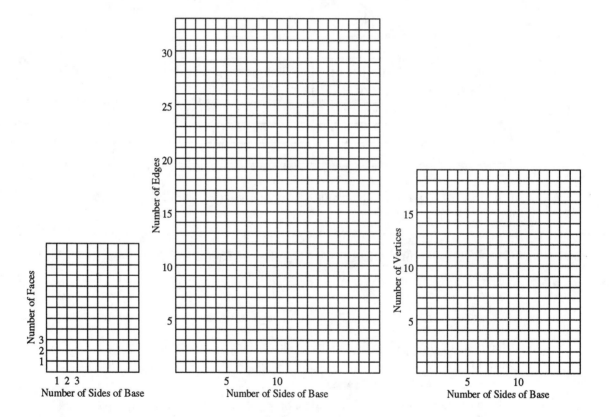

Add 3 new points to each graph following the established pattern.
Use the graphs to answer the following questions.

    a. If the base of the pyramid has 7 sides, how many edges does it have?

    b. If the pyramid has 8 vertices, how many sides does the base have?

    c. If the number of faces of the pyramid is 6, how many sides does the base have?

6. Imagine a pyramid with 12 faces. How many sides does the base have? Explain.

7. Imagine a pyramid with 12 vertices. How many sides does the base have? Explain.

8. Imagine a pyramid with 12 edges. How many sides does the base have? Explain.

Thinking Graphically I Quiz

Time & Distance

Name _____

1. Sketch the time-distance graph for a trip from home to a friend's house in Funtown, 170 miles away. Your total distances from home for various times are provided in the table.

Time Travelled (hours)	Total Distance Travelled (miles)
0	0
1	40
2	50
2.5	90
3	100
3.5	110
4	125
5	170

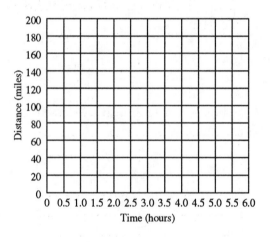

2. How far did you travel during the first 2 hours?

3. What was the total time it took for you to drive to Funtown?

4. It gets dark at about 9 p.m. during the summer in the area through which you were driving. You started your trip at 4:30 p.m. Did your driver have to turn on the car lights during the trip?

5. How far did you travel during each of the following time intervals?
   a. the first hour
   b. from time = 2 hours to time = 4 hours.
   c. from time = 1 hour to time = 5 hours.

6. You started the trip with a full tank of gas. The car you are driving gets only 12 miles per gallon of gas. If the gas tank holds 13 gallons, did you have to stop for gas before reaching Funtown?

Thinking Graphically II
Quiz

Time & Speed

Name _____

1. Sketch the time-distance graph for a trip from home to a friend's house in Bergsville. Your total distances from home for various times are provided in the table.

Time Travelled (hours)	Total Distance Travelled (miles)
0	0
1	20
2	80
2.5	85
3	100
3.5	120
4	140
5	180

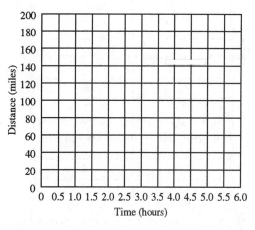

2. What was the average speed for the time interval from time = 3 hours to time = 5 hours?

3. During which one-hour time interval was your average speed the greatest?
   Hint: Look for the steepest parts of your graph.

4. What was your average speed during the time interval from number 3?

5. During which $\frac{1}{2}$ hour time interval was your average speed the slowest?

6. What was your average speed during the time interval from number 5?

Explorations with Perimeter
Quiz

Name _____

1. The length of one side of a square is $6\frac{1}{2}$". Find the perimeter of the square. Show your work.

2. The perimeter of a square is 60 cm. Find the length of one side of the square. Show your work.

3. On the graph paper below, draw two rectangles whose perimeter is 20 units, but whose lengths and widths are different.

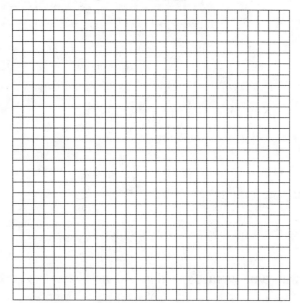

4. A rectangular lot measures 150 ft. by 200 ft.
   a. What is the perimeter of the lot? Show your work.

   b. A particular type of fence costs $3 per foot. How much will it cost to enclose the lot with this type of fence? Show your work.

5. A rectangle has a perimeter of 44 units and a width of 7 units.

    a. Draw this rectangle on the graph paper below.

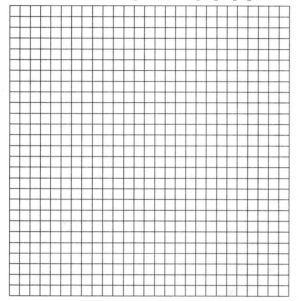

    b. What is the length of the rectangle?

    c. Write a formula that describes perimeter, P, in terms of width, w, and length, l.

    d. Write an equation that you could solve to determine the length of a rectangle whose perimeter is 44 units and whose width is 7 units.

        What is the solution of your equation?

6. a. A rectangular city block is 300 yards wide and 500 yards long. If Tom jogs once around the block, how far will he go?

    b. A mile is 1760 yards. If Tom jogs once around the block, will he jog more than a mile or less than a mile?

BONUS

Refer to question 6. Tom's coach requires that Tom jog at least 5 miles. How many times must Tom jog around this block to satisfy the coach's requirement? Show your work.

Explorations with Area
Quiz

Name _____

1. Find the area of a rectangle whose width is 10 ft. and whose length is 14 ft. Show your work.

2. On the graph paper below, draw 2 rectangles whose area is 24 square units, but whose widths and lengths are different.

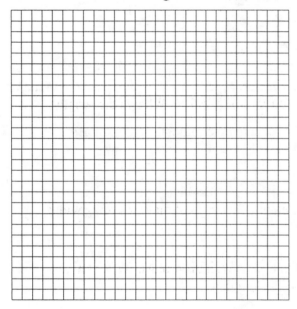

3. On the graph paper below, draw a square whose area is 36 square units. What is the length of one side of the square?

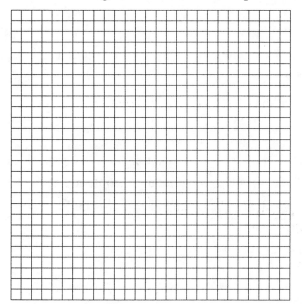

4. The area of a rectangle is 40 sq. ft. and its width is 5 ft. What is the length of the rectangle? Show your work.

5. Write a formula that describes the area of a rectangle, A, in terms of its width, w, and its length, l.

6. The area of a rectangle is 60 sq. units and its width is 4 units. Write an equation that you could solve to find the length.

What is the solution to your equation?

7. The Wilsons are going to remodel their rectangular living room. They plan to buy new carpet and wallpaper. The floor measures 12 feet by 15 feet and the ceilings are 7 feet high.

a. How many square feet of carpet will they need to buy?

If the carpet costs $14 per square foot, how much will it cost to carpet the living room? Show your work.

b. To determine the amount of wallpaper to buy, the Wilsons calculated the amount of wall space in the living room. They included the area occupied by the windows and the door, reasoning that they would rather have extra paper than not enough. How many square feet of wallpaper did the Wilsons decide to buy? Show your work.

Area and Perimeter
Quiz

Name _____

The following questions refer to the diagram below:

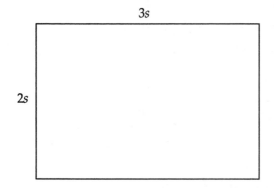

1. Determine the perimeter and area of the above rectangle in terms of *s*.

2. Complete the following table by looking at various values of *s*.

s	Perimeter	Area
$\frac{1}{2}$		
1		
$\frac{3}{2}$		
2		
3		

   a. What is the perimeter if *s* equals 4?

      What is *s* if the perimeter is 45 units?

   b. If the area is 96 square units, what is the value of *s*?

3. Plot the data points from your table using *s* and "Area."

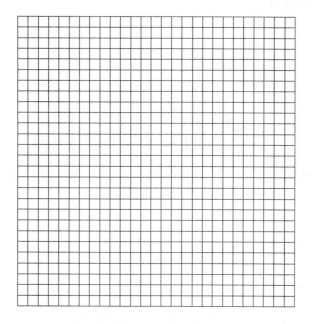

4. Using your graph, approximate the value of *s* if the area is 36 square units.

5. Plot the data points from your table using *s* and "Perimeter."

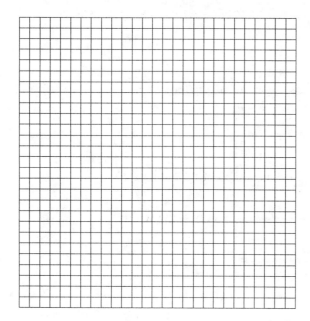

6. Using your graph, approximate the value of *s* if the perimeter is 35 units.

Rectangular Garden
Quiz

Name _____

Janet has 20 feet of fencing. She wants to plant a rectangular garden then enclose
it with the fencing.

1. Janet decides she would like the width of the garden to be 3 feet.
    a. What would be the length of the garden?
    b. What would be the area of the garden?
    c. Draw this rectangle below labeling the length and the width.

2. The graph below shows the relationship between the possible widths and
    lengths of Janet's garden. Use the graph to answer the following questions.

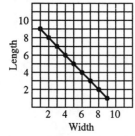

    a. If you know the width is 4 feet, how could you find the length?
        What is the length?
    b. If you know the length is 9 feet, how could you find the width?
        What is the width?

3. Refer to the graph from Exercise 2 to fill in the following table.

Width (ft)	Length (ft)	Area (ft^2)
1		
	8	
	7	
4		
5		
	4	
	3	
8		
9		

4. Use the data from the table in Exercise 3 to make a graph with width on the horizontal axis and area on the vertical axis.

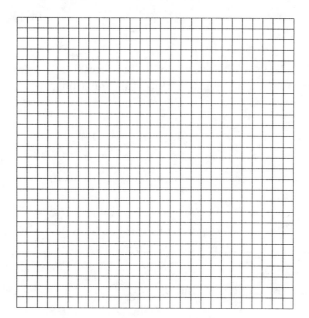

5. **a.** What width should Janet make her garden if she wants it to have the greatest possible area?

   b. What would the length of this garden be?

   c. What is the greatest area of Janet's garden?

   d. What is the name of the shape of this garden?

Counting Cubes
Quiz

Name _____

You decide to paint only the top and bottom of a block of cubes. Thus, only two sides of the block would be painted.

1. Fill in the following table.

Length of Edge	Block Dimensions	Number of Cubes in Block	Number of Cubes with No Paint	Number of Cubes with One Painted Side
2	$2 \times 2 \times 2$			
3	$3 \times 3 \times 3$			
4	$4 \times 4 \times 4$			

2. Plot your data points using the columns "Length of Edge" and "Number of Cubes with No Paint" on one of the grids below.

3. Predict how many cubes are not painted for a $5 \times 5 \times 5$ block. Fill in the appropriate column in the table. Plot your data point on the graph.

4. Plot your data points using the columns "Length of Edge" and "Number of Cubes with One Painted Side" on the grid you haven't used.

5. Predict how many cubes are painted on one side for a $5 \times 5 \times 5$ block. Fill in the appropriate column in the table. Plot your data point on the graph.

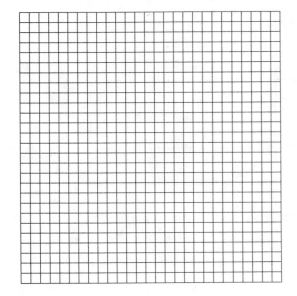 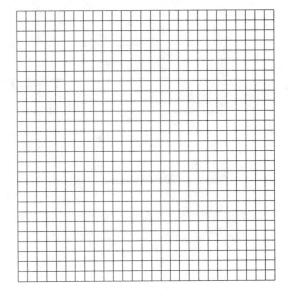

Probability
Quiz

Name _____

1. Suppose you roll one die. List all possible outcomes for your experiment.
    a. What is the probability of rolling a 2?
    b. What is the probability of *not* rolling a 2?
    c. What is the probability of rolling an odd number?
    d. What is the probability of rolling a 7?
    e. What percent of the time can you expect to roll a 5?

2. Suppose you roll one die 30 times.
    a. How many times can you expect to roll a 2?
    b. How many times can you expect to roll an odd number?

3. a. Complete the chart below with the outcomes for the sum of two dice.

First Die Outcome	Second Die Outcome					
	1	2	3	4	5	6
1						
2						
3						
4						
5						
6						

    b. What is the total number of possible outcomes when 2 dice are rolled?

c. List the possible outcomes that give a sum of 9 in the table below.

1st die	2nd die

Suppose you roll two dice.

d. What is the probability that the sum of the dice is 9?

e. What is the probability that you will roll doubles (that is, both dice have the same number)?

4. Suppose you roll 2 dice 72 times.

How many times would you expect that the sum of the 2 dice would be 9? Show your work.

5. If you roll 2 dice, what sum has the highest probability of occurring?

Coin Toss Experiments
Quiz

Name

1. Suppose you toss a coin 2 times. Using the tree diagram below, it is possible to determine all of the possible outcomes.

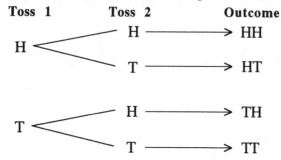

| Toss 1 | Toss 2 | Outcome |

H → HH
HT
TH
TT

   a. What is the probability of tossing two heads?
   b. What is the probability of tossing 2 tails?
   c. What is the probability of tossing one head and one tail?

2. Suppose you toss a coin 3 times.

   a. Complete the tree diagram below to determine all of the possible outcomes. List all possible outcomes under the heading "Outcome."

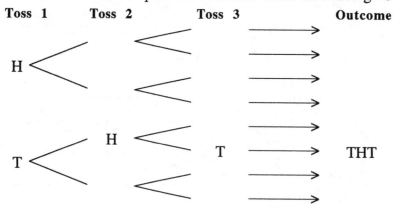

   b. What is the probability of obtaining 2 heads and 1 tail?
   c. What is the probability of obtaining 2 tails and 1 head?
   d. What is the probability of obtaining 3 tails?
   e. What is the probability of obtaining 3 heads?

3. Suppose that you "toss a coin 3 times" for a total of 24 trials. Refer to your answers to Question 2 to help you answer the following questions.

    a. How many times would you expect to obtain 2 heads and 1 tail?

    b. How many times would you expect to obtain 3 heads?

4. Pascal's Triangle can be used to determine the number of possible outcomes when a coin is tossed 4 times, 5 times, *etc*.

    a. Fill in the missing rows of Pascal's Triangle.

		Number of possible outcomes
Toss a coin 0 times	1	1
Toss a coin 1 time	1 1	2
Toss a coin 2 times	1 2 1	4
Toss a coin 3 times	1 3 3 1	8
Toss a coin 4 times		
Toss a coin 5 times		

    b. Observe the pattern in the first two tables and fill in the last two tables.

Toss a coin 2 times

Outcome	Probability
2H's	$\frac{1}{4}$
1H and 1T	$\frac{2}{4}$
2T's	$\frac{1}{4}$

Toss a coin 3 times

Outcome	Probability
3H's	$\frac{1}{8}$
2H's and 1T	$\frac{3}{8}$
1H and 2T's	$\frac{3}{8}$
3T's	$\frac{1}{8}$

Toss a coin 4 times

Outcome	Probability
4H's	
3H's and 1T	
2H's and 2T's	
1H and 2T's	
4T's	

Toss a coin 5 times

Outcome	Probability
5H's	
4H's and 1T	
3H's and 2T's	
2H's and 2T's	
1H and 2T's	
5T's	

What's Your Chance I
Quiz

Name _____

1. Suppose that a local restaurant offers ham sandwiches, chicken sandwiches and fish sandwiches. The customer may order a sandwich with either ketchup or special sauce on either bread or a roll. Using a tree diagram, list all of the different sandwiches that a customer could order.

   How many different sandwiches could a customer order?

2. The Pedal Power Bike Shop sells 3 kinds of bikes: 3 speed, 10 speed and 15 speed. The customer has a choice of 5 colors for any bike purchased: blue, red, yellow, green, and orange. For a limited time the shop also offers a complimentary headband or water bottle with each purchase.

   a. Make a "carefully ordered list" of all the different choices that a customer has. The list has been started for you.

   3BH
   3BW

   b. Use the Multiplication Counting Principle to determine the number of different choices that a customer has. Show your work.

   c. Suppose that the shop will randomly select a bike and a complimentary gift to offer as a prize for the local carnival. What is the probability that the selected prize is a green 3-speed bike and a water bottle?

BONUS

What is the probability that the prize includes the green 3-speed bike?

What's Your Chance II
Quiz

Name _____

1. At a party, Jason has a choice of 5 kinds of pizza: pepperoni, sausage, mushroom, olive and anchovy. He decides that he will eat one slice of each type of pizza.

    a. In how many different orders can he eat the pizza?

    Describe the method that you used to determine your answer.

    b. If Jason decides that he will eat the slice of anchovy pizza last, in how many different ways can he eat the remaining slices?

    Describe the method that you used to determine your answer.

    Write the answer using factorial notation.

2. In the Summer Olympics, 8 finalists will compete for the gold, silver, and bronze medals in the 110 meter high hurdle race.

    a. How many different slates of winners are possible?

    Describe the method that you used to determine your answer.

    b. Write your answer to part a by filling in the blanks:

    $_{\_}P_{\_}$ = _____ = _____

                expression   value

3. Fill in the table below.

	Expression	Value
	6!	
$_7P_3$		
$_6P_1$		
$_4P_4$		

What's Your Chance III
Quiz

Name _____

1. Explain the difference between a combination and a permutation.

2. The manager of a swim club must hire 2 new lifeguards for next summer. Megan, Laura, Coy, Kevin, and Andreas apply for the job.

    a. Make a carefully ordered list of the different pairs of lifeguards that can be chosen keeping in mind that the pair ML(Megan, Laura) is the same as the pair LM(Laura, Megan).

    How many different pairs are there?

    b. Write your answer to part a by filling in the blanks.

$$ _{\_}C_{\_} = \underset{\text{expression}}{\underline{\hspace{3cm}}} = \underset{\text{value}}{\underline{\hspace{2cm}}} $$

3. Fill in the table below.

	Expression	Value
$_7C_3$		
$_5C_4$		
$_6C_2$		

4. There are 5 eighth grade positions on the varsity cheerleading squad. If 12 students try out, how many different groups of 5 students could make the squad? Show your work.

Get Ready, Get Set
Quiz

Name _____

1. Refer to the Venn Diagram to answer the following questions.

   E = the set of students registered for an English class
   M = the set of students registered for a math class

   a. What is the total number of students in the freshman class at State University?

   b. Find the following. For the probabilities, assume that one student is chosen at random from the freshman class.

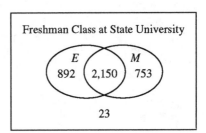

$N(E) =$	$P(E) =$
$N(M) =$	$P(M) =$
$N(\text{NOT } E) =$	$P(\text{NOT } E) =$
$N(\text{NOT } M) =$	$P(\text{NOT } M) =$
$N(E \text{ AND } M) =$	$P(E \text{ AND } M) =$
$N(E \text{ OR } M) =$	$P(E \text{ OR } M) =$
$N(E \cup M) =$	$P(E \cup M) =$
$N(E \cap M) =$	$P(E \cap M) =$

   c. Jay is a member of the set $E \cup M$. What does this tell you about Jay?

   d. Johanna is a member of the set $E \cap M$. What does this tell you about Johanna?

   e. What does the expression $P(E \cup M)$ mean?

2. a. Draw a Venn Diagram for the following.

   In the eighth grade class,

   • 12 students are on the basketball team

   • 25 students are on the soccer team

   • 8 students are on the soccer team and the basketball team

   b. How many students are on the soccer team or the basketball team?

3. Draw a Venn Diagram of 2 sets that are disjoint. Label one set A and the other B.

4. In Ms. Ricci's class, the following data was collected:

- 9 students play the piano
- 3 students play the guitar and the piano
- 14 students play the guitar or the piano

How many students play the guitar? Show your work.

5. Fill in the blanks with the symbols $N(A)$, $N(B)$, and $N(A \cap B)$ to make a true statement:

$N(A \cup B) = $ _____ $+$ _____ $-$ _____

When can you omit the subtraction and still get a true statement?

6. Fill in the blanks with the symbols $P(A)$, $P(B)$, and $P(A \cap B)$ to make a true statement:

$P(A \cup B) = $ _____ $+$ _____ $-$ _____

When can you omit the subtraction and still get a true statement?

Independent and Dependent Events Quiz

Name _____

1. Three soccer players and two tennis players have been nominated to win two awards: the Best Athlete Award and the Good Sport Award. The Awards Committee has decided that 2 different athletes will win the awards. First, they will choose the Best Athlete and then they will choose the Good Sport Award winner from the remaining candidates.

   a. The Awards Committee wants to look at all possible outcomes. Help them by completing the modified tree diagram below. We named the three soccer players S1, S2, and S3 and the two tennis players T1 and T2.

Choose Best Athlete	Choose Good Sport	Outcome
S1		$\longrightarrow$
S2		$\longrightarrow$
S3		$\longrightarrow$
T1		$\longrightarrow$
T2		$\longrightarrow$

   b. To answer the questions below, assume that all outcomes listed above have an equal chance of occurring.

   i. What is the probability that a soccer player will win the Best Athlete Award and a soccer player will win the Good Sport Award?

   ii. What is the probability that a soccer player will win the Best Athlete Award and a tennis player will win the Good Sport Award?

   iii. What is the probability that a tennis player will win the Best Athlete Award and a soccer player will win the Good Sport Award?

   iv. What is the probability that a tennis player will win the Best Athlete Award and a tennis player will win the Good Sport Award?

   v. What is the sum of the four probabilities found above?

2. Suppose the Awards Committee will allow the same athlete to win both awards.

    a. The Awards Committee wants to look at all possible outcomes. Help them by completing the modified tree diagram below. We named the three soccer players S1, S2, and S3 and the two tennis players T1 and T2.

Choose Best Athlete	Choose Good Sport	Outcome
S1		$\longrightarrow$
S2		$\longrightarrow$
S3		$\longrightarrow$
T1		$\longrightarrow$
T2		$\longrightarrow$

    b. To answer the questions below, assume that all outcomes listed above have an equal chance of occurring.

        i. What is the probability that a soccer player will win the Best Athlete Award and a soccer player will win the Good Sport Award?

        ii. What is the probability that a soccer player will win the Best Athlete Award and a tennis player will win the Good Sport Award?

        iii. What is the probability that a tennis player will win the Best Athlete Award and a soccer player will win the Good Sport Award?

        iv. What is the probability that a tennis player will win the Best Athlete Award and a tennis player will win the Good Sport Award?

        v. What is the sum of the four probabilities found above?

3. a. In Question 1, are the events "Choose a soccer player for Best Athlete" and "Choose a soccer player for the Good Sport Award" independent or dependent? Explain your reasoning.

    b. In Question 2, are the events "Choose a soccer player for Best Athlete" and "Choose a soccer player for the Good Sport Award" independent or dependent? Explain your reasoning.

Geometry and Probability Quiz

Name _____

Use geometric probability to estimate the area of the peanut-shaped region below.

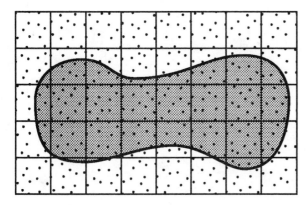

1. Count the dots inside the peanut-shaped region.

2. Count the dots in the whole figure.

3. What is the area of the whole figure?

4. Use the information found above to estimate the area of the peanut-shaped region. Show your work.

Teaching Notes

Conducting a Survey

Teaching Notes

PRE-ALGEBRA/ALGEBRA CONTENT

Part-whole concept
Equivalent fractions
Relationship between fractions and decimals
Percent
Developing and using tables and graphs to describe situations
Interpreting different mathematical representations

STATISTICS CONTENT

Frequency of Event A = the number of times that Event A occurs

Relative Frequency of Event A $= \dfrac{\text{Frequency of Event A}}{\text{Total Number of Events}}$

Create frequency tables and frequency bar graphs
Interpret frequency tables and frequency bar graphs

SUGGESTIONS FOR TEACHING

1. Introduce students to the vocabulary *frequency* and *relative frequency* by using the Activity.

2. Collect survey data by secret ballot and tally the data on a blackboard.

3. Have students work in small groups on the lesson.

EXTENSIONS

1. Have students bring in a frequency table or a bar graph from a newspaper. Each student group must write an article (no more than one page) about the data.

2. Repeat this lesson with a survey involving numeric data. For example, survey each member of the class to determine the number of children in his/her family.

3. Have students design their own survey question, carry out the survey and analyze the data. The topic might be a school or community issue.

4. Ask questions about the frequency tables that involve "not" and "or" such as:

   a. How many students in the survey prefer vanilla *or* strawberry?

   b. How many students in the survey do *not* prefer chocolate?

Ask students about the relationship between their answers to parts a and b.

5. Have students look for boy-girl differences in flavor preference and fill out a table such as the following:

Frequency of Student Flavor Preferences

	Boy	Girl	Total
Vanilla			
Chocolate			
Strawberry			
Total			

Ask questions such as the following.

   a. What percent of the boys prefer vanilla?

   b. What percent of the girls prefer chocolate?

   c. What percent of the students in the class prefer vanilla?

   d. Do boys and girls in your class appear to have different flavor preferences? Explain your answer.

   e. How many students in the class prefer vanilla *or* strawberry?

   f. How many students in the class do *not* prefer chocolate?

   g. How many students in the class are girls *and* prefer chocolate? Explain how to use the frequency table to find this answer.

   h. How many students in the class are girls *or* prefer chocolate? Explain how to use the frequency table to find this answer.

6. Have students use a compass and a protractor to construct a pie chart for your class and for Ms. Ryan's class.

Survey Worksheet

Name _____

Describe the survey that you conducted.

Fill in the following frequency table based on your survey.

Category	Frequency	Relative Frequency Fractional Form		Relative Frequency Decimal Form to nearest 100th	Percent
		Unreduced	Reduced		
Totals					

Complete each bar graph below based on the information in your table. Label your categories on the horizontal axis. Write three to five numbers along the Frequency axis to show your scale.

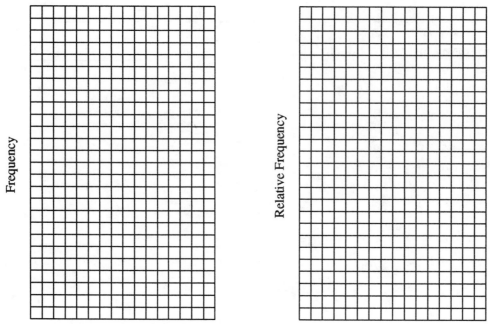

Describe the results of your survey in paragraph form.

The Meaning Of Mean

Teaching Notes

PRE-ALGEBRA/ALGEBRA CONTENT

Part-whole concept
"Fair share" model for division
The concept of fraction
Number line: distance between 2 points

STATISTICS CONTENT

Using tables to display data
Using tables to analyze data
The concept of (arithmetic) mean
Discovery of a method for computing the mean of a set of numbers

SUGGESTIONS FOR TEACHING

1. Activity 1: Distribute index cards so that each group has a total of 12 or 24 cards. The mean will then be easy to calculate. Be sure that students record the original number of cards each person received before pooling. Each group should report their results to the class to reinforce the idea that different sets of 3 (or 4) numbers with a sum of 24 have a mean of 8 (or 6). Similarly, sets of 3 (or 4) with a sum of 12 have a mean of 4 (or 3). Have students note that different distributions result in the same mean. Students should be able to discover a formula for calculating the mean:
$$\frac{\text{total number of cards}}{\text{size of group}} = \text{mean}$$
   Or, more generally,
$$\frac{\text{sum of numbers}}{\text{number of numbers}} = \text{mean}$$
   If students have difficulty discovering the formula, repeat Activity 1 with 36 cards per group.

2. In Exercise 3, adding one index card to the group will result in a non-integral mean. Thus, students will have to divide a single index card evenly. A ruler and scissors may be needed. This activity reinforces the concept of fraction.

Building Foundations

3. Activity 2: Here groups of students are given the mean and are asked to determine the total number of index cards necessary to obtain that mean. Students should discover the following:

   total number of cards = size of group · mean.

   Point out the relationship between this equation and the first equation in Suggestion 1.

4. This lesson introduces a visual representation which we call a *number line diagram* to help students see the mean as a balance point among the numbers in a data set. To construct a number line diagram, plot each data point, compute the mean of the data set, and indicate the mean as shown in the example in the lesson. Ask students to construct a number line diagram for a data set in which 2 or more numbers are equal. Allow students to be creative. Two possible diagrams appear below for the data set consisting of 2, 8, and 8:

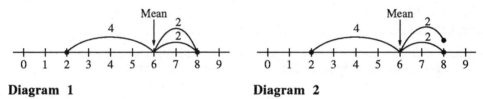

   Diagram 1   **Diagram 2**

   We prefer Diagram 2 because the vertical arrangement of the 2 points at 8 suggests describing the frequency of the number 8 on a vertical axis, which is precisely what is done in a histogram.

CAUTION

Some students may mistakenly believe that the number of data points above the mean must equal the number of data points below the mean. Rather, the total **distances** from the mean on one side must be equal to the total distances from the mean on the other side. You may want to introduce the concept of *median* to clarify this issue. In fact, the number of data points above the median must equal the number of data points below the median.

EXTENSIONS

1. Have students look for articles in newspapers or magazines that quote a mean.

2. Ask students to determine the mean number of pets or children in their families.

3. Have students determine what their next quiz or test score needs to be in order to have an average grade of 85.

4. Introduce the concept of median and contrast it with mean. (See the discussion above under CAUTION.)

5. Students who have studied integers could fill in a table such as the following.

Name	Original Number of cards	Mean (Fair Share)	Original Number – Mean of Cards
Hank	11	6	5
Sally	2	6	-4
Jo	3	6	-3
Roberto	9	6	3
Nakia	5	6	-1
Totals	30	30	0

Compare this table with the one in Exercise 8.

Ratios and Rates

Teaching Notes

PRE-ALGEBRA/ALGEBRA CONTENT

Rates expressed as fractions and decimals
Ratios expressed as fractions and decimals
Rates and ratios expressed concretely using icons (pictures or symbols)

SUGGESTIONS FOR TEACHING

1. Have students give examples of rates and ratios from real life. Emphasize that **units** are important.

   Examples

   30 miles/hour, 70 heartbeats/minute, 2.1 children/family, etc.

2. Have students gain experience in computing rates and ratios from real life.

   Examples

   Take pulse and compute beats per minute.

   Compare price per ounce (or gram) for a brand name product *versus* the store brand equivalent, or for different sized packages of the same product.

EXTENSIONS

1. The Equivalent Fractions lesson can be used as a related topic.

2. If you have students do the comparison shopping examples above, have groups of students compete to find the biggest **percent increase**. Prices must be verified and students must demonstrate the percent increase calculation in front of the class.

   Example

   Product 1: 10¢/oz. vs. 14¢/oz. gives a 4¢/oz. increase, which represents a 4/10 = 0.4 = 40% increase

   Product 2: 20¢/oz. vs. 25¢/oz. gives a 5¢/oz. increase, which represents a 5/20 = 0.25 = 25% increase

   Thus, although Product 1 has a smaller increase in price per ounce, it has a larger percent increase. Students who correctly demonstrate the Product 1 percent increase would be declared the winners.

Equivalent Fractions

Teaching Notes

Pre-Algebra/Algebra Content

Rates and ratios expressed in table form
Rates and ratios expressed concretely using icons (pictures or symbols)
Rates and ratios expressed by graphing ordered pairs
The concept of equivalent fractions
Solving an equivalent fraction equation (proportion)
Solving word problems by setting up and solving an equivalent fraction equation

Suggestions for Teaching

1. Make liberal use of the Icon-Table-Graph Worksheet until students understand the concepts of rate, ratio and equivalent fractions. Refer students back to the worksheet if they run into difficulty, especially with word problems.

2. In this lesson, students should be taught **why** the procedures they use are legal. For instance, to solve the equation

$$\frac{5}{6} = \frac{?}{24}$$

students should understand that they are multiplying $\frac{5}{6}$ by 1 in the guise of $\frac{4}{4}$, and therefore obtain an **equal** fraction.

$$\frac{5}{6} \cdot 1 = \frac{5}{6} \cdot \frac{4}{4} = \frac{20}{24}$$

This "legalizes" the procedure of multiplying both numerator and denominator of the original fraction by 4.

To solve the equation

$$\frac{?}{6} = \frac{20}{24}$$

students should understand that they are simply reversing the above process.

$$\frac{20}{24} = \frac{5}{6} \cdot \frac{4}{4} = \frac{5}{6} \cdot 1 = \frac{5}{6}$$

3. In this lesson, all solutions to equivalent fraction equations are positive integers. Thus, students should be able to determine an appropriate "multiplier" or "divider" by inspection.

4. Encourage students to label all four entries, including the unknown, in an equivalent fraction equation.

5. The NCTM *Standards* explicitly suggests that students not be taught to solve proportions (equivalent fraction equations) using cross-multiplication until they have the background to understand why cross-multiplication is legal. We agree with this suggestion and thus provide you and your students with alternative procedures for solving proportions **with understanding** in this lesson.

6. Point out the difference in representing "part to part" and "part to whole" rates and ratios.

   Example

   "3 nurses for every 10 patients" is a "part to part" relationship requiring 13 icons per box.

   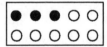

   "3 out of every 10 nurses" is a "part to whole" relationship requiring only 10 icons per box.

EXTENSIONS

1. Have students solve equivalent fractions in which the "multiplier" or "divider" is not a positive integer.

2. Have students exchange the word problems that they wrote in Exercise 5. Have them work in pairs to refine the statement of the problem, if necessary, and share the best problems and their solutions with the class.

3. The Similar Figures lesson can be used as a related topic.

4. The Capture-Recapture Experiment lesson can be used as a related topic.

Similar Figures

Teaching Notes

PRE-ALGEBRA/ALGEBRA CONTENT

Ratios expressed in fraction and decimal form
Solving an equivalent fraction equation

GEOMETRY CONTENT

Concept of similar figures: same shape, corresponding angles have the same
  measure, the scale factor for all pairs of corresponding sides is the same
  number.
Measurement to obtain scale factor
Use of protractor to measure angles
Concept of "stretcher": scale factor greater than 1
Concept of "shrinker": scale factor less than 1

SUGGESTIONS FOR TEACHING

1. The following lessons should be done as prerequisites:
   Rates and Ratios
   Equivalent Fractions

2. The method used in this lesson is consistent with the method used in the
   Equivalent Fractions lesson. However, in this lesson, we avoid dividing both
   numerator and denominator by the same number by using a scale factor
   (multiplier) that is less than 1. We believe that consistent use of the scale
   factor as a multiplier may be easier for students than having to decide
   between multiplication and division.

3. The word "corresponding" is used but not defined in this lesson. You may
   need to explain to students that "corresponding" means "matching", in a
   sense, and illustrate with several examples.

4. To find missing sides in similar figures, once students calculate a scale factor, they do not actually need to set up a proportion. In fact, they need only multiply a side in the original figure by the scale factor to obtain the corresponding side in the new figure. However, we recommend that students do a few problems using proportions to preview the method frequently used in high school geometry classes.

5. Students should be exposed to the following definition of similar figures, which is more formal mathematically.

> Two figures are **similar** if and only if corresponding sides are proportional and corresponding angles are congruent.

EXTENSIONS

1. The Graph Paper Art lesson can be used as a related lesson.

2. Have students investigate perimeters and areas of similar figures. For example, students could draw a 2 by 3 rectangle for an original figure and copy it with scale factors of 2, 3, and 4. Then students could fill in the following table. They might predict the values for a scale factor of 5 and verify their answers by drawing the figure.

Scale factor	Width	Length	Perimeter	Area
1	2	3	10	6
2				
3				
4	8	12	40	96
5				

Have students investigate:

a. ratio of corresponding sides vs. ratio of perimeters

Solution: If one figure has length of a side S_1 and perimeter P_1, and another figure has S_2 and P_2, respectively, then $\dfrac{S_2}{S_1} = \dfrac{P_2}{P_1}$

b. ratio of corresponding sides vs. ratio of areas

Solution: If one figure has length of a side S_1 and area A_1, and another figure has S_2 and A_2, respectively, then $\left(\dfrac{S_2}{S_1}\right)^2 = \dfrac{A_2}{A_1}$

Graph Paper Art

Teaching Notes

PRE-ALGEBRA/ALGEBRA CONTENT

Use of a coordinate plane
Ratios expressed in fraction form
Equivalent fractions

GEOMETRY CONTENT

Concept of similar figures
Scale factor for similar figures
Measurement

SUGGESTIONS FOR TEACHING

1. In all questions dealing with drawing similar figures on graph paper, have students make a list of the coordinates of the original figure's vertices and a corresponding list for the similar figure.

2. Suggest that the design in Exercise 6 be colored in or painted. The best ones can be displayed around your classroom.

3. The design in Exercise 6 may be a good candidate for a student's portfolio.

EXTENSIONS

1. Begin with a relatively simple figure, such as a triangle, on graph paper. Have students investigate what happens if you multiply the coordinates of the vertices by –1 and then plot and connect the corresponding points. Repeat this exercise using a multiplier of –2.

2. Use the idea of "rise over run" to draw similar figures on graph paper. To create the larger triangle, we chose a scale factor of 3 and made 3 consecutive copies of each side of the original triangle.

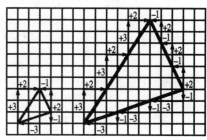

Capture-Recapture Experiment

Teaching Notes

PRE-ALGEBRA CONTENT

Part to whole concept
Ratios expressed as fractions and decimals
Scale factor
Solving an equivalent fractions equation (proportion)

STATISTICS CONTENT

Relative frequency
Sample vs. population
Sampling techniques—randomization
Pooling sample data
Effect of sample size on estimate of population

SUGGESTIONS FOR TEACHING

1. The following lessons should be done as prerequisites:

   Conducting a Survey (ratio concept and relative frequency)

   Ratios and Rates, Equivalent Fractions (solving an equivalent fraction equation)

   Similar Figures (scale factor and non-integer multiplier)

2. Possible substitutes for beans:

   goldfish crackers
   small styrofoam objects used for packing boxes

   Tag using a marker

   Possible substitutes for coffee can:

   shoe box with reasonably tight lid
   cereal box — tape shut to shake for randomization

3. Be sure that students take only one sample at a time. If they take more than one, the population that they are trying to estimate will change in size.

4. To choose a sample of 100 beans, a group of 4 (or 5) students should remove approximately $\frac{1}{4}$ cup of beans from the population and place them on a table. Each student should count the 25 (or 20) beans closest to him/her. Care must be taken to ensure that neither type of bean is "favored" in the counting.

5. For samples of size 100, you might want to use the idea of percent. Suppose your sample has 23 navy beans and your population has 207 navy beans:

Sample: $\frac{23}{100} = 23\%$ navy beans

207 is 23% of what number?

$207 = 0.23x$ Multiply mystery number by 0.23 to get 207.

$\frac{207}{0.23} = x$ Therefore, divide 207 by 0.23 to get the mystery number.

$900 = x$

Of course, you can also use the idea of percent for samples of different sizes.

6. We deliberately used the idea of scale factor to solve equivalent fraction equations in this lesson. Think of the scale factor as "stretching" the sample, or enlarging it to correspond to the size of the population—just as we used scale factors greater than 1 to stretch a geometric figure into a larger one.

7. If your students are not familiar with negative numbers, you may want them to calculate the "Difference" column in Exercise 7 by subtracting the smaller number from the greater.

EXTENSIONS

Create a large population of beans, for example 925, and tag it with 200 beans. A student can then take one sample consisting of 50 beans and estimate the population based on that sample, then return the sample to the population for the next student.

Prepare a frequency bar graph and have each student add his or her population estimate to the appropriate category. Using ranges such as 650 to 700, 700 to 750, *etc.*, will illustrate the point better than using individual quantities. The bar graph should approximate the shape of a normal curve with mean approximately equal to the total number of beans in the population.

If this experiment is repeated with a larger sample size, the population estimates should cluster more toward the mean; with a smaller sample size, the population estimates should spread out from the mean. This should illustrate that larger sample sizes result in more accurate estimations.

Getting the Picture

Teaching Notes

PRE-ALGEBRA/ALGEBRA CONTENT

Concept of variable as pattern generalizer in a table
Concept of variable as place holder in an equation
Concept of variable as a quantity which varies

Translate from narrative description of a relationship to a picture of the
relationship
Translate from a picture of a relationship to a narrative description of the
relationship

Given a narrative description of a relationship between two quantities:
Construct a table of ordered pairs
Describe the function rule in words
Describe the relationship using the variable symbol x
Given one quantity, find the other
Graph the ordered pairs in a coordinate plane
Given one quantity, find the other using the graph

Given a Cartesian graph to describe a relationship between two quantities:
Construct a table of ordered pairs
Describe the function rule in words
Describe the relationship using the variable symbol x
Given one quantity, find the other

Given x and an expression involving x to describe a relationship between two
quantities:
Construct a table of ordered pairs
Describe the function rule in words
Given one quantity, find the other
Give a narrative description of the relationship

SUGGESTIONS FOR TEACHING

1. Have extra graph paper handy.

2. Have students work in small groups on the lesson.

3. Exercises 2 and 5: Point out that many different answers are possible.

4. Exercise 6: It may be helpful to write the following equations.

Joseph's age = x
Serafina's age = $x + 2$

This allows the following:

If Joseph's age = 20
then Serafina's age = 20 + 2 = 22

5. When students solve problems graphically, arrows may be helpful (see figure). However, this process should not be purely mechanical; in Exercise 6, students should understand that the height of the point represents Serafina's age. The left arrow is not really necessary; we need only look to the left to determine the height. However, we draw the left arrow to help our eyes look straight to the left.

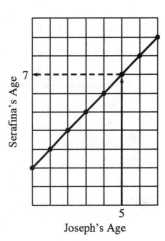

Joseph's Age

6. Point out that the quantity in the left column of the table is always measured on the horizontal axis and that the quantity in the right column of the table is always measured on the vertical axis.

EXTENSIONS

1. Use relationships that involve more than one operation.

Examples

5 more than 2 times x
5 less than 2 times x

2. Play "Guess My Rule"

Preparation:

Each student gets 2 cards and puts a rule, such as $y = 3x + 1$, on each card. Collect and shuffle the cards. Divide the class into groups of 3 or 4 and give each person 2 cards, face down. Group members should sit in a circle.

Play:

One person selects a rule card.

Beginning with the student to the left of the selector and continuing clockwise, the other group members take turns giving the selector a number to substitute for *x*.

The selector gives the corresponding value for *y*.

Group members should record data in a table:

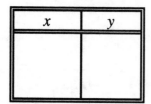

x	*y*

Each member has a chance to guess the rule after each row is added to the table, beginning with the member who chose the *x* value and continuing clockwise.

The 1st correct guesser becomes the next selector.

3. The lesson Explorations with Prisms can be used as a related topic.

4. The lesson Explorations with Pyramids can be used as a related topic.

Explorations With Prisms

Teaching Notes

PRE-ALGEBRA/ALGEBRA CONTENT

Looking for patterns
Concept of variable as pattern generalizer in a table
Concept of variable as a quantity which varies
Use of coordinate graphs to describe relationships
Given a graph and a particular x value, find y
Given a graph and a particular y value, find x

GEOMETRY CONTENT

Constructing 3-dimensional figures by cutting out and folding 2-dimensional figures
Vocabulary: prism, face, vertex, edge, base
Concrete experience with prisms - counting faces, vertices and edges

SUGGESTIONS FOR TEACHING

1. The lesson Getting the Picture should be done as a prerequisite.

2. Have students work in groups of 4. Each student will be responsible for assembling one prism.

3. Have students set up equations and solve them by inspection. For example: If a prism has 24 edges, how many sides does its base have?

    Solution: From Exercise 7, part b

    x = number of sides of base
    $3x$ = number of edges
    $3x = 24$

    $\therefore\ x = 8$

4. Consider using the Explorations with Pyramids lesson as a quiz for this lesson.

EXTENSIONS

1. Have students investigate properties of regular polygons using the 2-dimensional figures at the end of the lesson. For example, for each regular polygon, they could measure the angles and determine the sum of the measures. Have them make a table similar to the following.

Regular Polygons

Number of Sides	Measure of Each Angle	Sum of Angle Measures
3		
4		
5		
6		

Students can then look for patterns and predict more table values.

2. Have students write a paragraph about the life and accomplishments of Leonhard Euler.

3. The Explorations with Pyramids lesson can be used as a related topic.

4. Have students compare and contrast formulas in this lesson with the formulas for pyramids found in the Explorations with Pyramids Lesson.

TRIANGULAR PRISM

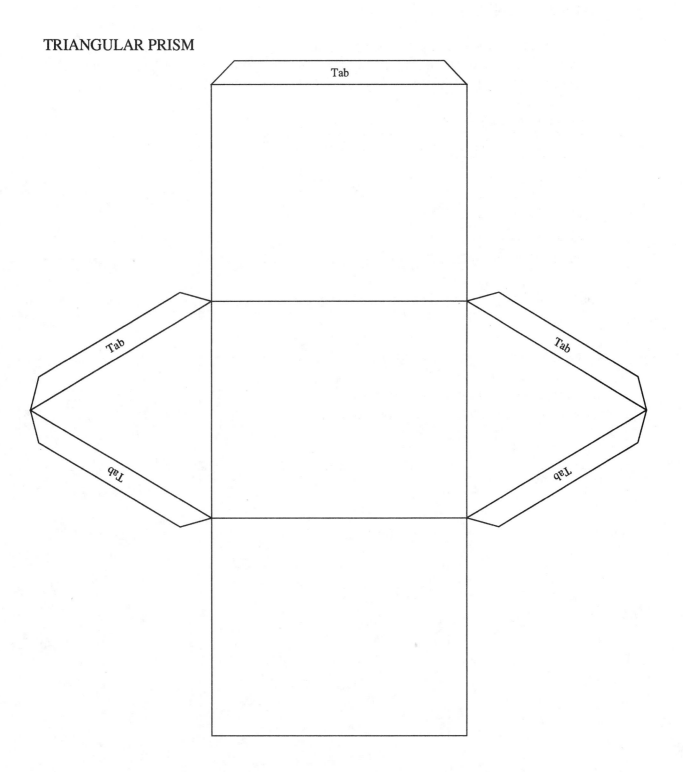

Tab

Tab

Tab

Tab

Tab

RECTANGULAR PRISM

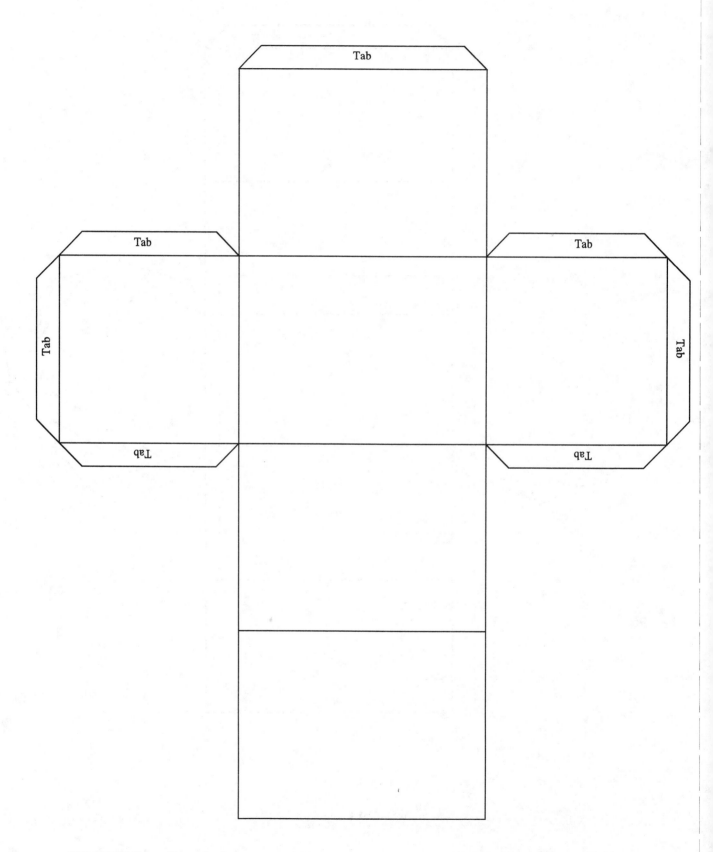

PENTAGONAL PRISM

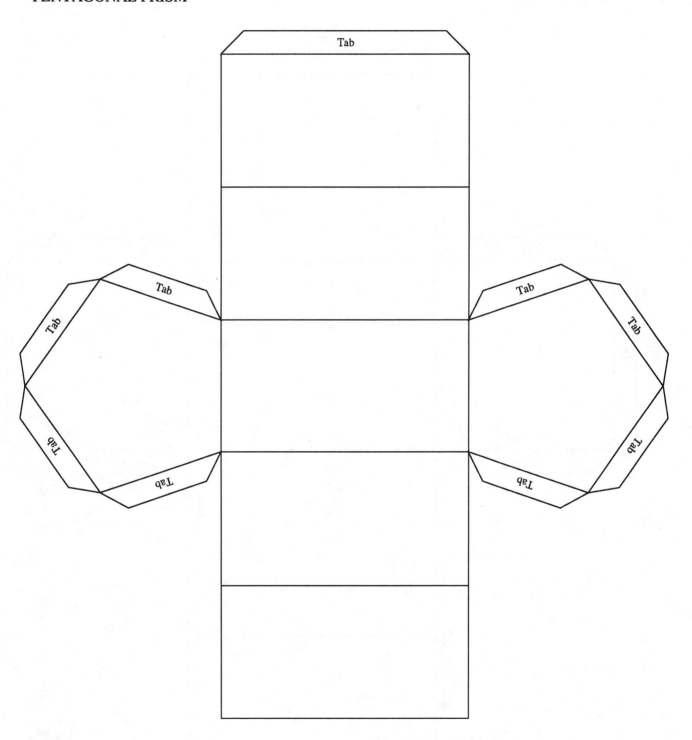

HEXAGONAL PRISM

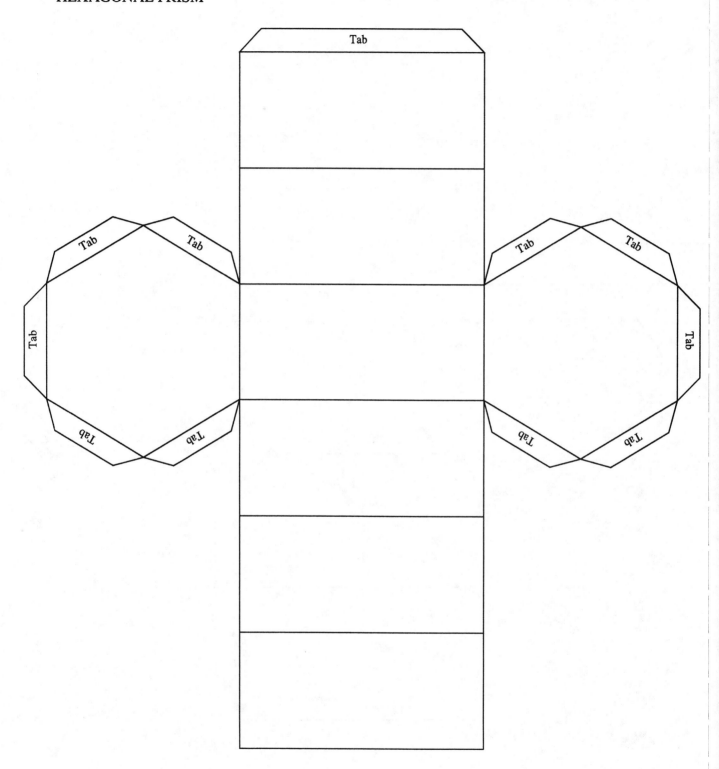

Explorations With Pyramids

Teaching Notes

PRE-ALGEBRA/ALGEBRA CONTENT

Looking for patterns
Concept of variable as pattern generalizer in a table
Concept of variable as a quantity which varies
Use of coordinate graphs to describe relationships
Given a graph and a particular x value, find y
Given a graph and a particular y value, find x

GEOMETRY CONTENT

Constructing 3-dimensional figures by cutting out and folding 2-dimensional
   figures
Vocabulary: pyramid, face, vertex, edge, base
Concrete experience with pyramids - counting faces, vertices, and edges

SUGGESTIONS FOR TEACHING

1. The lesson Getting the Picture should be done as a prerequisite.

2. Have students work in groups of 4. Each student will be responsible for
   assembling one pyramid.

3. Have students set up equations and solve them by inspection. For example:
   If a pyramid has 24 edges, how many sides does its base have?

   Solution: From Exercise 7, part b

   x = number of sides of base
   $2x$ = number of edges
   $2x = 24$
   $\therefore\ x = 12$

4. Consider using the Explorations with Prisms lesson as a quiz for this
   lesson.

EXTENSIONS

1. Have students investigate properties of regular polygons using the 2-dimensional figures at the end of the lesson. For example, for each regular polygon, they could measure the angles and determine the sum of the measures. Have them make a table similar to the following.

Regular Polygons

Number of Sides	Measure of Each Angle	Sum of Angle Measures
3		
4		
5		
6		

Students can then look for patterns and predict more table values.

2. Have students write a paragraph about the life and accomplishments of Leonhard Euler.

3. The Explorations with Prisms lesson can be used as a related topic.

4. Have students compare and contrast formulas in this lesson with the formulas for prisms found in the Explorations with Prisms Lesson.

5. Have students research the pyramids of ancient Egypt and write a short paper describing their findings.

TRIANGULAR PYRAMID

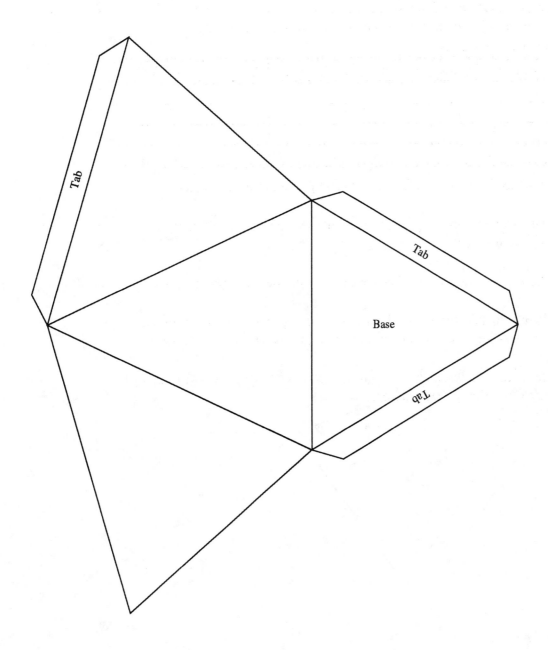

RECTANGULAR PYRAMID

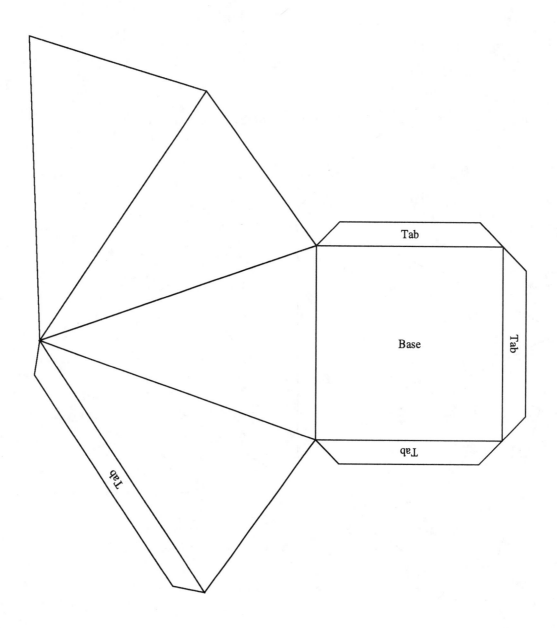

PENTAGONAL PYRAMID

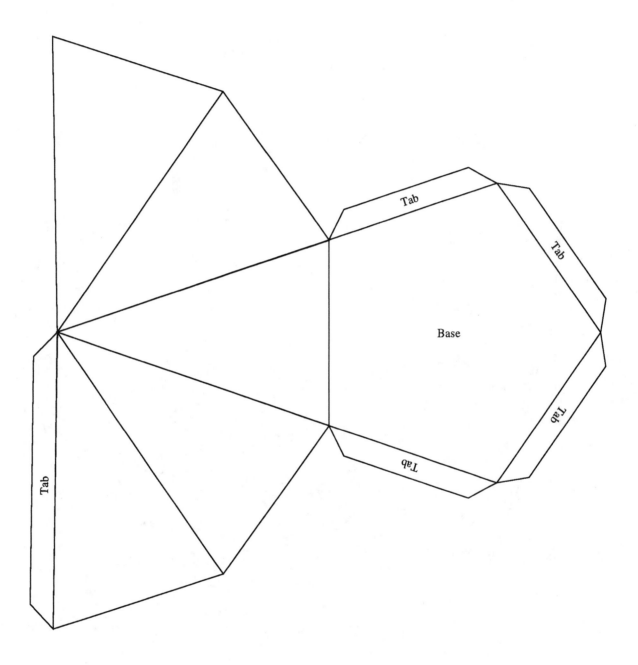

HEXAGONAL PYRAMID

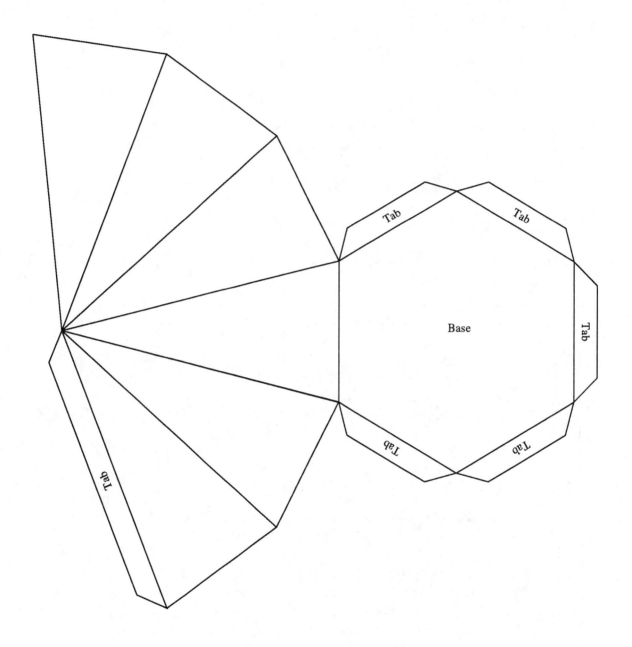

Thinking Graphically I

Time & Distance

Teaching Notes

PRE-ALGEBRA CONTENT

Developing and using tables and graphs to describe situations
Use of a coordinate plane
Concept of an interval
Connecting mathematics to real-world situations

SUGGESTIONS FOR TEACHING

1. Have students work in pairs on the lesson.

2. Please let your students work through this lesson on their own. Then, after they have had a chance to discover the concepts presented, discuss it as a class.

3. During discussion either before or after the students work on the lesson, emphasize the overall situation the graph represents, not just the specific points and their coordinates.

CAUTION

1. Initially, students may take the term *graph* to mean the coordinate grid. To help eliminate this possible misconception, the term *coordinate plane* is emphasized to distinguish the coordinate grid from the graph.

2. Considering a graph to be a picture of an event is a very common misconception for students. The graphs provided in the lesson are not the route for the trip. A nice summary of that misconception was developed in a project at the University of Maryland with Dr. Anna Graeber as the project director, funded by the National Science Foundation.

EXTENSIONS

1. Have students write interesting tasks that are more easily done by thinking about them graphically. This may be an opportunity for them to write in their journals or to create graphs for their tasks to put in a portfolio.

2. The lesson Thinking Graphically II is a natural extension for this lesson.

Thinking Graphically II

Time & Speed

Teaching Notes

Pre-Algebra/Algebra Content

Developing and using tables and graphs to describe situations
Use of a coordinate plane
Concept of an interval
Connecting mathematics to real-world situations
Interpretation of steepness (*i.e.* slope)

Suggestions for Teaching

1. The Thinking Graphically I lesson should be used as a prerequisite.

2. Have students work in pairs on the lesson.

3. Please let your students work through this lesson on their own. Then, after they have had a chance to discover the concepts presented, discuss it as a class.

4. During discussion either before or after the students work on the lesson, emphasize the overall situation the graph represents, not just the specific points and their coordinates.

5. If *rates* have been discussed previously, you may want to point out that speed is sometimes called the rate of movement.

Extensions

1. Give students the following definition of *slope*. For two points on a graph having coordinates (x,y) and (u,v), the *slope* of the line segment through them is the difference between their second coordinates divided by the difference between their first coordinates, *i.e.*

$$\text{slope} = \frac{y-v}{x-u}.$$

Then ask them the following questions:

a. What is the average speed from (1, 40) to (1.5, 80)? How does this compare to the slope?

b. Determine the slope of the line segment in the graph which connects the two points where time = 3 and time = 3.5 hours.

Note. Be careful about students' inferences about slopes of lines based upon this example. All the line segments here have non-negative slopes. You may want to give students more varied examples, including segments with slopes that are negative, and undefined (vertical lines). It may be interesting for them to try to interpret these slopes as speeds.

Explorations with Perimeter

Teaching Notes

Concept of variable as pattern generalizer in a table
Review of fraction and decimal arithmetic
Use of formulas:

$$P = 2l + 2w \text{ for a rectangle}$$

Substitute known values and solve the resulting equation by inspection
Use of graphs to estimate solutions:

for a fixed perimeter, given one dimension, estimate the other

Geometry Content

Concept of perimeter for squares and rectangles
Develop the formula $P = 2l + 2w$ by drawing several rectangles and finding a
pattern

Suggestions for Teaching

1. The lesson Getting the Picture should be done as a prerequisite.

2. Encourage students to think of figures whose perimeter can be easily
calculated, such as the perimeters of their desks. You could bring in various
objects and have students measure their perimeters using a ruler.

3. Have plenty of graph paper. Students who have difficulty determining
entries in the tables can use graph paper to draw an appropriate figure and
count units.

4. Some familiarity with the coordinate plane is necessary here. Students
should be able to create graphs on a piece of graph paper specifying each
axis and the scale. In Exercise 2, part e, students are given the scale for the
vertical axis. The horizontal axis should go up to 16. For the second graph,
in Exercise 10, students are told what each axis represents but they must
choose a scale. Both of the dimensions should go up to 14.

Building Foundations 205

EXTENSIONS

1. Have students find perimeters for figures that are not rectangles.

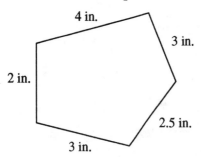

2. Work from a known perimeter back to finding a missing side.

Perimeter = 20 feet

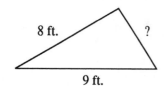

3. The Explorations with Area lesson can be used as a related topic.

4. The Rectangular Garden lesson can be used as a related topic.

Explorations with Area

Teaching Notes

PRE-ALGEBRA/ALGEBRA CONTENT

Concept of variable as pattern generalizer
Non-linear relationships: graphing ordered pairs and connecting points with a
   smooth curve
Use of exponent: Area of square = side^2
Problem-solving applications involving rates

GEOMETRY CONTENT

Concept of area for squares and rectangles
Compare and contrast area and perimeter
Given a fixed area, draw several rectangles having this area and determine the
   relationship between the length and width

SUGGESTIONS FOR TEACHING

The following lessons should be done as prerequisites:

Getting the Picture

Explorations with Perimeter

EXTENSIONS

1. The Rectangular Garden lesson can be done as a related topic.

2. Have students investigate areas of triangles using graph paper.
    a. Begin with areas of right triangles.

    Area $= \frac{1}{2} \cdot 4 \cdot 3 = 6$

b. Extend to areas of acute triangles

Area = Area small right Δ + Area larger right Δ

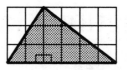

$$= \frac{1}{2} \cdot 2 \cdot 3 \ + \frac{1}{2} \cdot 4 \cdot 3$$

$$= 3 + 6 = 9$$

c. Extend to areas of obtuse triangles

Area = Area large right Δ – Area small right Δ

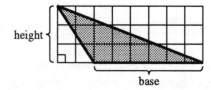

$$= \frac{1}{2} \cdot 8 \cdot 3 - \frac{1}{2} \cdot 2 \cdot 3$$

$$= 12 - 3 \ = 9$$

Notice that in all 3 cases, Area $= \frac{1}{2} \cdot b \cdot h$

Rectangular Garden

Teaching Notes

PRE-ALGEBRA/ALGEBRA CONTENT

Cause and effect relationship among variables
Developing and using tables and graphs to describe situations
Interpreting different mathematical representations
Looking for patterns and developing rules based on the patterns
Solving a maximization problem through the use of tables and graphs
Approximating solutions for a quadratic equation through the use of tables and graphs

GEOMETRY CONTENT

Concept of perimeter – measure in linear units
Concept of area – measure in square units
Concrete experiences in drawing rectangles with a fixed perimeter but with different areas

SUGGESTIONS FOR TEACHING

Review the ideas of perimeter and area.

The following situations deal with perimeter:

1. Janet jogs around an oval track

2. Marie puts baseboard molding in her living room

3. Rob places a lace border around his picture frame

The following situations deal with the idea of area:

1. Mark carpets his living room

2. The city of Philadelphia sponsors a concert on the infield of J.F.K. Stadium

3. Juanita paints her garage door

EXTENSIONS

1. **a.** Find the solution to the problem if Mrs. Wilson has 60 ft of fencing instead of 40 ft.

   b. Find the solution to the problem if Mrs. Wilson has 10 ft of fencing instead of 40 ft.

2. Find the solution to the original problem, except a wall of her house is used for one side of the garden.

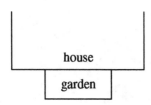

3. Find the solution to the original problem, except two sides of the garden are against the house.

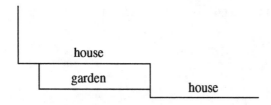

4. Given 12 inches of string, what type of geometric figure gives the maximum area? Have students use 12-inch lengths of string to outline the following figures on a piece of $\frac{1}{4}$ inch graph paper or geoboard: equilateral triangle, square, regular hexagon, circle. Estimate the number of squares inside each figure and fill in the following table.

Figure	Approximate Area
Equilateral Triangle	
Square	
Regular Hexagon	
Circle	

Which figure gives the maximum area?

Counting Cubes

Teaching Notes

This lesson was developed around a problem from the NCTM's *Curriculum and Evaluation Standards for School Mathematics* (March, 1989) on page 99:

> "Investigate what happens when different-sized cubes are constructed from unit cubes, the surface area is painted, and the large cube is then disassembled into its original unit cubes. How many of the $1 \times 1 \times 1$ cubes are painted on three faces, two faces, one face and no faces?"

PRE-ALGEBRA/ALGEBRA CONTENT

Looking for patterns
Concept of variable as pattern generalizer
Linear and non-linear relationships: generating data from concrete experiences, plotting ordered pairs and connecting points with a smooth curve
Using a graph to estimate solutions: given x, estimate y

GEOMETRY CONTENT

Concrete experience with 3-dimensional objects
Concept of volume of a cube
Concept of surface area of a cube

SUGGESTIONS FOR TEACHING

1. The following lessons should be done as prerequisites;

   Getting the Picture

   Explorations with Prisms

2. We recommend that you have plastic or wooden unit cubes or sugar cubes and colored chalk available so that students can construct and "paint" the different-sized cubes (blocks).

3. In Exercises 4 through 8, students are asked to make smooth cirves through data points. You may want to start a discussion regarding whether a fraction of a cube (such as $2\frac{1}{2}$) makes sense, and how the students might want to interpret such points. The functions studied are discrete rather than continuous, and students should realize there are limitations to their graphs.

EXTENSIONS

1. Point out that the volume of each block is the number of cubes in the block.

2. Point out that the surface area of each block is the total number of painted faces. Have students look for different methods to compute surface area.
   Example using a $5 \times 5 \times 5$ block

   Method A
   6 faces, each face is a 5×5 square
   $6 \cdot 25$ square units = surface area
   150 square units = surface area

   Method B
   Add up the number of painted faces given in the table.
   8 cubes with 3 faces painted   = 24 faces painted
   36 cubes with 2 faces painted   = 72 faces painted
   54 cubes with 1 face painted   = 54 faces painted

                                                        150 faces painted

   $\therefore$ surface area = 150 square units

Probability

Teaching Notes

Pre-Algebra Content

Part-whole concept
Percent
Relationships among fractions, decimals, and percents
Developing and using tables and graphs to describe situations

Statistics Content

Create frequency tables and bar graphs
Interpret frequency tables and bar graphs

Probability Content

Definition of probability of an event
Probabilities expressed as fractions, decimals, and percents
Performing experiments and comparing the experimental probability of an event
 with its theoretical probability
Properties of probability:
 As the number of trials of an experiment increases, the experimental probability of
  an event more closely approximates its theoretical probability.
 The sum of the probabilities of the possible outcomes for a given experiment is 1.
 The probability of an event is a number between 0 and 1, inclusive.

Suggestions for Teaching

1. The Conducting a Survey lesson should be done as a prerequisite.

2. Have dice available for experiments. To cut down on noise, have students
 shake dice in their hands and roll the dice onto a paper towel.

3. Parts c and d of Exercise 2 lead to a general principle.

 $P(\text{Event } A) + P(\text{not Event } A) = 1$

 You might want to give students supplementary problems to help them
 discover this principle.

4. To see that the largest possible value for a probability is 1, ask students questions such as the following.

If I draw one card from a deck of 52 cards, what is the probability that the card will be red or black? Is any event *more likely* to happen?

5. To see that the smallest possible value for a probability is 0, ask students questions such as the following:

If I draw one card from a deck of 52 cards, what is the probability that the card will be green? Is any event *less likely* to happen?

EXTENSIONS

1. Use spinners with different numbers of divisions, say 4, 10(digits) or 12(hours).

Example

4-color spinner:

What is P(landing on red)?
What is P(not landing on red)?

Carnival game:

Put a dime on red.
If red comes up, you win a dime.
If red does not come up, you lose a dime.

Suppose you play the game 20 times.

a. How many times do you expect to win?
Theoretically, how much money would you win?

b. How many times do you expect to lose?
Theoretically, how much money would you lose?

c. Theoretically, if you play 20 games, how much money would you win/lose overall?

2. Discuss *odds*

In the example above, the odds of landing on red

$$\frac{\text{no. of successes}}{\text{no. of failures}} = \frac{\text{red outcomes}}{\text{not red outcomes}} = 1 \text{ to } 3 \text{ or } \frac{1}{3}$$

vs. the probability of landing on red

$$\frac{\text{no. of successes}}{\text{total no. of outcomes}} = \frac{\text{red outcomes}}{\text{total no. of possible outcomes}} = \frac{1}{4}$$

3. The Coin Toss Experiments lesson can be used as a related topic.

Coin Toss Experiments

Teaching Notes

PRE-ALGEBRA CONTENT

Part-whole concept
Developing tables to organize data
Looking for patterns

STATISTICS CONTENT

Creating a frequency table

PROBABILITY CONTENT

Performing experiments and comparing theoretical frequencies with experimental
  frequencies
Using tree diagrams to describe possible outcomes from an experiment
Using the probability of an event to predict its experimental frequency
Using Pascal's Triangle to predict outcomes for a coin toss experiment

SUGGESTIONS FOR TEACHING

1. Use nickels for the experiments. Their size and color make them easier to
   find if dropped onto the floor. To cut down on noise, have students deposit
   the coin onto a paper towel or carpet.

2. To save time, instead of having three students each toss the same coin, you
   may have each of the three students toss a different coin—mathematically
   the results should be the same.

3. To explain the top line in Pascal's Triangle, Toss a Coin 0 Times, have
   students think about a coin sitting on a table. There is only one possible
   outcome. H if the coin is already face-up. T if the coin is already face-
   down.

4. You may want to point out to students that in order to get a tree diagram for tossing $n + 1$ coins (*e.g.* tossing 4 coins) they can simply add an additional column to the tree diagram for tossing n coins (tossing 3 coins). This method is an example of a useful problem-solving technique:

Solve a simpler problem and use your solution to help solve the current problem.

EXTENSIONS

1. Have students use tree diagrams to solve a variety of counting problems such as the following.

Anne Marie has 5 blouses and 3 skirts.
How many possible outfits does she have?

This particular problem is an excellent lead-in to the What's Your Chance I lesson.

2. Have students draw a tree diagram to answer the following question.

In a family of three children, what is the probability that there are 2 boys and 1 girl?

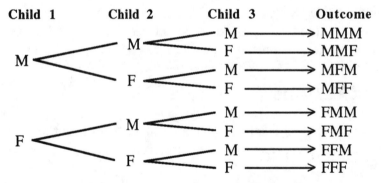

Point out that this tree diagram has the same structure as the tree diagram for "Toss a coin 3 Times"—simply replace H with M(Male) and T with F(Female).

Have students use the tree diagrams and tables that they already constructed for 4 coins to answer questions such as the following:

In a family of 4 children, what is the probability that there are 3 girls and 1 boy?

What's Your Chance I

Teaching Notes

COMBINATORICS CONTENT

Multiplication Counting Principle
Use of tree diagrams
Use of carefully ordered lists

PROBABILITY CONTENT

Use of the Multiplication Counting Principle to count elements in a sample space
and compute probability

PRE-ALGEBRA/ALGEBRA CONTENT

A new model for multiplication
A new look at the decimal number system

Example

How many whole numbers can be represented using the 1's, 10's and 100's decimal places?

$\underline{10} \cdot \underline{10} \cdot \underline{10} = 1000$

SUGGESTIONS FOR TEACHING

1. The Probability lessons should be done as a prerequisite.

2. Young students might benefit from using physical models.
Examples
Cut out pictures of objects such as articles of clothing
Use index cards labeled with names of objects

EXTENSIONS

1. The What's Your Chance II and What's Your Chance III lessons can be used as related topics. We suggest they be done in order.

What's Your Chance II

Teaching Notes

COMBINATORICS CONTENT

Use of the Multiplication Counting Principle to find the number of permutations of n objects

Use of the Multiplication Counting Principle to find the number of permutations of n objects taken r at a time

Use of tree diagrams

Use of carefully ordered lists

$_nP_r$ notation

Factorial notation

PROBABILITY CONTENT

Use of permutations to find the number of elements in a sample space, followed by the computation of a related probability

SUGGESTIONS FOR TEACHING

1. The following lessons should be done as prerequisites:
   Probability I
   Probability II
   What's Your Chance I

2. Have students illustrate permutations as follows.

   To list permutations of 4 CD's, choose 4 students to stand in front of the class, each holding a letter representing a CD: D(Dance), R(Rap), H(Hard Rock), and S(Soft Rock). Students change places to illustrate new permutations.

   a. Begin with alphabetical order.

   b. Exchange letters from the right side, keeping ones on the left stationary as long as possible.

   c. When you must change a letter, replace it with the one that occurs next in the alphabet. For example:

DHRS
DHSR   Must change H, candidates are R and S
DRHS
DRSH   Must change R, only candidate is S
DSHR
DSRH   Must change D, candidates are H, R, and S
HDRS

Now look for 6 permutations with H first, 6 more with R first, and 6 more with S first, for a total of 24 permutations

3. Do not emphasize a formula for $_nP_r$. Rather, students should be encouraged to think about the Multiplication Counting Principle: multiply r consecutive counting numbers, the largest of which is n.

	n choices	$n-1$ choices	$n-2$ choices	...	$n-r+1$ choices
	1st item	2nd item	3rd item	...	rth item
$_nP_r =$	n $\cdot$	$(n-1)$ $\cdot$	$(n-2)$ $\cdot$	... $\cdot$	$(n-r+1)$

Notice that there are precisely r counting numbers from $n-r+1$ through n, inclusive.

Students should do many examples with specific values for n and r so that they understand the concept of $_nP_r$.

EXTENSIONS

1. The What's Your Chance III lesson can be used as a related topic.

Building Foundations 219

What's Your Chance III

Teaching Notes

COMBINATORICS CONTENT

Combinations
$_nC_r$ notation
Permutations
The difference between combinations and permutations

The relationship between combinations and permutations: $_nC_r = \dfrac{_nP_r}{r!}$

PROBABILITY CONTENT

Use of combinations to count elements in a sample space followed by the computation of a related probability

SUGGESTIONS FOR TEACHING

1. The following lessons should be done as prerequisites.

   Probability I
   What's Your Chance I
   What's Your Chance II

2. If students have difficulty, suggest that they begin by writing a carefully ordered list.

3. Do not emphasize a formula for $_nC_r$. Rather, students should be encouraged to think about computing all the different arrangements of r objects, $_nP_r$, and then divide by $r!$ to remove duplicate combinations that differ only by order, thus getting the number of combinations.

   Note that we are using the following formula.

   $$_nC_r = \frac{_nP_r}{r!} = \frac{n \cdot (n-1) \cdot \ldots \cdot (n-r+1)}{r!}$$

   This is equivalent to

   $$_nC_r = \frac{_nP_r}{r!} = \frac{n \cdot (n-1) \cdot \ldots \cdot (n-r+1)}{r!} \cdot \frac{(n-r)!}{(n-r)!} = \frac{n!}{r!(n-r)!}$$

4. Be sure that students understand the difference between combinations and permutations. A different order of the same objects does make a new permutation but does not make a new combination. Use the example of slates of officers vs. committees to illustrate this point.

With slates of officers, a different order of people does make a different slate. Therefore, this is a permutation problem.

With committees, a different order of people does not make a different committee. Therefore, this is a combination problem.

EXTENSIONS

1. Give students a mixed list of permutation and combination problems to solve. A useful technique is to ask whether a given problem is like the slates of officers problem or like the committees problem. Students might also ask whether a new order of the same objects should add to their count. If the answer is "yes," they have a permutations problem. But if the answer is "no," they have a combinations problem.

2. The Handshake Problem (Recommended in the NCTM's *Standards*.)

Seven people are at a party. If each person shakes hands with every other person at the party, how many handshakes will occur?

Encourage many different solutions.

Method 1

Model the problem and count the handshakes.

Method 2

This problem is like counting committees of size 2 chosen from 7 people: $_7C_2 = \dfrac{7 \cdot 6}{2 \cdot 1} = 21$

Method 3

Make a carefully ordered list.
AB, AC, AD, AE, AF, AG; BC, BD, BE, BF, BG; CD, CE, CF, CG; DE, DF, DG; EF, EG; FG
21 handshakes

Method 4

Make a table of hand shakes as people arrive.

Number of People	2	3	4	5	6	7
Number of Handshakes	1	3	6	10	15	21

$$+2 \quad +3 \quad +4 \quad +5 \quad +6$$

Each new arrival at the party must shake hands with each person present.

Get Ready, Get Set

Teaching Notes

PRE-ALGEBRA/ALGEBRA CONTENT

Part-whole concept
Percent
Addition and subtraction of fractions

SET THEORY CONTENT

Concept of union of two sets—use of OR and $\cup$
Concept of intersection of two sets—use of AND and $\cap$
Concept of complement of a set—NOT(A)
Counting elements in the union of two sets
Guided discovery of the relationship

$$N(A \cup B) = N(A) + N(B) - N(A \cap B)$$

Counting elements in the intersection of two sets
Counting elements in the complement of a set
Overlapping vs. disjoint sets
Venn diagrams

PROBABILITY CONTENT

Count outcomes of an event within a sample space
Guided discovery of the relationship

$$P(A \cup B) = P(A) + P(B) - P(A \cap B)$$

SUGGESTIONS FOR TEACHING

1. The Probability I lesson should be done as a prerequisite.

2. Students should be guided to a discovery of the general principle
$$N(A \cup B) = N(A) + N(B) - N(A \cap B)$$

and use it for all related problems. Since the special case for disjoint sets is an immediate consequence of this general principle, students need not learn a separate formula for it. Some textbooks begin with the special case, leaving students with the erroneous impression that they must learn two separate formulas and a rule for when to use which one.

Similarly, students should be guided to the general principle

$$P(A \cup B) = P(A) + P(B) - P(A \cap B)$$

and use it for all related problems.

EXTENSIONS

1. The Independent and Dependent Events lessons can be used as related topics.

2. Use real-world examples with 3 categories and have students construct Venn diagrams to solve related problems.

Independent and Dependent Events

Teaching Notes

PRE-ALGEBRA/ALGEBRA CONTENT

Part-whole concept
Multiplication of fractions

PROBABILITY CONTENT

Count outcomes of an event within a sample space
Conditional probability: $P(B \mid A)$, the probability of B given A
Guided discovery of the relationship

$$P(A \cap B) = P(A) \cdot P(B \mid A)$$

Independent events: $P(B \mid A) = P(B)$
Guided discovery of the special case for independent events:

$$P(A \cap B) = P(A) \cdot P(B)$$

SUGGESTIONS FOR TEACHING

1. The following lessons should be done as prerequisites.
   Probability I
   Probability II
   Get Ready, Get Set

2. Theoretical probabilities for Experiment 1 can be found using the following probability tree.

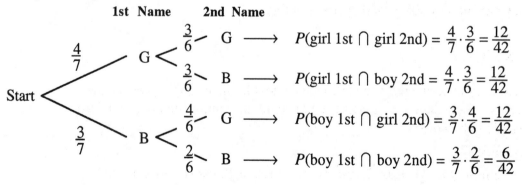

3. Theoretical probabilities for Experiment 2 can be found using the following probability tree.

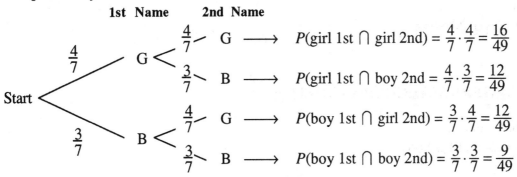

$P(\text{girl 1st} \cap \text{girl 2nd}) = \frac{4}{7} \cdot \frac{4}{7} = \frac{16}{49}$

$P(\text{girl 1st} \cap \text{boy 2nd} = \frac{4}{7} \cdot \frac{3}{7} = \frac{12}{49}$

$P(\text{boy 1st} \cap \text{girl 2nd}) = \frac{3}{7} \cdot \frac{4}{7} = \frac{12}{49}$

$P(\text{boy 1st} \cap \text{boy 2nd}) = \frac{3}{7} \cdot \frac{3}{7} = \frac{9}{49}$

4. We recommend that students use the general principle

$$P(A \cap B) = P(A) \cdot P(B \mid A)$$

for all $P(A \cap B)$ problems. Computation of $P(B \mid A)$ forces the student to consider the independence vs. dependence issue. Too many students use $P(A \cap B) = P(A) \cdot P(B)$ without considering the independence vs. dependence issue, and consequently get an incorrect answer.

5. You may want to run several experiments similar to Experiments 1 and 2 so that students get a clear idea of the difference between dependent and independent events. You can simply change the numbers of names in the hat at the beginning of the experiments. Once students get the idea, instead of actually running an experiment, you can ask, "If there were 5 girls' names and 4 boys' names to start with, find $P(\text{girl 1st} \cap \text{girl 2nd})$ without replacement, as you did in Experiment 1." Then you can repeat this question with replacement, as done in Experiment 2.

6. As a general principle for probability problems, if students have any doubt about how to proceed, they can draw a tree diagram (or at least a partial tree diagram) or make a carefully ordered list (or at least a partial one) so that they can literally see what they are counting.

EXTENSIONS

1. Card deck experiments provide a nice context for investigating dependent events. Make sure your students understand the composition of a standard deck first, however.

Example

Suppose you are dealt 2 cards from a deck of 52 cards. What is the probability that you will be dealt a pair of jacks?

Solution: $P(\text{jack 1st} \cap \text{jack 2nd}) = P(\text{jack 1st}) \cdot P(\text{jack 2nd} \mid \text{jack 1st})$

$$\frac{4}{52} \cdot \frac{3}{51}$$

As a check, you may also view this as a combinations problem:

$$P(\text{jack 1st} \cap \text{jack 2nd}) = \frac{\text{number of pairs of jacks}}{\text{number of pairs of cards}}$$

$$= \frac{_4C_2}{_{52}C_2} = \frac{(4 \cdot 3)/(2 \cdot 1)}{(52 \cdot 51)/(2 \cdot 1)} = \frac{4 \cdot 3}{52 \cdot 51}$$

2. Revisit the Coin Toss Experiments lesson. The coin toss experiments provide a nice context for independent events.

Example

Suppose a coin is tossed 4 times. What is the probability of getting 4 heads?

Solution: $P(\text{head 1st} \cap \text{head 2nd} \cap \text{head 3rd} \cap \text{head 4th}) =$

$P(\text{head 1st}) \cdot P(\text{head 2nd}) \cdot P(\text{head 3rd}) \cdot P(\text{head 4th}) =$

$$\frac{1}{2} \cdot \frac{1}{2} \cdot \frac{1}{2} \cdot \frac{1}{2} = \frac{1}{16}$$

Geometry and Probability

Teaching Notes

PRE-ALGEBRA/ALGEBRA CONTENT

Ratios expressed in fraction form and in decimal form
Equivalent fractions

GEOMETRY CONTENT

Concept of area as measuring the interior of a figure
Estimating areas of figures using random dots
Guided discovery of a formula for area of a triangle
Guided discovery of a formula for area of a circle
Estimating π using areas of circles

PROBABILITY CONTENT

Count outcomes of an event within a sample space
Basic concepts in geometric probability

$$\frac{\text{dots in shaded region}}{\text{dots in whole figure}} \approx \frac{\text{area of shaded region}}{\text{area of whole figure}}$$

$$\frac{\text{area of shaded region}}{\text{area of whole figure}} = \begin{array}{l}\text{probability that a dot selected at}\\\text{random from the whole figure is}\\\text{in the shaded region}\end{array}$$

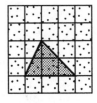

SUGGESTIONS FOR TEACHING

1. Counting dots is not an exact science. Three different conventions can be used.

   a. If a dot is on a border, do not count it as inside or outside the figure, that is, totally ignore it.

   b. If a dot is on a border, count it as inside the figure.

   c. Count all dots on a given border and categorize half of them as inside and half of them as outside the figure.

   We have chosen option (a) for use in this lesson.

2. The supplied random dot transparency is not very dense; therefore, you should expect results to be rough approximations. We recommend that groups of students pool data to obtain better approximations.

3. Use of the random dot transparency.
   a. Trace the perimeter of the whole figure and the perimeter of the interior figure with an overhead pen.
   b. As you count points, go through the whole figure either by rows or by columns to keep track of where you are. Count all points inside the interior figure, then count all points outside the interior figure. Use two different colored overhead pens to distinguish the two sets of points.
   c. Be sure to add the counts for the "inside" and "outside" points together to get the total points for the whole figure.
   d. When two or more students pool data, each student should use a different section of the random dot transparency.

4. The Activity at the end (the carnival game) may be omitted for the class. It can then be used as an Extension for students who finish early.

EXTENSIONS

A Variation on the Carnival Problem

Assume that you do not know the radius of a penny but wish to estimate it using geometric probability. Repeat the experiment of dropping a penny onto a paper mat consisting of $1\frac{1}{2}$" squares and reason as follows:

$$\frac{\text{winning drops}}{\text{total number of trials}} \approx \frac{\text{area of "safe" region for centers}}{\text{area of } 1\frac{1}{2}\text{" square}}$$

For example, suppose the number of winning drops is 53 and the total number of trials is 200. Let r be the radius of a penny. Note that the "safe" region is a square whose side is 1.5–2r. Thus, the area of the safe region is $(1.5-2r)^2$. This gives

$$\frac{53}{200} \approx \frac{(1.5-2r)^2}{(1.5)^2}$$

$$\frac{53}{200} \cdot (1.5)^2 \approx (1.5-2r)^2$$

$$0.59625 \approx (1.5-2r)^2$$

$$\sqrt{0.59625} \approx 1.5-2r$$

$$0.36 \approx r$$

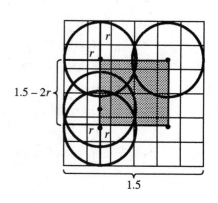

Thus, our approximation for the radius of a penny is 0.36".

RANDOM DOTS

Answers

Conducting A Survey Lesson

ACTIVITIES

A–H. Answers may vary. Examples are given based on the data in step A.

A.

Flavor	Frequency	Relative Frequency Fractional Form		Relative Frequency Decimal Form	Percent
		Unreduced	Reduced	to nearest 100th	
Vanilla	3	$\frac{3}{22}$	$\frac{3}{22}$	0.14	14
Chocolate	12	$\frac{12}{22}$	$\frac{6}{11}$	0.55	55
Strawberry	7	$\frac{7}{22}$	$\frac{7}{22}$	0.32	32
Totals	22	$\frac{22}{22}$	1	1.01	101

B.

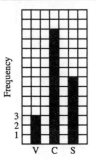 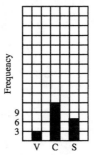

C.

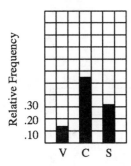

D. i. Chocolate

ii. Find the largest number in the "Frequency" column.

iii. Find the tallest bar.

E. i. 5 votes

ii. From the frequency column, subtract the largest number minus the second-largest number. In this case, $12 - 7 = 5$.

iii. From the frequency bar graphs, take the difference in the heights of the 2 tallest bars.

F. 22. This represents the number of students who responded to the survey.

G. 1

H. i. 101

ii. 100

iii. They are almost the same. The difference is due to rounding the decimal form.

EXERCISES

1. Answers may vary. Examples are based on Activity data.

a. Vanilla: 46; Chocolate: 179; and Strawberry: 104.

b. No; answers are rounded up to avoid having too few.

c. Answers may vary.

2. Vanilla: 3 students; Chocolate: 18 students; and Strawberry: 11 students.

3. 32 students

Answers

4. Mrs. Ryan's class

Flavor	Frequency	Relative Frequency Fractional Form		Relative Frequency Decimal Form	Percent
		Unreduced	Reduced	to nearest 100th	
Vanilla	3	$\frac{3}{32}$	$\frac{3}{32}$	0.09	9
Chocolate	18	$\frac{18}{32}$	$\frac{9}{16}$	0.56	56
Strawberry	11	$\frac{11}{32}$	$\frac{11}{32}$	0.34	34
Totals	32	$\frac{32}{32}$	1	0.99	99

5. 1. They are equal.

6. **a.** 1

b. If the numbers do not add up to 1, there must be an error in the table.

7. **a.** 99

b. 100

c. The difference is due to rounding the decimal form.

8. **a.** 7 students

b. 6 students

c. 8 students

9. Mr. Allen's class

Flavor	Frequency	Relative Frequency
Vanilla	3	$\frac{1}{8}$
Chocolate	15	$\frac{5}{8}$
Strawberry	6	$\frac{2}{8}$
Totals	24	$\frac{8}{8} = 1$

10. Ms. Thompson's class

Flavor	Frequency	Relative Frequency Fractional Form		Relative Frequency Decimal Form	Percent
		Unreduced	Reduced	to nearest 100th	
Vanilla	3	$\frac{3}{30}$	$\frac{1}{10}$	0.1	10
Chocolate	18	$\frac{18}{30}$	$\frac{3}{5}$	0.6	60
Strawberry	9	$\frac{9}{30}$	$\frac{3}{10}$	0.3	30
Totals	30	$\frac{30}{30}$	1	1.0	100

11. Mr. Brown's class

Flavor	Frequency	Relative Frequency
Vanilla	5	$\frac{1}{4}$
Chocolate	12	$\frac{3}{5}$
Strawberry	3	$\frac{3}{20}$
Totals	20	1

12. **a.** 10 students

b. 12 students

c. $\frac{10}{20} = 0.5 = 50\%$.

d. $\frac{12}{30} = 0.4 = 40\%$.

e. Class A. Explanations may vary.

Conducting a Survey Quiz

1.

Pet	Frequency	Relative Frequency Fractional Form		Relative Frequency Decimal Form	Percent
		Unreduced	Reduced	to nearest 100th	
Dog	11	$\frac{11}{24}$	$\frac{11}{24}$	0.46	46
Cat	8	$\frac{8}{24}$	$\frac{1}{3}$	0.33	33
Gerbil	5	$\frac{5}{24}$	$\frac{5}{24}$	0.21	21
Totals	24	$\frac{24}{24}$	1	1.00	100

2.

3.
  a. Dog

  b. 3 votes

  c. 6 students

4. 19 dogs

5. **a.** 31

  b. 1

  c. 100

6. 12 students

BONUS: 28 students responded to the survey in Ms. Washington's class.

The Meaning of Mean Lesson

ACTIVITY 1

Tables may vary. An example is given.

Name	Number of Index Cards
Saja	12
Joe	5
Mikel	7

A. Answers may vary. For the table above, the total is 24.

B. Methods may vary. For example, collect all cards and deal them out.

C. Answers may vary. For the table above, the fair share is 8.

D. Answers may vary.

E. Tables may vary. An example is given.

Group	Numbers of Cards	Group Size	Total Number of Cards	Mean
Group 0	7, 3, 9, 5	4	24	6
Group 1	12, 5, 7	3	24	8
Group 2	10, 5, 4	3	24	8

F. Answers may vary. For example, if 4 are in a group, 6 is the mean, but if 3 are in a group, 8 is the mean.

EXERCISES

1. Total number of cards divided by the number of people in the group.

2. Answers may vary. Examples include: {6, 2, 10, 6}, {8, 3, 5, 8}, and {6, 6, 6, 6}.

3. Answers may vary. Examples are given.

  a. 25 cards

  b. $8\frac{1}{3}$ cards

  c. $8\frac{1}{3}$ cards. $25 \div 3 = 8\frac{1}{3}$.

  d. Yes.

4. **a.** $9 + 7 + 8 = 24$; $24 \div 3 = 8$.

  b. $5 + 10 + 6 + 9 = 30$; $30 \div 4 = 7.5$.

  c. $8 + 8 + 8 + 8 + 8 = 40$; $40 \div 5 = 8$.

ACTIVITY 2

A. 21 cards (group of 3) or 28 cards (group of 4)

B. 7 cards

C. Tables may vary. An example is given.

Name	Number of Index Cards
Saja	10
Joe	3
Mikel	8
Total	21

D. Students' work may vary. The mean is still 7.

E. Yes. You could change the total number of cards or the number of people to get a mean other than 7.

Answers

EXERCISES

5. 55 cards.

6. 67 cards. Methods may vary. There must be a total of 3 · 40 = 120 cards. Carlos and Anita together have 23 + 30 = 53 cards, so Michael must have 120 − 53 = 67 cards.

7. a. Explanations may vary. For example, Jen must have a total of 4 · 80 = 320 points. The three scores that are legible total 254 points, so the missing score must be 320 − 254 = 66.

b. No.

8. Tables may vary. An example is given based on sample data for Activity 1.

Name	Number of Index Cards	Mean (Fair Share)	Number of Cards Above the Mean	Number of Cards Below the Mean
Saja	12	8	4	
Joe	5	8		3
Mikel	7	8		1
Total	24	24	4	4

Answers may vary. For example, the totals are the same.

9. a. Answers may vary. An example is given using data from Exercise 8.

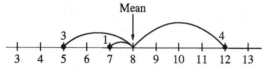

Mean

b. 4 cards

c. 4 cards

d. Yes.

10. a. 14. Explanations may vary. For example, the sum of the distances to the right of the mean must be 10, the same as the sum of the distances to the left of the mean. The other distance to the right of the mean must be 10 − 7, or 3. Plotting the number 14 gives this distance.

b. 11. Yes.

11. a. No. Explanations may vary. For example, many different sets of 3 numbers can have a mean of 33.

b. Predictions and explanations may vary. For example, 3 · 33 = 99; no, because the average (mean) is 33 but some packages may have a few more or a few less than 33.

12. a. No, some planes will be older and others younger.

b. Yes.

c. The sum of the ages is divided by the number of planes.

13. a. The sum of Marvin's grades so far is 369.

Tomorrow's Quiz Score	New Mean
75	$\frac{444}{6} = 74$
80	$\frac{449}{6} = 74.8$
85	$\frac{454}{6} = 75.7$

The score that Marvin will need is between 80 and 85. A score of 81 on the sixth quiz will give Marvin a mean of exactly 75.

b. See the diagram below. The total of the distances to the left of the mean is 18. The total of the distances to the right of the mean is 13. A score of 81 will make the total to the right 18.

c. The total that Marvin would need on his six quizzes is 6 · 75 = 450. He has a total of 369 on the first five quizzes, so he needs 450 − 369 = 81 on the sixth quiz.

d. Yes.

e. Answers may vary.

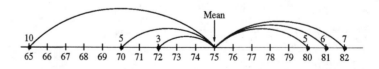

Mean

The Meaning of Mean Quiz

1. **a.** No. The distribution could include some people who spend more than $2.93 and some people who spend less than $2.93.

b. Barry had to spend more than $2.93. Therefore, he spent more than Evan.

2. **a.** The mean of Joan's exam grades was an 81.

b. Joan needs a total of $4 \cdot 85 = 340$ points. She has 243 points now, so she needs $340 - 243 = 97$ points on tomorrow's exam.

3. Answers may vary. Possible answers include {70, 72, 75, 83} or {75, 75, 75, 75}.

4. **a.** $1 + 5 + 7 + 10 + 17 = 40$; $40 \div 5 = 8$.

b. See the diagram below.

c. 11.

d. 11.

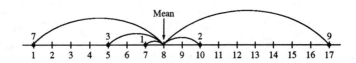

Ratios and Rates Lesson

EXERCISES

1. **a.** $\frac{10}{6}$ or $\frac{5}{3}$

b. $\frac{6}{10}$ or $\frac{5}{3}$

2. **a.** $\frac{20}{25}$ or $\frac{4}{5}$

b. 0.8

c. 20:25 or 4:5

d. $\frac{25}{20}$ or $\frac{5}{4}$

e. 1.25

f. 25:20 or 5:4

3. **a.** $\frac{3}{4}$

b. 0.75

c. 75%

d. 0.75(20) = 15 days.

4. Answers may vary. Examples are given.

a. $\frac{15}{10}$ or $\frac{3}{2}$

b. $\frac{10}{15}$ or $\frac{2}{3}$

c. The fractions are reciprocals.

d. $\frac{15}{25}$ or $\frac{3}{5}$

e. $\frac{10}{25}$ or $\frac{2}{5}$

f. Sum is $\frac{25}{25} = 1$. Each student is counted for both the numerator and the denominator of the fraction.

5. **a.** Miles per gallon and gallons per mile

b. $\frac{180}{15} = \frac{12}{1} = 12.0$ miles per gallon

c. $\frac{15}{180} = \frac{1}{12} = 0.083$ gallons per mile

6. **a.** Dollars per hour and hours per dollar

b. $2.50

c. Answers may vary. $2.50 per hour; 2.50 dollars per hour; $2.50/hr.

d. $\frac{2}{5}$ hr

7. **a.** 2 canteloupes

b. $\frac{2}{4} = \frac{1}{2} \frac{\text{dollar}}{\text{canteloupes}}$

c. $0.50

d. 7 canteloupes

ACTIVITY
Table and answers may vary.

Rates and Ratios Quiz

1. **a.** $\frac{60}{5} = \frac{12}{1} = 12.0 \frac{\text{cents}}{\text{minute}}$

b. $\frac{5}{60} = \frac{1}{12} = 0.083 \frac{\text{cents}}{\text{minute}}$

2. **a.** $\frac{50}{10} = \frac{5}{1} = 5.0$

b. $\frac{10}{50} = \frac{1}{5} = 0.2$

c. $\frac{20}{10} = \frac{5}{1} = 2.0$

d. $\frac{30}{10} = \frac{3}{1} = 3.0$

e. $\frac{20}{30} = \frac{2}{3} \approx 0.67$

f. $\frac{30}{20} = \frac{3}{2} = 1.5$

3. Answers may vary.

4. **a.** 15 swimmers

   b. 14 swimmers

   c. Answers may vary. For example, Midvale is safer because each lifeguard at Midvale is responsible for fewer swimmers.

Equivalent Fractions Lesson

EXERCISE

1. **a.**

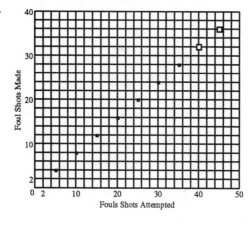

   b.

Foul Shots Attempted	Foul Shots Made	Foul Shots Made / Foul Shots Attempted	
		Fraction	Decimal
5	4	4/5	0.8
10	8	8/10 = 4/5	0.8
15	12	12/15 = 4/5	0.8
20	16	16/20 = 4/5	0.8
25	20	20/25 = 4/5	0.8
30	24	24/30 = 4/5	0.8
35	28	28/35 = 4/5	0.8

Additional rows for part f:

40	32	32/40 = 4/5	0.8
45	36	36/45 = 4/5	0.8

   c. 80%

   d. 24 shots were made. Explanations may vary; for example, look down the "Foul Shots Attempted" column until you see the value 30. Then look across to the "Foul Shots Made" column.

   e.

(graph: Foul Shots Made vs. Fouls Shots Attempted)

5. **a.** $\dfrac{10}{5}$ or $\dfrac{2}{1}$

   b. $\dfrac{5}{15} = \dfrac{1}{3} = 0.33$

   c. $\dfrac{10}{15}$ or $\dfrac{2}{3}$

   f. The first point is (40, 32)—32 shots made out of 40 attempted. The second point is (45, 36)—36 shots made out of 45 attempted. See parts b and e for table and graph.

EXERCISES

2. **a.** $\dfrac{7}{10} = \dfrac{56}{80}$

   b. $\dfrac{4}{3} = \dfrac{36}{27}$

   c. $\dfrac{4}{5} = \dfrac{16}{20}$

   d. $\dfrac{6}{8} = \dfrac{30}{40}$

   e. $\dfrac{10}{15} = \dfrac{2}{3}$

   f. $\dfrac{9}{24} = \dfrac{3}{8}$

3. Seven out of every 10 doctors surveyed preferred Stickem bandages. There were actually 140 doctors in the survey who preferred Stickems.

   a. Answers may vary. An example is given. Here, a "Y" represents a doctor who uses Stickems and an "N" represents one who does not.

Y Y Y Y	Y Y Y Y	Y Y Y Y
Y Y Y	Y Y Y	Y Y Y
N N N	N N N	N N N

   b. 20 boxes are needed. Explanations may vary; for example, there are 7 icons representing doctors who use Stickems in each box. $7 \cdot 20 = 140$, so 20 boxes are needed.

   c. 200 doctors

   d. $\dfrac{7}{10}\dfrac{\text{Stickem Drs}}{\text{Total Drs}} = \dfrac{140}{?}\dfrac{\text{Stickem Drs}}{\text{Total Drs}}$. 200 doctors.

4. **a.** 2.5 miles per hour

   b. 8 hours

5. Answers may vary.

Equivalent Fractions Quiz

1. **a.** $2

    b. $3

2.

S S W W W	S S W W W	S S W W W	S S W W W
S S W W W	S S W W W	S S W W W	S S W W W
S S W W W	S S W W W	S S W W W	S S W W W

3.

Total	Special Olympics
$ 5	$2
$10	$4
$15	$6

4.

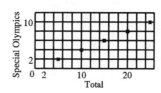

5. $20

6. **a.** $\frac{2}{5}$

    b. $\frac{3}{5}$

7. $32

8. $100

9. $24

10. $20

BONUS: $10

Similar Figures Lesson

EXERCISES

1.

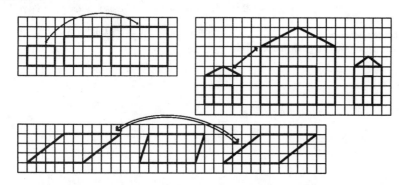

2.

Triangle	Short Side	Medium Side	Long Side	$\dfrac{\text{Short Side}}{\text{Medium Side}}$	$\dfrac{\text{Short Side}}{\text{Long Side}}$	$\dfrac{\text{Medium Side}}{\text{Long Side}}$
(1)	3	4	5	$\dfrac{3}{4}$	$\dfrac{3}{5}$	$\dfrac{4}{5}$
(2)	6	8	10	$\dfrac{6}{8}=\dfrac{3}{4}$	$\dfrac{6}{10}=\dfrac{3}{5}$	$\dfrac{8}{10}=\dfrac{4}{5}$
(3)	9	12	15	$\dfrac{9}{12}=\dfrac{3}{4}$	$\dfrac{9}{15}=\dfrac{3}{5}$	$\dfrac{12}{15}=\dfrac{4}{5}$

Additional row for Exercise 4:

(4)	12	16	20	$\dfrac{12}{16}=\dfrac{3}{4}$	$\dfrac{12}{20}=\dfrac{3}{5}$	$\dfrac{16}{20}=\dfrac{4}{5}$

3. Answers may vary. For example, in the $\dfrac{\text{Short Side}}{\text{Medium Side}}$ column, all fractions equal $\dfrac{3}{4}$. In the $\dfrac{\text{Short Side}}{\text{Long Side}}$ column, all fractions equal $\dfrac{3}{5}$. In the $\dfrac{\text{Medium Side}}{\text{Long Side}}$ column, all fractions equal $\dfrac{3}{4}$.

4. See Exercise 2 for table.

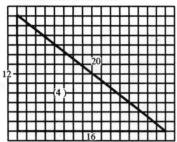

5. **a.** Measurements may vary. An example is given.

Triangle	Small Angle	Medium Angle	Large Angle
(1)	38°	52°	90°
(2)	38°	52°	90°
(3)	38°	52°	90°

Additional row for part b:

(4)	38°	52°	90°

   b. Predictions may vary, depending on measurements given in the table.

6. Answers may vary. For example, they have the same measure.

ACTIVITY

A. Measurements may vary. For example, short side measures 4.6 cm, medium side 4.8 cm, and long side 6 cm.

Similar Figures Quiz

1. They must have the same shape.

2. They must have the same size as well as the same shape.

3. **a.** $\frac{48}{30} = 1.6$

   b. $24 (1.6) = 38.4$

Graph Paper Art Lesson

EXERCISES

	Triangle	Short Side	Medium Side	Long Side	$\frac{\text{Short Side}}{\text{Medium Side}}$	$\frac{\text{Short Side}}{\text{Long Side}}$	$\frac{\text{Medium Side}}{\text{Long Side}}$
1.	Small	1.0	1.6	2.2	$\frac{1.0}{1.6} \approx 0.63$	$\frac{1.0}{2.2} \approx 0.45$	$\frac{1.6}{2.2} \approx 0.73$
	Large	3.0	4.8	6.6	$\frac{3.0}{4.8} \approx 0.63$	$\frac{3.0}{6.6} \approx 0.45$	$\frac{4.8}{6.6} \approx 0.73$

2. 3; the ratio of corresponding sides, $\frac{\text{new triangle}}{\text{original triangle}} = \frac{1.0}{3.0}$ $= \frac{1.6}{4.8} = \frac{2.2}{6.6} = 3$.

3. They are the same.

Graph Paper Art Quiz

1. Check students' drawings.

2. **a.** About 2.5 cm

   b. About 5 cm

B. Answers may vary. For example, yes; if you multiply the long side of the original triangle by 1.20, you get 6.

C. Medium side length is 4.8 cm and short side length is 4.56≈4.6 cm.

D. Answers may vary.

EXERCISES

7. **a.** Short side: 3.

   b. Long side: 21; short side: 15.

   c. 3

   d. 0.25

   e. Long side 17.5; short side 12.5.

8. Measurements may vary. Examples are given.

   a. 1.3

   b. 0.7

9. **a.** Scale factor < 1: photocopy is smaller than original

   b. Scale factor = 1: photocopy is congruent to original

   c. Scale factor > 1: photocopy is larger than original

10. Answers may vary. For example, the measures of corresponding sides of congruent figures are equal, so in the ratio $\frac{\text{New}}{\text{Original}}$ the numerator is the same as the denominator, and the ratio, or scale factor, is 1.

11. Yes; scale factor for houses is $\frac{1}{2}$ and scale factor for rectangles is $\frac{1}{2}$. All corresponding angles have the same measure.

4. **a.** $\frac{5}{8} = 0.625$

   b. $7 (0.625) = 4.375 \approx 4.4$

4. Check students' drawings.

5. Answers may vary.

6. Answers may vary.

   c. $\frac{5}{2.5} = \frac{2}{1} = 2$.

   d. 2

   e. They are the same.

Capture-Recapture Experiment Lesson

PROCEDURE

Answers may vary. Examples are based on an actual experiment.

1. **a.** 189 pinto beans removed.
   b. Yes, they are the same size.
   c. There are 189 navy beans.

2. **b.** There are 19 pinto beans in the sample.
   c. There are 81 navy beans in the sample.
   d. Relative frequency is $\frac{19}{100}$.
   e. There are about 995 beans in population.

4.

Sample Number	Number of Navy Beans in Sample	Total Number of Beans in Sample	Proportion	Estimate of Total Number of Beans in Population
1	19	100	$\frac{19}{100} = \frac{189}{x}$	995
2	22	100	$\frac{22}{100} = \frac{189}{x}$	859
3	26	100	$\frac{26}{100} = \frac{189}{x}$	727
4	28	100	$\frac{28}{100} = \frac{189}{x}$	675
5	24	100	$\frac{24}{100} = \frac{189}{x}$	788

995 + 859 + 727 + 675 + 788 = 4044; 4044 ÷ 5 = 808.8; the average is about 809.

5. **a.** 119
   b. 500
   c. $\frac{119}{500} = \frac{189}{x}$
   d. About 795

   b. 809 − 802 = 7.
   c. 809 − 795 = 14.
   d. Yes; both estimates differ by a small amount.
   e. Answers may vary. Estimates should be close to actual populations.

6. **a.** The actual population is 802.

7. **a.**

Sample size	Number of Navy Beans in Sample	Total Number of Beans in Sample	Proportion	Estimate of Total Number of Beans in Population	Difference: Estimate − Population
25	9	25	$\frac{9}{25} = \frac{189}{x}$	525	−277
50	9	50	$\frac{9}{50} = \frac{189}{x}$	1050	248
100	19	100	$\frac{19}{100} = \frac{189}{x}$	995	193
200	50	200	$\frac{50}{200} = \frac{189}{x}$	756	−46
500	119	500	$\frac{119}{500} = \frac{189}{x}$	795	−7

   b. It seems to make the estimate more accurate.
   c. Answers may vary. Findings of other groups should support this theory.

Capture-Recapture Experiment Quiz

1. 800 fish
2. 750 fish
3. The sample with 100 fish. A larger sample size tends to give a better population estimate.

Pooled: 772 fish.

BONUS

Averaged: 775 fish.

Getting the Picture Lesson

EXERCISES

1. a. Sam's picture is on the left.

 b. Marie's picture is on the left.

 c. Sally's picture is on the top.

 d. Sari's picture is first, and Tom's picture is last.

2. Answers may vary. Examples are given.

 a.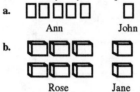

 b.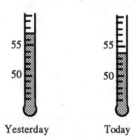

3. Answers may vary. Examples are given.

 a. 54°

 b. See diagram below.

 c. 57°

 d. Copy and color the "Yesterday" thermometer to illustrate the temperature for yesterday.

 Yesterday   Today

 e. The "Yesterday" thermometer would be colored one degree above the 50 mark.

4. a. Descriptions iii and iv are correct.

 b. Descriptions ii, iii, vi, and vii are correct.

5. Answers may vary. Examples are given.

 a. Alice has one more dollar than Tom.

 b. Darren is 4 times as old as Tanya.

6. a.

Joseph's age	Serafina's age
1	3
2	4
3	5
7	9
$8\frac{1}{2}$	$10\frac{1}{2}$
10	12
13	15
14	16

Additional row for part c:

x	$x + 2$

 b. Add two to the number in the first column.

 c. $x + 2$; see table in part a.

 d. Serafina is 22 years old. Explanations may vary. For example, substitute 20 for x in the expression for Serafina; $x + 2 = 20 + 2 = 22$.

 e. Joseph is 18 years old. $x + 2 = 20$.

 f.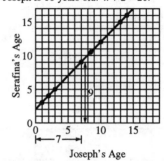

 g. See graph above. The graph is a straight line.

 h. Serafina is 7 years old. Explanations may vary. For example, start at 5 on the horizontal axis. Go up to the line representing the data points. Then go left to the vertical axis. The number on the vertical axis is Serafina's age.

 i. Joseph is 9 years old. Explanations may vary. For example, start at 11 on the vertical axis. Go right to the line representing the data points. Then go down to the horizontal axis. The number on the horizontal axis is Joseph's age.

7. a.

Number of Pounds Bought	Total Cost in dollars
0	0.00
1	3.00
2	6.00
3	9.00
6	18.00
7	21.00
$8\frac{1}{2}$	25.50
10	30.00

Additional row for part c:

x	$3x$

 b. Multiply the number in the first column by 3.

 c. $3x$; see table in part a.

 d. Total cost is $45. Explanations may vary. For example, substitute 15 for x in the expression for total cost: $3x = 3 \cdot 15 = 45$.

 e. 20 pounds; $3x = 60$.

f.

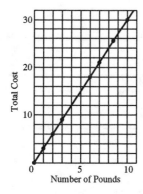

g. See table. The graph is a straight line.

h. The cost is $24. Explanations may vary. For example, start at 8 on the horizontal axis. Go up to the line representing the data points. Then go left to the vertical axis. The number on the vertical axis is the cost.

i. 5 pounds were bought. Explanations may vary. For example, start at 15 on the vertical axis. Go right to the line representing the data points. Then go down to the horizontal axis. The number on the horizontal axis is the number of pounds bought.

8. a.

Time Worked (hours)	Money Earned (dollars)
0	0
1	2
2	4
3	6
4	8
5	10

Additional rows for part b:

6	12
7	14
8	16
9	18

Additional row for part d:

Getting the Picture Quiz

1. The first picture represents Andrew.

2.

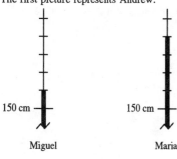

Miguel   Maria

x	$2x$

b. See table above.

c. Multiply the number in the first column by 2.

d. $2x$; see table.

e. $14. Explanations may vary. Students may use the table or the expression.

f. 8 hours. Explanations may vary. Students may use the table or the expression.

g. $2 per hour.

9. a.

Ari's age	Ned's age
4	0
7	3
12	8
13	9
x	$x-4$

b. Subtract 4 from the number in the first column.

c. Ned is 6 years old. Explanations may vary. For example, substitute 10 for x in the expression for Ned's age: $x-4 = 10-4 = 6$.

d. Ari is 9 years old. $x-4 = 5$.

e.

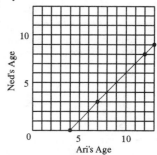

f. Ned is 7 years old. Explanations may vary. Students may use the expression or the graph.

g. Ari is 10 years old. Explanations may vary. Students may use the expression or the graph.

h. i. Ari is 4 years older than Ned.

ii. Ned is 4 years younger than Ari.

3. Answers may vary. For example, 3 times as many people voted for Brand Y as voted for Brand X.

4. Descriptions b, c, e, and g are correct.

5. a.

Number of Cards Owned by Lamar	Number of Cards Owned by Juan
1	2
2	4
3	6
5	10
8	16

Answers

b.

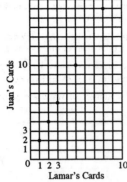

Juan's Cards / Lamar's Cards

c. Multiply the number in the first column by 2.

d. $2x$

e. 40 cards. Explanations may vary. For example, substitute 20 for x in the expression for Juan; $2x = 2 \cdot 20 = 40$.

f. 7 cards. $2x = 14$.

6. a.

Isabella's Weekly Salary	Antonio's Weekly Salary
25	29
36	40
x	$x + 4$

b. Add 4 to the number in the first column.

c. 14

d. 16

e. **i.** Antonio earns more money per week than Isabella.

ii. Isabella earns less money per week than Antonio.

7. a.

Megan's Age	Paulette's Age
3	0
4	1
5	2
6	3

b.

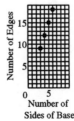

Paulette's Age / Megan's Age

c. Subtract 3 from the number in the first column.

d. $x - 3$

e. Paulette is 5 years old. Start at 8 on the horizontal axis. Go up to the data point directly above the 8. Go to the left to the vertical axis.

f. Megan is 7 years old. Start at 7 on the vertical axis. Go right to the data point directly to the right of the 4. Go down to the horizontal axis.

BONUS

a. 120 miles

b. 5 hours

c. 40 miles per hour

Explorations with Prisms Lesson

2.

Name of Shape of Base	Number of Sides of Base	Number of Faces	Number of Vertices	Number of Edges
Triangle	3	4	6	9
Rectangle	4	6	8	12
Pentagon	5	7	10	15
Hexagon	6	8	12	18

Additional row for Exercises 5–7:

	x	$x + 2$	$2x$	$3x$

3. Predictions may vary. The actual numbers are 10 faces, 14 vertices, and 21 edges, but allow some variations in a student's answers.

4. Predictions may vary. The actual numbers are 12 faces, 16 vertices, and 24 edges, but allow some variations in a student's answers.

5. a. Add 2 to the number of sides of the base.

b. $x + 2$. See the table in Exercise 2.

6. a. Multiply the number of sides of the base by 2.

b. $2x$. See the table in Exercise 2.

7. a. Multiply the number of sides of the base by 3.

b. $3x$. See the table in Exercise 2.

8.

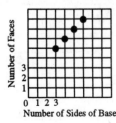

Number of Faces / Number of Sides of Base

Number of Vertices / Number of Sides of Base

Number of Edges / Number of Sides of Base

9. No.
10. **a.** 12 faces
    b. 7 sides
11. **a.** 10 sides
    b. 18 vertices
12. **a.** Octagon
    b. 27 edges

13. **a.** 22 faces. Explanations may vary. For example, add 2 to the number of sides of the base.
    b. 40 vertices. Explanations may vary. For example, multiply the number of sides of the base by 2.
    c. 60 edges. Explanations may vary. For example, multiply the number of sides of the base by 3.
14. **a.** number of faces + number of vertices = number of edges + 2.
    b. $F + V = E + 2$.

Explorations with Prisms Quiz

1.

Name of Shape of Base	Number of Sides of Base	Number of Faces	Number of Vertices	Number of Edges
Rectangle	4	6	8	12
Pentagon	5	7	10	15
Hexagon	6	8	12	18

2. **a.** 5 faces
   b. Add 2 to the number of sides of the base.
   c. $x + 2$

3. **a.** 6 vertices
   b. Multiply the number of sides of the base by 2.
   c. $2x$
4. **a.** 9 edges
   b. Multiply the number of sides of the base by 3.
   c. $3x$

5.

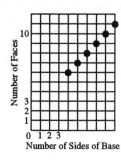 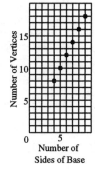 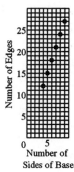

   a. 21 edges
   b. 4 sides
   c. 4 sides

6. 10 sides. Explanations may vary. For example, the number of faces is 2 more than the number of sides of the base so the number of sides is 2 less than the number of faces.

7. 6 sides. Explanations may vary. For example, the number of vertices is 2 times the number of sides of the base so the number of sides is half the number of vertices.

8. 4 sides. Explanations may vary. For example, the number of edges is 3 times the number of sides of the base so the number of sides is one-third the number of edges.

9. Yes

Answers

Explorations with Pyramids Lesson

2.

Name of Shape of Base	Number of Sides of Base	Number of Faces	Number of Vertices	Number of Edges
Triangle	3	4	4	6
Rectangle	4	5	5	8
Pentagon	5	6	6	10
Hexagon	6	7	7	12

Additional row for Exercises 5–7:

	x	x + 1	x + 1	2x

3. 8 faces, 8 vertices, and 14 edges.

4. 9 faces, 9 vertices, and 16 edges.

5. **a.** Add 1 to the number of sides of the base.
   b. x + 1. See the table in Exercise 2.

6. **a.** Add 1 to the number of sides of the base.
   b. x + 1. See the table in Exercise 2.

7. **a.** Multiply the number of sides of the base by 2.
   b. 2x. See the table in Exercise 2.

8.

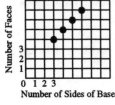 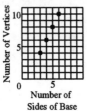 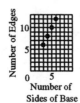

9. No.

10. Data points may vary.
   a. 11 faces
   b. 8 sides

11. Data points may vary.
   a. 10 sides
   b. 10 vertices

12. Data points may vary.
   a. Octagon
   b. 18 edges

13. **a.** 21 faces. Explanations may vary. For example, add 1 to the number of sides of the base.
   b. 21 vertices. Explanations may vary. For example, add 1 to the number of sides of the base.
   c. 40 edges. Explanations may vary. For example, multiply the number of sides of the base by 2.

14. **a.** number of faces + number of vertices = number of edges + 2.
   b. F + V = E + 2.

Explorations with Pyramids Quiz

1.

Name of Shape of Base	Number of Sides of Base	Number of Faces	Number of Vertices	Number of Edges
Triangle	3	4	4	6
Rectangle	4	5	5	8
Pentagon	5	6	6	10

2. **a.** 7 faces
   b. Add 1 to the number of sides of the base.
   c. x + 1

3. **a.** 7 vertices
   b. Add 1 to the number of sides of the base.
   c. x + 1

4. **a.** 12 edges
   b. Multiply the number of sides of the base by 2.
   c. 2x

5.

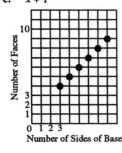 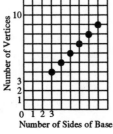 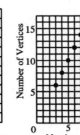

5. **a.** 14 edges

    b. 7 sides

    c. 5 sides

6. 11 sides. Explanations may vary. For example, the number of faces is 1 more than the number of sides of the base so the number of sides is 1 less than the number of faces.

7. 11 sides. Explanations may vary. For example, the number of vertices is 1 more than the number of sides of the base so the number of sides is 1 less than the number of vertices.

8. 6 sides. Explanations may vary. For example, the number of edges is 2 times the number of sides of the base so the number of sides is one-half the number of edges.

9. Yes

Thinking Graphically I Lesson

EXERCISES

1. 6 hours

2. 210 miles

3.

Time (hours)	Distance (miles)
0	0
1	40
2	110
3	120
4	160
5	190
6	210

4. **a.** 0 miles

    b. Answers may vary. For example, we may have stopped for lunch or to use restrooms.

5. **a.** About 3 hours

    b. About 3 hours 20 minutes

    c. Answers may vary. For example, the answer to part a could be found using the table. For part b, locate 140 on the veritcal axis of the graph. Go right to the line representing the trip. Then go down to the horizontal axis to find the time.

6. She would have to drive 50 miles. Explanations may vary. For example, we reached the park after 4 hours. The distance traveled was 160 miles. The distance for the total trip was 210 miles. We would have to return 210 – 160 = 50 miles. We probably couldn't convince her to drive us; she would have been tired!

7. (1, 40)

8. (4, 160)

9. Answers may vary. Any coordinate with *x*-coordinate between 2 and 2.5, inclusive, and *y*-coordinate of 110 is acceptable. For example, (2, 110), (2.25, 110), or (2.5, 110).

10. 100 miles

11. No.

12. (4, 160)

13. Answers may vary. For example, the distance traveled after 4 hours can be only *one* value. She can't be two different places at the same time!

14. From time = 2 to time = 3 hours.

15. The 6th interval

16. 40 miles

17. 70 miles

18. 50 miles

19.

Time Interval (hours)	Distance Traveled (miles)
0 – 1	40
1 – 2	70
2 – 3	10
3 – 4	40
4 – 5	30
5 – 6	20

Time Interval (hours)	Distance Traveled (miles)
0 – 2	110
2 – 4	50
4 – 6	50

Thinking Graphically I Quiz

1.

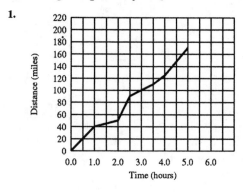

2. 50 miles

3. 5 hours

4. Yes. Explanations may vary. For example, we didn't arrive at Funtown until 9:30 p.m.

5. **a.** 40 miles

    b. 75 miles

    c. 130 miles

6. Yes. 12 · 13 = 156, so you can travel only 156 miles on 13 gallons and the total distance was 170 miles.

Answers

Thinking Graphically II Lesson

EXERCISES

1. **a.** 4 feet/second
   b. about 11.0 meters/second

2. **Table I. 1-hour time intervals**

Time Interval (hours)	Distance Traveled (miles)	Time Elapsed (hours)	Average Speed (miles/hour)
0 – 1	40	1	40
1 – 2	70	1	70
2 – 3	10	1	10
3 – 4	40	1	40
4 – 5	30	1	30
5 – 6	20	1	20

Table II. 2-hour time intervals

Time Interval (hours)	Distance Traveled (miles)	Time Elapsed (hours)	Average Speed (miles/hour)
0 – 2	110	2	55
2 – 4	50	2	25
4 – 6	50	2	25

3. From time = 1 hour to time = 2 hours, or during the second time interval.

4. Interval b: 1 – 2 hrs.

13. **a.**

Time Interval (hours)	Approx. Distance Traveled (miles)	Average Speed (miles/hour)
0 – 1/2	20	40
1/2 – 1	20	40
1 – 1 1/2	40	80
1 1/2 – 2	30	60
2 – 2 1/2	0	0
2 1/2 – 3	10	20

b.

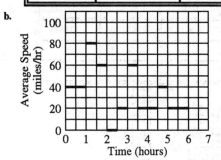

5. Answers may vary. For example, the steeper the graph is during a time interval, the greater the average speed in that interval.

6. They appear to have the same steepness.

7. Answers may vary. For example, since the steepness is greater in the first half hour, Ms. Swift probably slowed down during the second half hour.

8.

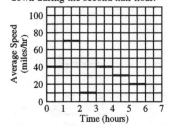

9. From time = 2 to time = 3, or the third time interval.

10. Yes; the interval with the least steep part of the graph has the smallest average speed.

11. **a.** 0 miles
    b. 0 miles/hour
    c. Answers may vary. For example, we may have stopped to have lunch, to use a restroom, or to fix a flat tire.

12. **a.** about 20 miles
    b. about 40 miles/hour

Time Interval (hours)	Approx. Distance Traveled (miles)	Average Speed (miles/hour)
3 – 3 1/2	30	60
3 1/2 – 4	10	20
4 – 4 1/2	10	20
4 1/2 – 5	20	40
5 – 5 1/2	10	20
5 1/2 – 6	10	20

14. **a.** 1 hour to 1.5 hours
    b. 3.5 to 4 hours
    c. 4 stops, from 1.5 to 2 hours, 2.5 to 3 hours, 4 to 4.5 hours, and 5 to 5.5 hours.
    d. 210 miles total distance; 6 hours total time; and average speed of 35 miles/hour.

Thinking Graphically II Quiz

1.
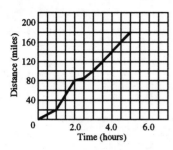

2. 40 miles/hour
3. 1 hour to 2 hours
4. 60 miles/hour
5. 2 hours to 2.5 hours
6. 10 miles/hour

Explorations with Perimeter Lesson

EXERCISES

1. **a.** Each side is 1 inch long; perimeter is 4 inches.
   b. Each side is $1\frac{1}{2}$ inches long; perimeter is 6 inches.
   c. Each side is 2 inches long; perimeter is 8 inches.

2. **a.**

Length of One Side	Perimeter of the Square
$\frac{1}{2}$ inches	2 inches
1 inch	4 inches
$1\frac{1}{2}$ inches	6 inches
2 inches	8 inches
$2\frac{1}{2}$ inches	10 inches
3 inches	12 inches

Additional row for part c and h:

x	4x
$\frac{p}{4}$	p

   b. Multiply each number in the first column by 4.
   c. 4x; see table in part a.
   d. 20 feet. Substitute 5 for x in the expression: $4x = 4 \cdot 5 = 20$.
   e.
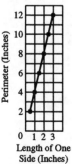

   f. The graph is a line.
   g. 14 inches; 16 inches.
   h. $\frac{p}{4}$ or p÷4; see table in part a.

3. **a.** Long side is 2 inches, short side is 1 inch. Perimeter is 6 inches.

   b. Long side is 3 inches, short side is 2 inches. Perimeter is 10 inches.

4. **a.** Answers may vary. An example is given.

w	l	p
1	2	6
5	8	26
3	9	24

Additional row for part b:

w	l	2w + 2l

   b. 2w + 2l, 2(w + l), or w + w + l + l; see table in part a.

5. **a.** 18 units
   b. Check students' drawings.
   c. Yes.
   d. 18 units; check students' drawings.
   e. They are the same.

6.
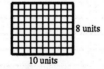
8 units
10 units

7.

Width	Length	Perimeter
8	10	36
12	6	36
15	3	36

8.
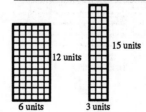
12 units
6 units
15 units
3 units

9. $36 = 2 \cdot 3 + 2w$ or $36 = 6 + 2w$.

Answers

10.

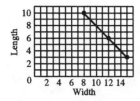

11. The graph is a straight line.
12. 14 units; 14 units.

Explorations with Perimeter Quiz

1. 26 inches.
2. 15 cm.
3. Answers may vary. Examples are given.

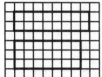

4. **a.** 700 ft.
  b. $2100

5. **a.**

  b. 15 units
  c. Formulas may vary. For example, $P = 2w + 2l$.
  d. $44 = 2 \cdot 7 + 2\,l$. The solution is 15 units.
6. **a.** 1600 yards
  b. Less than a mile

BONUS: 5.5 times. Methods may vary.

Explorations with Area Lesson

EXERCISES
1. **a.** 1 square foot
  b. 15 square feet
  c. 15 posters
2. **a.** 15 square inches
  b. 16 square feet
  c. 8 square inches
  d. 20 square yards
3.

4. **a.** Multiply the length times the width.
  b. $A = l \cdot w$.
5. 14 square inches
6. **a.**

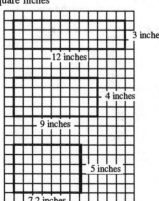

b.

Width inches	Length inches	Area square inches
1	36	36
1.5	24	36
2	18	36
9	4	36
7.2	5	36
24	1.5	36

Additional row for part d:

w	$\dfrac{36}{w}$	36

c.

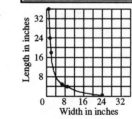

  d. $\dfrac{36}{w}$ or $36 \div w$; see table in part b.
  e. 3 inches; 3 inches
7. 9 square inches

8. a.

l	*A*
0.5	0.25
1	1
1.5	2.25
2	4
3	9

Additional row for part b:

s	s^2

b. $s \cdot s$ or s^2; see table in part a. Multiply the length of the side times itself, that is, square the length of the side.

c.

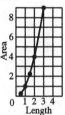

Explorations with Area Quiz

1. 140 square feet

2.

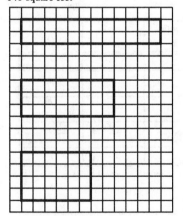

Area and Perimeter Quiz

1. Perimeter: $6s + 4s = 10s$.
Area: $(3s)(2s) = 6s^2$.

2.

s	Perimeter	Area
$\frac{1}{2}$	5	$\frac{6}{4}$ or $\frac{3}{2}$
1	10	6
$\frac{3}{2}$	15	$\frac{54}{4}$ or $\frac{27}{2}$
2	20	24
3	30	54

a. 40 units; 45 units

b. 4 units

d. 25 square inches. Explanations may vary. For example, find 5 on the horizontal axis. Go up to the curve, then go to the left and read your answer from the vertical axis.

e. about 3.5 inches

9. a. 60 feet

b. 1380 square feet

c. i. Area: $18 \cdot 23 = 414$ square feet; cost: $5.50 \cdot 414 = \$2,277$.

ii. Area: $3 \cdot 20 = 60$ square feet; cost: $5.50 \cdot 60 = \$330$.

iii. Area: $23 \cdot 22 = 506$ square feet; cost: $5.50 \cdot 506 = \$2,783$.

iv. $5.50A$

v. No, because the total cost is $\$2,277 + 330 + 2,783 = \$5,390$. I need $\$390$ more.

d. $25

e. i. $20A$

ii. Area: $10 \cdot 9 = 90$ square feet; cost: $20 \cdot 90 = \$1800$.

3. Length is 6 units.

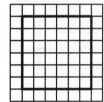

4. 8 feet

5. $A = l \cdot w$.

6. $60 = l \cdot 4$. $l = 15$ units.

7. a. 180 square feet

b. 378 square feet

c. 51 feet

3.

4.

5. About $3\frac{1}{2}$ or $\frac{7}{2}$

6. About $\frac{5}{2}$

Rectangular Garden Lesson

EXERCISES

1. **a.** Check students' drawings of rectangles.

Width ft	Length ft	Area ft^2
1	19	19
2	18	36
3	17	51
4	16	64
5	15	75
6	14	84
7	13	91
8	12	96
9	11	99
10	10	100
11	9	99
12	8	96
13	7	91
14	6	84
15	5	75
16	4	64
17	3	51
18	2	36
19	1	19
x	$20 - x$	$x(20 - x)$

Answers to parts b through f may vary. Examples are given.

b. Each time the width increases by 1 the length decreases by 1. The area increases as the width increases to 10 ft, then decreases in the same manner as the width increases from 10 to 19 ft.

c. Subtract the width from 20.

d. Multiply the width by 20 – width.

e. The length decreases.

f. The length increases.

g. The width and the length are both 10 ft.

h. 100 ft^2

i. A square

j. Between 4 and 5 ft, and between 15 and 16 ft.

2.

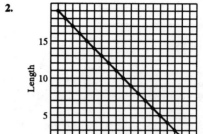

a. Answers may vary. For example, start at 7 on the horizontal axis. Go up to the line, then go left to the vertical axis. The number on the vertical axis is the length; 13 ft.

b. Answers may vary. For example, start at 17 on the vertical axis. Go right to the line, then go down to the horizontal axis. The number on the horizontal axis is the width; 3 ft.

c. Estimates may vary. For example, about $11\frac{1}{2}$ ft.

d. Estimates may vary. For example, about $16\frac{1}{2}$ ft.

e.

Width ft	Length ft	Area ft^2
1	19	19
$\frac{1}{2}$	$19\frac{1}{2}$	$9\frac{3}{4}$
$\frac{1}{10}$	$19\frac{9}{10}$	$1\frac{99}{100}$
$\frac{1}{100}$	$19\frac{99}{100}$	$\frac{1999}{10\,000}$
0	20	0

i. The length approaches 20.
ii. The area approaches 0.
iii. Yes.

f.

Width ft	Length ft	Area ft^2
19	1	19
$19\frac{1}{2}$	$\frac{1}{2}$	$9\frac{3}{4}$
$19\frac{9}{10}$	$\frac{1}{10}$	$1\frac{99}{100}$
$19\frac{99}{100}$	$\frac{1}{100}$	$\frac{1999}{10\,000}$
20	0	0

i. The length approaches 0.
ii. The area approaches 0.
iii. Yes.

3.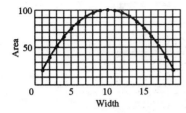

Answers for parts a through e may vary. Examples are given.

a. Yes, by locating the highest point on the curve.

b. Yes, from the highest point on the curve move down to the horizontal axis.

Rectangular Garden Quiz

1. a. 7 ft

b. 21 ft^2

c.

2. a. Start at 4 on the horizontal axis. Go up to the line, then go left to the vertical axis. The number on the vertical axis is the length; 6ft.

b. Start at 9 on the vertical axis. Go right to the line, then go down to the horizontal axis. The number on the horizontal axis is the width.

3.

Width (ft)	Length (ft)	Area (ft^2)
1	9	9
2	8	16
3	7	21
4	6	24
5	5	25
6	4	24
7	3	21
8	2	16
9	1	9

Counting Cubes Lesson

EXERCISES

1. No cubes will be painted on 4, 5, or 6 sides.

2. a. The interior of the block; there are 8.

b. The four middle cubes of each face; there are 24.

c. The two middle cubes of each edge; there are 24.

d. At the corners (vertices) of the block; there are 8.

c. Not directly. However, the graph will tell you the width and once you know the width, you can find the length.

d. Estimates may vary. For example, about 85 ft^2. Actual area is $81\frac{15}{16}$ ft^2.

e. Start at 70 on the vertical axis. Go right to the curve, then go down to the horizontal axis. The number on the horizontal axis is the width; about $4\frac{1}{3}$ ft or about $4\frac{1}{4}$ ft.

4.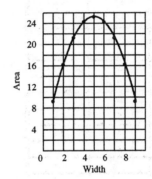

5. a. 5 ft

b. 5 ft

c. 25 ft^2

d. A square

Answers

3. **a.**

Length of Edge	Block Dimensions	Number of Cubes in Block	Number of Cubes with Paint On			
			3 Faces	2 Faces	1 Face	0 Faces
2	2x2x2	8	8	0	0	0
3	3x3x3	27	8	12	6	1
4	4x4x4	64	8	24	24	8
5	5x5x5	125	8	36	54	27
6	6x6x6	216	8	48	96	64

Additional rows for Exercises 4 to 9:

7	7x7x7	343	8	60	150	125
n	$nxnxn$	n^3	8	$12(n-2)$	$6(n-2)^2$	$(n-2)^3$

b. Answers may vary. For example, the number of cubes with 3 faces painted is the same for each block. The number of cubes with 2 faces painted increases by 12 as the length of the edge increases by 1. Starting with length of edge = 4, the "Number of Cubes with Paint On 0 Faces" column contains the same numbers as the "Number of Cubes in Block" column starting with length of edge = 2.

4. **a.**

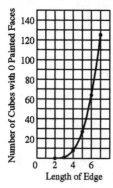

b. Predictions may vary. For example, 125; see table in Exercise 3, part a.

c. Answers may vary.

5. **a.**

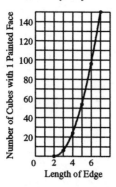

b. Predictions may vary. For example, 150; see table in Exercise 3, part a.

c. Answers may vary.

6. **a.**

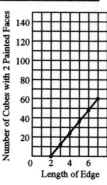

b. 60; see table in Exercise 3, part a.

c. Yes.

7. **a.**

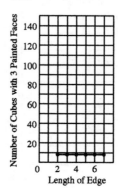

b. 8; see the table in Exercise 3, part a.

c. Yes.

8. a.

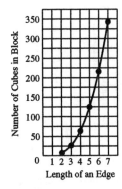

b. Predictions may vary. For example, 353; see the table in Exercise 3, part a.

c. Answers may vary.

9. a. See the table in Exercise 3, part a.

b. Multiply n times n times n; $n \cdot n \cdot n$ or n^3. See the table in Exercise 3, part a.

c. All blocks have 8 cubes with 3 faces painted. See the table in Exercise 3, part a.

d. Subtract 2 from n, then multiply by 12; $12(n-2)$. See the table in Exercise 3, part a.

e. 384 cubes.

f. Starting with length of edge = 4, the "Number of Cubes with Paint On 0 Faces" column contains the same numbers as the "Number of Cubes in Block" column starting with length of edge = 2. Subtract 2 from n and then cube the result.

Counting Cubes Quiz

1.

Length of Edge	Block Dimensions	Number of Cubes in Block	Number of Cubes with No Paint	Number of Cubes with One Painted Side
2	2x2x2	8	0	8
3	3x3x3	27	9	18
4	4x4x4	64	32	32
5	5x5x5	125	75	50

2.

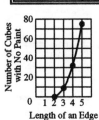

3. 75 cubes.

4.

5. 50 cubes.

Probability I Lesson

EXERCISES

1. a. $\frac{1}{6}$

b. $\frac{2}{6}$, or $\frac{1}{3}$

c. $\frac{3}{6}$, or $\frac{1}{2}$

d. $\frac{4}{6}$, or $\frac{2}{3}$

2. a. $\frac{26}{52}$, or $\frac{1}{2}$

b. $\frac{13}{52}$, or $\frac{1}{4}$

c. $\frac{4}{52}$, or $\frac{1}{13}$

d. $\frac{48}{52}$, or $\frac{12}{13}$

3. $\frac{1}{5}$

EXPERIMENT

Group Data Table

Answers may vary for experimental frequencies and probabilities; they have been omitted from this table.

Outcome	Theoretical Probability		Theoretical Frequency with 18 rolls
	Fraction	Percent	
1	$\frac{1}{6}$	16.7%	$\frac{1}{6} \cdot 18 = 3$
2	$\frac{1}{6}$	16.7%	3
3	$\frac{1}{6}$	16.7%	3
4	$\frac{1}{6}$	16.7%	3
5	$\frac{1}{6}$	16.7%	3
6	$\frac{1}{6}$	16.7%	3
Total	1	100.2%	18

A. i.

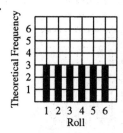

ii. Graphs may vary.

Class Data Table

Answers may vary. Theoretical probability column is identical to those in the Group Data Table. Theoretical frequency depends on the size of the class.

B. i. Graphs may vary.

ii. Graphs may vary.

C. Histograms for class data should be more alike.

D. The two new ones should be more alike.

E. The column in the Class Data table should be more alike.

F. The columns in the 1000-rolls table should be more alike.

Probability II Lesson

EXPERIMENT

A. Answers may vary for experimental frequencies and probabilities; they have been omitted from this table.

Group Data

Sum	Theoretical Probability		Theoretical Frequency 72 Rolls
	Fraction	Percent	
2	$\frac{1}{36}$	2.8%	$\frac{1}{36} \cdot 72 = 2$
3	$\frac{1}{18}$	5.6%	4
4	$\frac{1}{12}$	8.3%	6
5	$\frac{1}{9}$	11.1%	8
6	$\frac{5}{36}$	13.9%	10
7	$\frac{1}{6}$	16.7%	12

Sum	Theoretical Probability		Theoretical Frequency 72 Rolls
	Fraction	Percent	
8	$\frac{5}{36}$	13.9%	10
9	$\frac{1}{9}$	11.1%	8
10	$\frac{1}{12}$	8.3%	6
11	$\frac{1}{18}$	5.6%	4
12	$\frac{1}{36}$	2.8%	2
Total	1	100.1%	72

B. Answers may vary. Theoretical probability column is identical to those in the Group Data Table. Theoretical frequency depends on the size of the class.

C. About 11

D. Graphs may vary. Example below is based on 72 rolls.

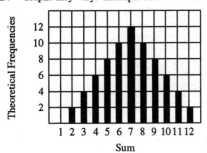

E. Graphs may vary.

F. Answers may vary. They should match more closely for the Class Data.

EXERCISES

4. The total is 1.

5. The total is close to 100%

6. The total equals the number of times the experiment is performed.

7. The total equals the number of times the experiment is performed.

8. The total should be close to 1.

9. The total should be close to 100%.

10. 0 and 1.

Probability Quiz

1. 1, 2, 3, 4, 5, and 6.

   a. $\frac{1}{6}$

   b. $\frac{5}{6}$

   c. $\frac{3}{6}$, or $\frac{1}{2}$

   d. 0

   e. About 16.7% of the time

2. **a.** $\frac{1}{6} \cdot 30 = 5$ times.

   b. $\frac{3}{6} \cdot 30 - 15$ times.

3. a.

First Die	Second Die					
	1	2	3	4	5	6
1	2	3	4	5	6	7
2	3	4	5	6	7	8
3	4	5	6	7	8	9
4	5	6	7	8	9	10
5	6	7	8	9	10	11
6	7	8	9	10	11	12

   b. 36 outcomes

   c.

1st die	2nd die
3	6
4	5
5	4
6	3

   d. $\frac{4}{36}$, or $\frac{1}{9}$

   e. $\frac{6}{36}$, or $\frac{1}{6}$

4. $\frac{1}{9} \cdot 72 = 8$ times.

5. 7

Coin Toss Experiment Lesson

EXPERIMENT 1

A. Answers and tables may vary.

B. See table; answers may vary.

Toss A Coin

Event	Probability	Theoretical Frequency with 20 Trials
H	$\frac{1}{2}$	$\frac{1}{2} \cdot 20 = 10$
T	$\frac{1}{2}$	$\frac{1}{2} \cdot 20 = 10$

C. Answers may vary.

D. Answers and tables may vary.

EXPERIMENT 2

A. Answers and tables may vary.

B. See table; answers may vary.

Toss a Coin 2 Times

Event	Probability	Theoretical Frequency with 20 Trials
2 H's	$\frac{1}{4}$	$\frac{1}{4} \cdot 20 = 5$
1H and 1T	$\frac{2}{4}$	$\frac{2}{4} \cdot 20 = 10$
2T's	$\frac{1}{4}$	$\frac{1}{4} \cdot 20 = 5$

C. Answers may vary.

D. Answers and tables may vary.

B. 8 events are listed. See table; answers may vary.

Toss a Coin 3 Times

Event	Probability	Theoretical Frequency with 20 Trials
3 H's	$\frac{1}{8}$	$\frac{1}{8} \cdot 20 = 2.5$
2H's and 1T	$\frac{3}{8}$	$\frac{3}{8} \cdot 20 = 7.5$
1H and 2T's	$\frac{3}{8}$	$\frac{3}{8} \cdot 20 = 7.5$
3T's	$\frac{1}{8}$	$\frac{1}{8} \cdot 20 = 2.5$

C. Answers may vary.

D. Tables and answers may vary.

ACTIVITY 1

A. See diagram; 16 outcomes are listed.

Coin Toss Experiments Quiz

1. **a.** $\frac{1}{4}$ **b.** $\frac{1}{4}$ **c.** $\frac{2}{4}$, or $\frac{1}{2}$

2. **a.** **Outcome**

b. $\frac{3}{8}$ **c.** $\frac{3}{8}$

d. $\frac{1}{8}$ **e.** $\frac{1}{8}$

B. See table; 240 times.

Toss a Coin 4 Times

Event	Probability
4 H's	$\frac{1}{16}$
3 H's and 1T	$\frac{4}{16}$
2H's and 2T's	$\frac{6}{16}$
1H and 3T's	$\frac{4}{16}$
4T's	$\frac{1}{16}$

ACTIVITY 2

A. To get a number in the interior, add the 2 closest numbers in the row above.

B. Number of Different Outcomes

1 5 10 10 5 1   32

1 6 15 20 15 6 1   64

C. Both patterns should hold.

D. **Toss a Coin 5 Times**

Outcome	Probability
5H's	$\frac{1}{32}$
4H's 1T	$\frac{5}{32}$
3H's 2T's	$\frac{5}{16}$
2H's 3T's	$\frac{5}{16}$
1H's 4T's	$\frac{5}{32}$
5T's	$\frac{1}{32}$

E. $\frac{5}{16} \cdot 640 = 200$ times.

3. **a.** 9 times **b.** 3 times

4. **a.** Number of Possible Outcomes

1	1
1 1	2
1 2 1	4
1 3 3 1	8
1 4 6 4 1	16
1 5 10 10 5 1	32

b. Toss a coin 4 times

Outcome	Probability
4H's	$\frac{1}{16}$
3H's and 1T	$\frac{4}{16}$
2H's and 2T's	$\frac{6}{16}$
1H and 2T's	$\frac{4}{16}$
4T's	$\frac{1}{16}$

Toss a coin 5 times

Outcome	Probability
5H's	$\frac{1}{32}$
4H's and 1T	$\frac{5}{32}$
3H's and 2T's	$\frac{10}{32}$
2H's and 2T's	$\frac{10}{32}$
1H and 2T's	$\frac{5}{32}$
5T's	$\frac{1}{32}$

What's Your Chance I Lesson

Exercises

1. See diagram; 28 different sundaes could be made.

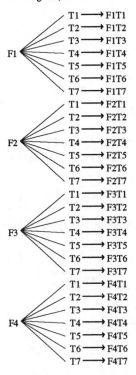

2. $10 \cdot 6 = 60$ combinations.

3. a. $52 \cdot 87 = 4524$ couples.

b. $\frac{1}{4524}$

4.

A1E1D1	A2E1D1	A3E1D1
A1E1D2	A2E1D2	A3E1D2
A1E2D1	A2E2D1	A3E2D1
A1E2D2	A2E2D2	A3E2D2
A1E3D1	A2E3D1	A3E3D1
A1E3D2	A2E3D2	A3E3D2
A1E4D1	A2E4D1	A3E4D1
A1E4D2	A2E4D2	A3E4D2

a. 24 meals

b. $3 \cdot 4 \cdot 2 = 24$ meals.

c. Yes.

5. a. $10 \cdot 10 = 100$ numbers.

b. $\frac{1}{100}$

6. a. $10 \cdot 10 \cdot 10 = 1000$ numbers.

b. $\frac{1}{1000}$

Answers

What's Your Chance I Quiz

1.
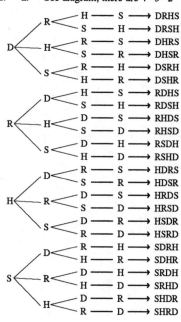

H ⟨ K ⟨ B → HKB
       R → HKR
    S ⟨ B → HSB
       R → HSR

C ⟨ K ⟨ B → CKB
       R → CKR
    S ⟨ B → CSB
       R → CSR

F ⟨ K ⟨ B → FKB
       R → FKR
    S ⟨ B → FSB
       R → FSR

2. **a.**

3BH	10BH	15BH
3BW	10BW	15BW
3RH	10RH	15RH
3YW	10YW	15YW
3YH	10YH	15YH
3GW	10GW	15GW
3GH	10GH	15GH
3OW	10OW	15OW
3OH	10OH	15OH

b. $3 \cdot 5 \cdot 2 = 30$ choices.

c. $\frac{1}{30}$

BONUS

$\frac{2}{30}$ or $\frac{1}{15}$

What's Your Chance II Lesson

EXERCISES

1. a. See diagram; there are $4 \cdot 3 \cdot 2 \cdot 1 = 24$ permutations.

D ⟨
  R ⟨ H — S → DRHS
      S — H → DRSH
  H ⟨ R — S → DHRS
      S — R → DHSR
  S ⟨ R — H → DSRH
      H — R → DSHR

R ⟨
  D ⟨ H — S → RDHS
      S — H → RDSH
  H ⟨ D — S → RHDS
      S — D → RHSD
  S ⟨ D — H → RSDH
      H — D → RSHD

H ⟨
  D ⟨ R — S → HDRS
      S — R → HDSR
  R ⟨ D — S → HRDS
      S — D → HRSD
  S ⟨ D — R → HSDR
      R — D → HSRD

S ⟨
  D ⟨ R — H → SDRH
      H — R → SDHR
  R ⟨ D — H → SRDH
      H — D → SRHD
  H ⟨ D — R → SHDR
      R — D → SHRD

b. $\frac{1}{24}$

2. a. $5 \cdot 4 \cdot 3 \cdot 2 \cdot 1 = 120$.

b. In 24 arrangements. This is $\frac{1}{5}$ of the total.

3. a. 362,880.

b. 5040.

4. a. $2 \cdot 1 = 2$.

b. $3 \cdot 2 \cdot 1 = 6$.

c. $4 \cdot 3 \cdot 2 \cdot 1 = 24$.

d. $5 \cdot 4 \cdot 3 \cdot 2 \cdot 1 = 120$.

e. $6 \cdot 5 \cdot 4 \cdot 3 \cdot 2 \cdot 1 = 720$.

5. a.

Factorial	Expression	Value
1!	1	1
2!	$2 \cdot 1$	2
3!	$3 \cdot 2 \cdot 1$	6
4!	$4 \cdot 3 \cdot 2 \cdot 1$	24
5!	$5 \cdot 4 \cdot 3 \cdot 2 \cdot 1$	120
6!	$6 \cdot 5 \cdot 4 \cdot 3 \cdot 2 \cdot 1$	720
7!	$7 \cdot 6 \cdot 5 \cdot 4 \cdot 3 \cdot 2 \cdot 1$	5040
8!	$8 \cdot 7 \cdot 6 \cdot 5 \cdot 4 \cdot 3 \cdot 2 \cdot 1$	40 320
9!	$9 \cdot 8 \cdot 7 \cdot 6 \cdot 5 \cdot 4 \cdot 3 \cdot 2 \cdot 1$	362 880
10!	$10 \cdot 9 \cdot 8 \cdot 7 \cdot 6 \cdot 5 \cdot 4 \cdot 3 \cdot 2 \cdot 1$	3 628 800

b. Answers are 2!, 3!, 4!, 5!, and 6!, respectively.

6. a. 5040 guesses · $0.19 per guess = $957.60.

b. No. Answers may vary, but it probably would be.

c. What is the probability that a single guess will be correct?

7. Each person should have $4 \cdot 3 = 12$ slates. Each group should have $5 \cdot 4 \cdot 3 = 60$ slates.

8.

Number of Records Nominated for Play	Number of Records Played	Number of Permutations (Expression)	Number of Permutations (Value)	Notation
10	1	10	10	$_{10}P_1$
10	2	$10 \cdot 9$	90	$_{10}P_2$
10	3	$10 \cdot 9 \cdot 8$	720	$_{10}P_3$
10	4	$10 \cdot 9 \cdot 8 \cdot 7$	5040	$_{10}P_4$
10	5	$10 \cdot 9 \cdot 8 \cdot 7 \cdot 6$	30 240	$_{10}P_5$
10	6	$10 \cdot 9 \cdot 8 \cdot 7 \cdot 6 \cdot 5$	151 200	$_{10}P_6$
10	7	$10 \cdot 9 \cdot 8 \cdot 7 \cdot 6 \cdot 5 \cdot 4$	604 800	$_{10}P_7$
10	8	$10 \cdot 9 \cdot 8 \cdot 7 \cdot 6 \cdot 5 \cdot 4 \cdot 3$	1 814 400	$_{10}P_8$
10	9	$10 \cdot 9 \cdot 8 \cdot 7 \cdot 6 \cdot 5 \cdot 4 \cdot 3 \cdot 2$	3 628 800	$_{10}P_9$
10	10	$10 \cdot 9 \cdot 8 \cdot 7 \cdot 6 \cdot 5 \cdot 4 \cdot 3 \cdot 2 \cdot 1$	3 628 800	$_{10}P_{10}$

9. All of the records are played.

10. **a.** $8 \cdot 7 \cdot 6$

   b. 336

   c. There are 8 objects are there to choose from; 3 are actually chosen. The corresponding expression contains 3 consecutive counting numbers, the largest of which is 8.

11. $_{12}P_3 = 1320$ outcomes.

12. **a.** Answers may vary.

   b. Answers may vary..

What's Your Chance II Quiz

1. **a.** 120 different orders. Methods may vary. Using permutations, $5 \cdot 4 \cdot 3 \cdot 2 \cdot 1 = 120$.

   b. 24 different orders. Methods may vary. Using permutations, $4 \cdot 3 \cdot 2 \cdot 1 = 24$. In factorial notation, 4!

2. **a.** 336 slates. Methods may vary. Using permutations, $8 \cdot 7 \cdot 6 = 336$.

   b. $_8P_3 = 8 \cdot 7 \cdot 6 = 336$

3.

	Expression	Value
6!	$6 \cdot 5 \cdot 4 \cdot 3 \cdot 2 \cdot 1$	720
$_7P_3$	$7 \cdot 6 \cdot 5$	210
$_6P_1$	6	6
$_4P_4$	$4 \cdot 3 \cdot 2 \cdot 1$	24

What's Your Chance III Lesson

ACTIVITIES

A. 2-member committes are AB, AC, AD, AE, BC, BD, BE, CD, CE, DE.

   i. 10 committees

   ii. The numbers are the same. For each committe of size 3, 2 students are not included, but these 2 students make a committee of size 2.

B. **i.** Committees: A, B, C, D, E, F. $_6C_1 = 6$.

   ii. Committees:

   AB BC CD DE EF
   AC BD CE DF
   AD BE CF
   AE BF
   AF

   $_6C_2 = 15$.

   iii. Committees: ABC ACD ADE AEF
   ABD ACE ADF
   ABE ACF
   ABF
   BCD BDE BED
   BCE BDF
   BCF
   CDE CEF
   CDF DEF

   $_6C_3 = 20$.

   iv. Committees: ABCD ACDE BCDE CDEF
   ABCE ACDF BCDF
   ABCF ACEF BCEF
   ABDE ADEF BDEF
   ABDF ABEF

   $_6C_4 = 15$.

   v. Committees: ABCDE ACDEF
   ABCDF BCDEF
   ABCEF ABDEF

   $_6C_5 = 6$.

vi. Committee: ABCDEF. $_6C_6 = 1$.

vii. $_6C_1 = {}_6C_5$; $_6C_2 = {}_6C_4$. Committees of size 1 (or 2) leave 5 (or 4) students out to create their own committee.

C. i.

ABC	BCD	CDE	DEF	EFG
ABD	BCE	CDF	DEG	
ABE	BCF	CDG	DFG	
ABF	BCG	CEF		
ABG	BDE	CEG		
ACD	BDF	CFG		
ACE	BDG	ACF	BEF	
ACG	BEG	ADE	BFG	
ADF	ADG	AEF	AEG	AFG

$_7C_3 = 35$.

ii. Predictions may vary.

EXERCISES

1. a. 120 committes.

b. $_{10}C_3$

2. a. The number of combinations of 17 things taken 5 at a time.

b. $\dfrac{17 \cdot 16 \cdot 15 \cdot 14 \cdot 13}{5 \cdot 4 \cdot 3 \cdot 2 \cdot 1}$

c. 6188

3.

Combinations	Expression	Value
$_6C_1$	$\dfrac{6}{1}$	6
$_6C_2$	$\dfrac{6 \cdot 5}{2 \cdot 1}$	15
$_6C_3$	$\dfrac{6 \cdot 5 \cdot 4}{3 \cdot 2 \cdot 1}$	20
$_6C_4$	$\dfrac{6 \cdot 5 \cdot 4 \cdot 3}{4 \cdot 3 \cdot 2 \cdot 1}$	15
$_6C_5$	$\dfrac{6 \cdot 5 \cdot 4 \cdot 3 \cdot 2}{5 \cdot 4 \cdot 3 \cdot 2 \cdot 1}$	6
$_6C_6$	$\dfrac{6 \cdot 5 \cdot 4 \cdot 3 \cdot 2 \cdot 1}{6 \cdot 5 \cdot 4 \cdot 3 \cdot 2 \cdot 1}$	1

4. Yes.

What's Your Chance III Quiz

1. A different order of the same items makes a different permutation but does not make a different combination.

2. a.

ML	MC	MK	MA
LC	LK	LA	
CK	CA		
KA			

b. $_5C_2 = \dfrac{5 \cdot 4}{2 \cdot 1} = 10$.

Get Ready, Get Set Lesson

EXERCISES

1. 40 students

2. a. 8 students

b. $\dfrac{8}{40}$, or $\dfrac{1}{5}$

5. a. MT, MW, MR, MF; TW, TR, TF; WR, WF; RF.

b. 10

c. $_5C_3$

d. $\dfrac{5 \cdot 4}{2 \cdot 1} = 10$; yes.

e. $\dfrac{4}{10} = \dfrac{2}{5}$

6. a.

AB	BC	CD	DE	EF	FG	GH
AC	BD	CE	DF	EG	FH	
AD	BE	CF	DG	EH		
AE	BF	CG	DH			
AF	BG	CH				
AG	BH					
AH						

b. 2 member committees; there are 8 people to choose from.

c. 28 games

d. $_8C_2$

e. $\dfrac{8 \cdot 7}{2 \cdot 1} = 28$; yes.

7. a. 3,838,380

b. $\dfrac{1}{3\,838\,380}$

c. Cash Stash; $\dfrac{1}{1\,947\,792} > \dfrac{1}{3\,838\,380}$, or $0.000000513 > 0.000000261$.

3.

	Expression	Value
$_7C_3$	$\dfrac{7 \cdot 6 \cdot 5}{3 \cdot 2 \cdot 1}$	35
$_5C_4$	$\dfrac{5 \cdot 4 \cdot 3 \cdot 2}{4 \cdot 3 \cdot 2 \cdot 1}$	5
$_6C_2$	$\dfrac{6 \cdot 5}{2 \cdot 1}$	15

4. $_{12}C_5 = \dfrac{12 \cdot 11 \cdot 10 \cdot 9 \cdot 8}{5 \cdot 4 \cdot 3 \cdot 2 \cdot 1} = 792$.

c. 20%

d. 32 students

e. 80%

3. **a.** 12 students

    b. 28 students

4. 17 students

5. 3 students

6. Overlapping

7. 5 students

8. 9 students

9. 23 students

10. **a.** $\dfrac{8}{40}, \dfrac{1}{5}$, or 0.2

    b. $\dfrac{12}{40}, \dfrac{3}{10}$, or 0.3

    c. $\dfrac{17}{40}$ or 0.425

    d. $\dfrac{3}{40}$ or 0.075

11. **a.** 30 students

    b. $N(C) = 10$ $N(C \text{ AND } H) = 6$

        $N(H) = 21$ $N(C \cap H) = 6$

        $N(C \text{ OR } H) = 25$ $N(\text{NOT } C) = 20$

        $N(C \cup H) = 25$ $N(\text{NOT } H) = 9$

    c. $P(C) = \dfrac{10}{30}$, or $\dfrac{1}{3}$ $P(C \text{ AND } H) = \dfrac{6}{30}$, or $\dfrac{1}{5}$

        $P(H) = \dfrac{21}{30}$, or $\dfrac{7}{10}$ $P(C \cap H) = \dfrac{6}{30}$, or $\dfrac{1}{5}$

        $P(C \text{ OR } H) = \dfrac{25}{30}$, or $\dfrac{5}{6}$ $P(\text{NOT } C) = \dfrac{20}{30}$, or $\dfrac{2}{3}$

        $P(C \cup H) = \dfrac{25}{30}$, or $\dfrac{5}{6}$ $P(\text{NOT } H) = \dfrac{9}{30}$, or $\dfrac{3}{10}$

    d. Helen is a cheerleader and an honor roll student.

    e. Tanya is a cheerleader, an honor roll student, or both.

    f. **i.** 31

         ii. 31 is greater than the total number of students in Mr. Nolan's class. 6 students were counted twice, namely those in both C and H.

12. **a.** $N(C \cup F) = 18; N(C \cap F) = 0.$

    b. $P(C \cup F) = \dfrac{18}{30}$, or $\dfrac{3}{5}; P(C \cap F) = 0.$

    c. Separate

13.

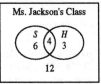

Ms. Jackson's Class

14. **a.**

Class	$N(A)$	$N(B)$	$N(A \cap B)$	$N(A \cup B)$
1	10	11	3	18
2	12	13	4	21
3	15	13	5	23
4	11	7	2	16
5	13	6	0	19
6	5	8	0	13

    b. Add $N(A)$ and $N(B)$, then subtract $N(A \cap B)$.

    c. $N(A \cup B) = N(A) + N(B) - N(A \cap B).$

    d. Subtraction is necessary when the sets overlap, because you have added the elements in the intersection twice.

15. **a.** 0

    b. $N(A) + N(B)$

16. **a.**

Class	$P(A)$	$P(B)$	$P(A \cap B)$	$P(A \cup B)$
1	$\dfrac{10}{28}$	$\dfrac{11}{28}$	$\dfrac{3}{28}$	$\dfrac{18}{28}$
2	$\dfrac{12}{27}$	$\dfrac{13}{27}$	$\dfrac{4}{27}$	$\dfrac{21}{27}$
3	$\dfrac{15}{34}$	$\dfrac{13}{34}$	$\dfrac{5}{34}$	$\dfrac{23}{34}$
4	$\dfrac{11}{28}$	$\dfrac{7}{28}$	$\dfrac{2}{28}$	$\dfrac{16}{28}$
5	$\dfrac{13}{34}$	$\dfrac{6}{34}$	$\dfrac{0}{34}$	$\dfrac{19}{34}$
6	$\dfrac{5}{31}$	$\dfrac{8}{31}$	$\dfrac{0}{31}$	$\dfrac{13}{31}$

    b. Add $P(A)$ and $P(B)$ then subtract $P(A \cap B)$.

    c. $P(A \cup B) = P(A) + P(B) - P(A \cap B).$

17. $P(A \cup B) = P(A) + P(B).$

18. Answers may vary.

19.

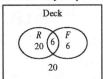

Deck

    a. $N(R) = 26$ $N(F) = 12$

        $N(R \cap F) = 6$ $N(R \cup F) = 32$

    b. $P(R) = 26$ $P(F) = 12$

        $P(R \cap F) = 6$ $P(R \cup F) = 32$

    c. **i.** True

         ii. True

20. Answers may vary.

21. Answers may vary.

22. a.

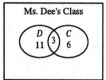

Ms. Dee's Class

D 11 (3) C 6

b.

Mr. Morris's Class

D 5 (2) C 13

c.

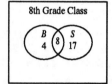

Ms. Chen's Class

D 10 (4) C 2

12

23. No; explanations may vary. For example, there could be overlap between the sets. Some students may participate in musical activity *and* participate in a physical education activity.

Get Ready, Get Set Quiz

1. a. 3818 students

b.

$N(E) = 3042$ $P(E) = \frac{3042}{2818}$

$N(M) = 2903$ $P(M) = \frac{2903}{3818}$

$N(\text{NOT } E) = 776$ $P(\text{NOT } E) = \frac{776}{3818}$

$N(\text{NOT } M) = 915$ $P(\text{NOT } M) = \frac{915}{3818}$

$N(E \text{ AND } M) = 2150$ $P(E \text{ AND } M) = \frac{2150}{3818}$

$N(E \text{ OR } M) = 3795$ $P(E \text{ OR } M) = \frac{3795}{3818}$

$N(E \bigcup M) = 3795$ $P(E \bigcup M) = \frac{2795}{3818}$

$N(E \bigcap M) = 2150$ $P(E \bigcap M) = \frac{2150}{3818}$

c. Jay is registered for Math, English, or both

d. Johanna is registered for both Math and English.

e. The probability that a student chosen at random is registered for Math, English, or both.

2. a.

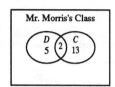

8th Grade Class

B 4 (8) S 17

b. 29 students

3.

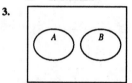

A B

4. 8 students play the guitar.

5. $N(A \bigcup B) = N(A) + N(B) - N(A \bigcap B)$. The subtraction can be omitted when the sets are disjoint, that is, when $N(A \bigcap B) = 0$.

6. $P(A \bigcup B) = P(A) + P(B) - P(A \bigcap B)$. The subtraction can be omitted when the sets are disjoint, that is, when $N(A \bigcap B) = 0$. In this case, $P(A \bigcap B) = 0$ as well.

Independent and Dependent Events Lesson
Dependent

EXPERIMENT 1
Answers may vary.

EXERCISES

1.

Choose 1st Name	Choose 2nd Name	Outcome
G1	G2, G3, G4, B1, B2, B3	G1G2, G1G3, G1G4, G1B1, G1B2, G1B3
G2	G1, G3, G4, B1, B2, B3	G2G1, G2G3, G2G4, G2B1, G2B2, G2B3
G3	G1, G2, G4, B1, B2, B3	G3G1, G3G2, G3G4, G3B1 G3B2, G3B3
G4	G1, G2, G3, B1, B2 ,B3	G4G1, G4G2, G4G3, G4B1 G4B2, G4B3

Choose 1st Name	Choose 2nd Name	Outcome
B1	G1, G2, G3, G4, B2, B3	B1G1, B1G2, B1G3, B1G4, B1B2, B1B3
B2	G1, G2, G3, G4, B1, B3	B2G1, B2G2, B2G3, B2G4, B2B1, B2B3
B3	G1, G2, G3, G4, B1, B2	B3G1, B3G2, B3G3, B3G4, B3B1, B3B2

2. a. 12 times   **b.** 42

   c. $\frac{12}{42}$ **d.** Answers may vary.

3. a. $4 \cdot 3 = 12$.

   b. $7 \cdot 6 = 42$.

   c. $\frac{12}{42}$

4. Yes.

5. **a.** There are 6 outcomes; the probability is $\frac{6}{42}$.

   b. There are 12 outcomes; the probability is $\frac{12}{42}$.

   c. There are 12 outcomes; the probability is $\frac{12}{42}$.

6. **a.** $P(\text{boy 1st} \cap \text{boy 2nd})$

   b. The probablility that a boy is chosen 2nd given that a girl was chosen 1st is $\frac{3}{6}$.

7. **a.** $\frac{4}{7}$ **b.** $\frac{3}{7}$

   c. $\frac{3}{6}$ **d.** $\frac{4}{6}$

   e. $\frac{3}{6}$ **f.** $\frac{2}{6}$

8. **a.** True   **b.** True

9. $(12,42)$ $\cdot\frac{3}{7}=\frac{4}{6}$.

10. $P(\text{boy 1st} \cap \text{boy 2nd}) = \frac{6}{42}$ by counting outcomes, or

   $P(\text{boy 1st} \cap \text{boy 2nd}) = P(\text{boy 1st}) \cdot P(\text{boy 2nd} \mid \text{boy 1st}) = \frac{3}{7} \cdot \frac{2}{6}$.

11. **a.** $P(\text{girl 1st} \cap \text{girl 2nd}) = P(\text{girl 1st}) \cdot P(\text{girl 2nd} \mid \text{girl 1st}) = \frac{5}{7} \cdot \frac{4}{6} = \frac{20}{42}$.

   b. $P(\text{boy 1st} \cap \text{boy 2nd}) = P(\text{boy 1st}) \cdot P(\text{boy 2nd} \mid \text{boy 1st}) = \frac{5}{7} \cdot \frac{4}{6} = \frac{20}{42}$.

Independent and Dependent Events Lesson

Independent

EXPERIMENT 2

Answers may vary.

EXERCISES

1.

Choose 1st Name	Choose 2nd Name	Outcome
G1	G1, G2, G3, G4, B1, B2, B3	G1G1, G1G2, G1G3, G1G4, G1B1, G1B2, G1B3
G2	G1, G2, G3, G4, B1, B2, B3	G2G1, G2G2, G2G3, G2G4, G2B1, G2B2, G2B3
G3	G1, G2, G3, G4, B1, B2, B3	G3G1, G3G2, G3G3, G3G4, G3B1, G3B2, G3B3
G4	G1, G2, G3, G4, B1, B2, B3	G4G1, G4G2, G4G3, G4G4, G4B1, G4B2, G4B3
B1	G1, G2, G3, G4, B1, B2, B3	B1G1, B1G2, B1G3, B1G4, B1B1, B1B2, B1B3
B2	G1, G2, G3, G4, B1, B2, B3	B2G1, B2G2, B2G3, B2G4, B2B1, B2B2, B2B3
B3	G1, G2, G3, G4, B1, B2, B3	B3G1, B3G2, B3G3, B3G4, B3B1, B3B2, B3B3

2. **a.** 16 times

   b. 49

   c. $\frac{16}{49}$

   d. Answers may vary.

3. **a.** $4 \cdot 4 = 16$.

   b. $7 \cdot 7 = 49$.

   c. $\frac{16}{49}$

4. Yes.

5. **a.** $\frac{4}{7}$ **b.** $\frac{4}{7}$

   c. $\frac{16}{49}$ **d.** True

6. Mr. Indy put the 1st name back before choosing the 2nd name. Preferences may vary.

7. $\frac{16}{49} = \frac{4}{7} \cdot \frac{4}{7}$.

8. $P(\text{boy 1st} \cap \text{boy 2nd}) = P(\text{boy 1st}) \cdot P(\text{boy 2nd}) = \frac{3}{7} \cdot \frac{3}{7} = \frac{9}{49}$.

9. **a.** $\frac{25}{49}$ **b.** $\frac{4}{49}$

   c. $\frac{10}{49}$ **d.** $\frac{10}{49}$

   e. $\frac{49}{49}$ or 1

10. **a.** The student is in both the art club and the band.

   b. $\frac{3}{40}$ **c.** $\frac{8}{40}$

   d. $\frac{12}{40}$ **e.** $\frac{3}{8}$

   f. No; $\frac{3}{40} \neq \frac{8}{40} \cdot \frac{12}{40}$.

   g. Yes; $\frac{3}{40} = \frac{8}{40} \cdot \frac{3}{8}$.

   h. Dependent; $P(B) \neq P(B \mid A)$.

11. **Rule 2:** $P(X \cap Y) = P(X) \cdot P(Y \mid X)$; X and Y must be independent events.

12. This is an independent event, so $\frac{3}{4} \cdot \frac{8}{10} = \frac{24}{40}$.

13. Dep represents *dependent* and Indy represents *independent*.

Independent and Dependent Events Quiz

1. a.

Choose Best Athlete	Choose Good Sport		Outcome
S1	S2, S3, T1, T2	$\longrightarrow$	S1S2, S1S3, S1T1, S1T2
S2	S1, S3, T1, T2	$\longrightarrow$	S2S1, S2S3, S2T1, S2T2
S3	S1, S2, T1, T2	$\longrightarrow$	S3S1, S3S2, S3T1, S3T2
T1	S1, S2, S3, T2	$\longrightarrow$	T1S1, T1S2, T1S3, T1T2
T2	S1, S2, S3, T1	$\longrightarrow$	T2S1, T2S2, T2S3, T2T1

b.

i. $P(\text{S 1st} \cap \text{S 2nd}) = \frac{3}{5} \cdot \frac{2}{4} = \frac{6}{20}.$

ii. $P(\text{S 1st} \cap \text{T 2nd}) = \frac{3}{5} \cdot \frac{2}{4} = \frac{6}{20}.$

iii. $P(\text{T 1st} \cap \text{S 2nd}) = \frac{2}{5} \cdot \frac{3}{4} = \frac{6}{20}.$

iv. $P(\text{T 1st} \cap \text{T 2nd}) = \frac{2}{5} \cdot \frac{1}{4} = \frac{2}{20}.$

v. $\frac{20}{20}$, or 1.

2. a.

Choose Best Athlete	Choose Good Sport		Outcome
S1	S1, S2, S3, T1, T2	$\longrightarrow$	S1S1, S1S2, S1S3, S1T1, S1T2
S2	S1, S2, S3, T1, T2	$\longrightarrow$	S2S1, S2S2, S2S3, S2T1, S2T2
S3	S1, S2, S3, T1, T2	$\longrightarrow$	S3S1, S3S2, S3S3, S3T1, S3T2
T1	S1, S2, S3, T1, T2	$\longrightarrow$	T1S1, T1S2, T1S3, T1T1, T1T2
T2	S1, S2, S3, T1, T2	$\longrightarrow$	T2S1, T2S2, T2S3, T2T1, T2T2

b.

i. $P(\text{S 1st} \cap \text{S 2nd}) = \frac{3}{5} \cdot \frac{3}{5} = \frac{9}{25}.$

ii. $P(\text{S 1st} \cap \text{T 2nd}) = \frac{3}{5} \cdot \frac{2}{5} = \frac{6}{25}.$

iii. $P(\text{T 1st} \cap \text{S 2nd}) = \frac{2}{5} \cdot \frac{3}{5} = \frac{6}{25}.$

iv. $P(\text{T 1st} \cap \text{T 2nd}) = \frac{2}{5} \cdot \frac{2}{5} = \frac{4}{25}.$

v. $\frac{25}{25}$, or 1

3. a. Dependent; reasons may vary. For example, $P(\text{Soccer player wins Good Sport} \mid \text{Soccer player wins Best Athlete}) = \frac{2}{4}.$ $P(\text{Soccer player wins Good Sport}) = \frac{12}{20}.$ Since the probabilities above are not equal, the events must be dependent.

b. Independent; reasons may vary. For example, $P(\text{Soccer player wins Good Sport} \mid \text{Soccer player wins Best Athlete}) = \frac{3}{5}.$ $P(\text{Soccer player wins Good Sport}) = \frac{15}{25} = \frac{3}{5}.$ Since the probabilities above are equal, the events must be independent.

Geometry and Probability Lesson

EXERCISES

1. Answers will vary. Examples are given.

   a. $\frac{3}{9}, \frac{1}{3}, 0.33$

   b. $\frac{4}{9}$ or 0.44

   c. $\frac{1}{9}$ or 0.11

2. a. $\frac{16}{45}$, or about 0.36

   b. $\frac{19}{45}$, or about 0.42

   c. $\frac{5}{45}, \frac{1}{9}$, or about 0.11

3. a. $\frac{3}{9}, \frac{1}{3}$, or about 0.33

   b. $\frac{4}{9}$ or about 0.44

   c. $\frac{1}{9}$ or about 0.11

4. All the answers are about the same.

5. $\frac{1}{9}$ or about 0.11

ACTIVITY 1

A. Answers may vary.

B. $\frac{6}{25}$, or 0.24

C. Answers may vary.

D. $\frac{6}{25}$

E. They are the same.

F. $\frac{6}{25} \cdot 400 = 96$; about 96 dots should land inside the shaded region.

EXERCISES

6. Answers may vary. For example, play game B because the probability of hitting the shaded region is greater.

7. Estimates may vary. Actual answers are given.

   a. 1.5 square units

   b. 3 square units

   c. 4.5 square units

   d. 6 square units

   e. 1.5 square units

   f. 3 square units

   g. 4.5 square units

   h. 6 square units

8. Answers may vary. Examples based on actual areas: a and c, b and f, c and g, d and h.

9.

Figure	Class Area Estimate	Base	Height
a	1.5	3	1
b	3	3	2
c	4.5	3	3
d	6	3	4
e	1.5	3	1
f	3	3	2
g	4.5	3	3
h	6	3	4

10. Multiply the base and height and then divide by 2.

11. $A = \dfrac{b \cdot h}{2}$.

12. **a.** 20 square units

   b. 12 square units

   c. 4 square units

13. Estimates may vary. Examples given are based on calculated areas.

   a. 3.1 square units

Geometry and Probability Quiz

1. Approximately 140 dots

2. Approximately 340 dots

3. 40 square units

4. $\dfrac{140}{340} = \dfrac{?}{40}$; $? \approx 16.5$. The area of the peanut-shaped region is approximately 16.5 square units.

b. 12.6 square units

c. 28.3 square units

14. **a.** Final column is for part d:

Figure	Radius	(Radius)^2	Class Area Estimate	$\dfrac{\text{Area}}{(\text{radius})^2}$
a	1	1	3.1	3.1
b	2	4	12.6	3.2
c	3	9	28.3	3.1

   b. Predictions may vary. For example, about 48 square units.

   c. About 3 times

   d. See table; averages may vary. For example, 3.1.

   e. 50.2 square units; comparisons may vary.

ACTIVITY

A. Answers may vary.

B. Answers may vary.

C. Answers may vary.

D. **i.**

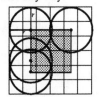

   ii. The shaded region is a square; the area is 0.5625 in^2.

   iii. $P(\text{win}) = \dfrac{0.5625}{2.25} = \dfrac{1}{4} = 0.25$.

E. Approximately 0.39

F. 0.0625

G. The area of the shaded square is 0, so the probability is 0.